DEAD MAN
WINS
ELECTION

DEAD MAN WINS ELECTION

Bizarre but true politics from around the world

Phil Mason

BOOKS

First published in Great Britain in 2010 by
JR Books, 10 Greenland Street, London NW1 0ND
www.jrbooks.com

ISBN 978-1-906779-98-6

1 3 5 7 9 10 8 6 4 2

Printed by Clays Ltd, St Ives Plc

CONTENTS

For Ally, but for whose long (and mainly silent) suffering this volume would not have seen the light of day.

In putting up with my persistent flight from domestic life for endless days and nights, she has perhaps approached knowing what it must be like to be a politician's wife – a husband who is never around when needed, who appears to be engaged in a tedium the merits of which she cannot begin to fathom and, worse, one which relies on the wisdom of untold strangers whom we'll never know for its success.

So here's to all you strangers, too!

Introduction

In November 2000, voters from Missouri elected a dead man as their Senator. Former Governor Mel Carnahan had died in an air crash three weeks before election day. But he still won by a 2 per cent margin. Unusual as Carnahan's achievement may sound, he is by no means unique. You will encounter seven others in these pages who have gained this ultimate accolade just in recent times, including one who won over 90 per cent of the vote, and one who won on the toss of a coin. Another, although he lost, amassed over half a million votes.

You will encounter many more strange episodes within these covers, from the candidate for mayor who got his twin brother to stand in for him at a city parade that clashed with his campaign rally to the environment minister who used a stretch limo to ride to a conference to make a speech on excessive car use; from the Canadian province that found all its laws passed in 95 years to be invalid to the Australian state that discovered in 2002 that it was still officially at war with Japan; and from the legislators of West Virginia who engaged in a protracted dispute as to whether the official state musical instrument should be the fiddle or the dulcimer to the local council in Wales that kept 'temporary' traffic lights in place for 28 years.

These, and hundreds more, are deeds that may redefine your view of politics, politicians and the trade they ply on our behalf. *Dead Man Wins Election* collects the best of the worst of politicians' extraordinary antics over the last three decades (and a bit more besides). We will come across incompetence and audacity, egotism and brazenness, largesse and myopia, the mad and the bad, the feckless and the luckless: enough perhaps to make us truly wonder whether we are sane in holding on to the idea that we elect our politicians on the basis of some feeling of trust that our futures lie safe in their hands. The practice recounted here would suggest a very different story.

Politics is a rich terrain for idiosyncrasy and the unexpected. By its nature, it is a risky business. Careers rest uneasily on the periodic judgement of voters. A glittering path can be snuffed out in a single adverse turn of electoral fortune. What certainties can they look to? 'All political lives…end in failure, because that is the nature of politics and of human affairs.' So, in 1977, wrote British politician Enoch Powell, who is generally regarded as having crashed his own career with a single ill-judged phrase in a single speech, as he summed up another exploded reputation, that of Joseph Chamberlain.

So if that is the prospect, how can we expect more from our entrusted leaders? They might be forgiven their short cuts and their short-term outlooks. They might be forgiven their duplicities, for the chances of permanently avoiding calamity are virtually non-existent. A frequently told Westminster story perhaps gives a clue to the essential powerlessness of a politician operating always at the mercy of 'events'. A cabinet minister, arriving at his new desk on the day of his appointment, finds three brown envelopes left by his predecessor, numbered one to three, with a note: 'Open only when in trouble.' Nine months into his job, the first crisis hits. The minister opens the first envelope. Inside is a slip that reads: 'Blame your predecessor.' He does, and the emergency is successfully overcome. A few months later, the next disaster hits. He opens the second envelope. The slip reads: 'Reorganise your department.' He does so, with a fanfare sufficient to distract attention, and he survives again. When the third calamity strikes, he turns to the third envelope, to be told: 'Write out three envelopes...'

This collection will give you a completely fresh perspective on politics and its propensity for the outrageous, the extreme and the just plain unbelievable. We will explore parliaments, the task of government, elections, the responsibilities of office and diplomacy as well as the often unfathomable world of local and parish council politics and the mad, modern world of health and safety. We'll also portray the best and funniest political wisdom.

Most of our tales are from the last 30 years. Lest this should lend credence to any impression that political insanity is merely a modern phenomenon, we bring up the rear in each chapter with a selection of the choicest snippets from the pages of history to restore the balance. Politics has been the magnet for the unhinged since the dawn of civilisation. That much, if little else, is clear.

What emerges from it all? Perhaps just that anything, literally anything, can be expected from our politicians. As characters they range from the out-of-control egotist who excels in repelling those they come into contact with to the fish-out-of-water ingénue who simply mystifies us all in how or why they got involved in the first place. And there are shades at all points in between, examples of whom you are about to meet.

Two illustrations of these extremes serve to set the scene. For brazenness there can be no better example than the driven, and some would say power-crazy, political machine that was Lyndon Johnson. As newly appointed Vice-President under John F. Kennedy after an already long career on Capitol Hill, he made his mark on senators in his usual ferocious way. One day he spotted a face in a Congress corridor, shouted, 'You, I've been looking for you,' and pulled the unfortunate senator into his room to begin an animated pep talk about how important the legislator was to the Administration. As he barrelled along, he scribbled something on a piece of paper and pressed a buzzer for his secretary, who came in and took it away. Johnson kept up an unremitting torrent of political puff. A few minutes later, the secretary returned and gave the paper back to him. He glanced at it without interrupting his flow, screwed it up and threw it in the bin, and hurtled on. A journalist afterwards discovered what Johnson had written on the paper: 'Who is this I'm talking to?'

At the other end of the scale lie the likes of Ernest Bevin. We see in Chapter 7 how this former trade union leader and genial embodiment of the working class, whom Attlee remarkably made Foreign Secretary in the post-war Labour government of 1945–51, defused ambassadorial pomposity with his common touch. Shortly after taking up his post at the Foreign Office, Bevin returned to his office on a Friday afternoon to find that his Private Secretary had left on his desk a huge pile of papers, on top of which was a carefully penned note: 'The Secretary of State may care to peruse these at his leisure before Monday.' Without looking at his homework, Bevin penned an equally short and obliging note and left for the weekend: 'A kindly thought, but erroneous.'

He perhaps also epitomises the gap that oft-times exists between politics as the personal endeavour and politics as 'the system', the machine that controls. It is this gap, and a politician's success or failure (and desire) in bridging it, that makes politics such a rich territory for oddity, and the terrain that we explore here.

Dead Man Wins Election ought to sow doubt in your minds about anyone standing for political office. When you reach the end, you too may conclude that the Americans, who like to think of themselves as the world's fullest exponents of the democratic creed, were perhaps saying more than they knew when they chose as their national motto, 'In God we trust'. For as sure as anything, they and we have been taking a risk with our earthly rulers ever since.

Phil Mason

THE BEAST WITHIN – POLITICIANS

When Harold Macmillan became Prime Minister in 1957, his appointment took second place on the front page of his local paper in Sussex, beaten by a report of a Brighton and Hove Albion football match. He kept the cutting on his desk at No. 10 in order, he said, to guard against the temptation towards self-importance. Most politicians are not like Macmillan. As they seek to climb the greasy pole, the animal inside is all too often revealed in bizarre ways.

Dodgy characters

Paul Reitsma, a Liberal Party member of the British Columbia legislative assembly in Canada, appeared to enjoy wide support among his Vancouver Island constituents if the local papers were anything to go by. They were always carrying letters to the editor from the community praising his performance. Reitsma's world collapsed in 1998 when one of the local organs used handwriting comparisons to show that he had been writing them himself. He confessed to being responsible for penning dozens of self-praising letters over a 10-year period, sending them under fictitious names to laud his own work and cast aspersions on his opponents. He was promptly expelled from the party, although he refused to resign his seat. Over 25,000 outraged local voters signed a petition for his dismissal under a new provincial recall procedure. After hanging on for two months, he resigned, shortly before he would have become the first Canadian politician to be forcibly removed from office by the procedure.

DEAD MAN WINS ELECTION

ANOTHER CANADIAN POLITICIAN, this time from the national House of Commons, came a cropper in January 2001 for his own bizarre attempt to deceive. Rahim Jaffer, MP for Edmonton and chairman of the Opposition Canadian Alliance Party's small business committee, was impersonated by his assistant for nearly an hour for a radio interview after a diary mix-up meant that Jaffer was unavailable for the talk show. The station, tipped off by suspicious listeners, contacted Jaffer afterwards to confirm it had been him. He initially maintained that he had done the interview, before later confessing that his aide had fulfilled the commitment. By way of contrition, he told listeners that his assistant had resigned. Although his party suspended him for several months, he hung on to his seat until losing it in the 2008 election.

BOURNEMOUTH LOCAL COUNCILLOR Ben Grower was unmasked in 2009 as having submitted internet postings under a disguised identity to praise his own performance. As he was one of only a handful of Labour members on the 54-seat council, generating publicity evidently required extra help. He turned to leaving laudatory comments on the website of his local newspaper, the Daily Echo, under several pseudonyms extolling the contribution he was making to services. Examples of his comments were published by the paper when it traced the posts back to an address owned by Grower. He left comments like, 'At least two councillors seem to be concerned about this mess. Well done Cllrs Ratcliffe and Grower,' and 'Just shows that the area does have councillors who care about their residents. Well done Ted Taylor, Ben Grower and Beryl Baxter.' Another purported to come from a detached observer: 'I have friends who live in the area. They say councillors Ted Taylor and Ben Grower fought hard against the proposals.' Initially denying the claims, Grower eventually acknowledged the ruse, saying that other councillors were also doing the same to get their names in the media.

GLOUCESTER LIBERAL DEMOCRAT councillor Jeremy Hilton, trying to whip up support for his campaign to become the local MP, was caught in March 2010 trying to write his own fan mail. He was caught out e-mailing scripts of letters to others, asking them to 'cut and paste' them into letters which they would send to the county's newspaper under their own names. They would proclaim him as the best man for representing the city at the coming general election. The ruse only came to light in a way that questioned his organisational attributes for the role he aspired to – he mistakenly fired off the obsequious e-mail to the newspaper itself. More woe followed at the May election – he came a distant third.

JULIAN CASTRO, campaigning to become mayor of San Antonio, Texas, in 2005, threw away his chances when he dealt with a clash of schedules by getting his identical twin brother to stand in for him at a civic parade while he attended a campaign meeting. Leading in the opinion polls at the time, he had brother Joaquin, a state legislator, walk in the city's high-profile annual River Parade, waving to the crowds, while he attended his meeting. Claiming afterwards that he had never intended to deceive, and blaming a parade announcer for misidentifying his brother as himself, Castro failed to survive the controversy. It did not help that the brothers had previous form, Julian having been accused of impersonating his brother when Joaquin ran for his state legislator seat.

Julian lost the election 51 per cent to 49. 'I don't think he was ready to become mayor,' said his victorious opponent, diplomatically. He bounced back, however, and eventually won the mayoralty in 2009.

THE 500-ODD RESIDENTS of the small Maryland community of Friendsville (motto: 'the friendliest little town in Maryland') have lived up to their name by re-electing their mayor, Spencer Schlosnagle, 13 times in succession from 1986 despite his wayward record in public decorum. He has been convicted on three separate occasions, in 1992, 1993 and 1995, for exposing himself in public. For the 1993 offence, he had to undertake 30 days' community work, returning to jail each night. Then, in 2004, he was fined $100 for leading police on a car chase when being apprehended for speeding. His political standing, however, did not seem to suffer. He still went on to win re-election in 2006, and at the time of writing is still mayor, up for election again in February 2012.

ILLINOIS ASSEMBLYMAN Roger McAuliffe, a former policeman, successfully introduced legislation in 1995 that enabled all former police officers who went on to serve in the State Assembly to be eligible to draw pensions from both the police and the legislature. At the time of its introduction, the measure benefited precisely one person – himself. There may have been divine justice, however. The following year, McAuliffe drowned in a boating accident. He was a day short of his 58th birthday, and never got to draw on the benefits he had craftily created.

THE NEW ZEALAND Prime Minister, Helen Clark, was discovered in 2002 to have signed a painting done by an unknown artist as her own work for a charity auction. The piece, described as 'a splashy abstract landscape', had been done three years earlier when Clark was Leader of the Opposition, for an animal welfare charity who had sought daubings from celebrity figures. A staff member had quietly commissioned an obscure artist, Lauren Fouhey, to do one for her. Clark then signed both the front and the back of the picture, and it successfully earned $1,000 at the event. 'I was trying to be helpful when I didn't have the time,' she explained when the disgruntled businessman who had bought the picture as a potential investment found out the truth. Adding to her embarrassment, Clark was by then also Minister for Arts and Culture, a post she had awarded herself days after winning office in 1999, saying that her personal pet project was furthering the arts. Although fraud offences carried a punishment of up to 10 years in jail, police authorities decided after looking into the case for three months that a prosecution was 'not in the public interest'.

Image problems

American President Bill Clinton, who portrayed his presidency as the watershed period for the modern 'Information Age', was revealed after he left office to have been a little less of a pioneer than he purported to be. In 1998, for example, in a speech to the Massachusetts Institute of Technology, he lauded how the information technology that had been harnessed and promoted by his Administration had been responsible for more than a third of America's economic expansion and confidently gushed how 'all students should feel as comfortable with a keyboard as a chalkboard, as comfortable with a laptop as a textbook'. Three years after his departure from the White House, staff at his Presidential Library archiving the President's records disclosed that of the 40 million or so e-mails that his office had produced, Clinton himself had sent just … two. One of these did not officially qualify as it was a test message to check that he knew where the 'send' button was. In actuality, it appeared that he only sent one real message – to orbiting astronauts in a publicity stunt. Skip Rutherford, the library's president, commented, seemingly unnecessarily, that Clinton was 'not a techno-klutz'.

MITT ROMNEY, former Massachusetts Governor, got off to a rocky start on his 2008 Presidential campaign as he tried to establish a profile for himself as a man of the common people. Declaring himself in April 2007 to have been a hunter 'pretty much all my life', it later transpired that this amounted to going hunting twice – once when he was 15 years old and not again until the previous year. He dropped out of the race within a month of the first primary votes in early 2008.

ITALIAN FOREIGN MINISTER Franco Frattini was caught by journalists buying a fake Rolex watch during a visit to China in October 2003. Frattini, who was head of a European Union delegation at the time, was in Beijing for an EU–China summit – on combating counterfeiting. His Prime Minister, Silvio Berlusconi, tried to dig his top diplomat out of the hole by claiming that Frattini had been acting with professional interest at heart, saying it was 'logical that a minister charged with speaking about the fight against pirated goods should have proof of their existence'. However, Frattini had already confessed to the press that he had succumbed to temptation and bought the watch 'for an absurdly low price'.

ISRAELI NEWSPAPERS HAD a field day in February 2007 when Defence Minister Amir Peretz, who had been widely criticised since his appointment the previous year for his lack of military background, was photographed looking through binoculars with the lens caps still on. Of particular hilarity was the fact that he raised the glasses to his eyes three times, nodding in acknowledgement each time as the Chief of Staff drew his attention to objects on the horizon, giving no apparent sign he was having difficulty seeing what his guide was pointing out. He quit the post four months later.

DURING A RECORD drought in Victoria, Australia, in 1982, the state Premier hosted a morale-boosting press visit to the worst-affected farms. As the media set up in the middle of a remote, parched field for a press conference to be carried live on early-evening news, almost on cue a dramatic rainstorm broke. The Premier persevered, and the scene was captured for posterity of 30 politicians and local dignitaries bemoaning the effects of the drought – in the middle of a muddy field huddled under umbrellas and the odd sodden newspaper.

Mistakes that reveal

A morale-boosting communications drive by Britain's Labour Party headquarters to help MPs keep on-message with the leadership backfired in early 2005 when some members failed to read the material fully before despatching thousands of copies of a self-promoting letter around their constituencies. Draft pro forma letters containing a fulsome account of the government's achievements were sent to all MPs, littered with uplifting sentiments such as 'And nowhere can we be more proud than here in...' with helpful markers indicating '(insert constituency name here)'. Unfortunately, at least nine MPs simply cut and pasted the text unamended on to their own letter-headed paper and sent them on their way.

IRKED BY A POLITICAL opponent who had called him a liar, California Governor Arnold Schwarzenegger succumbed to temptation in October 2009 when he wrote back to the lawmaker vetoing his proposed legislation. Encoded in the official-looking response to San Francisco Democrat Tom Ammiano was an obscene message. Reading vertically downwards, the first letter of each line spelled out *'fuck you'*. Officially, Schwarzenegger's press spokesman was 'surprised' at the 'strange coincidence'.

Doing it my way

Stefano Bottini became one of the unlikeliest politicians to reach Parliament when he was appointed a socialist party member of the Italian lower house in 1992. The 36-year-old was both deaf and mute, and communicated to fellow members by a sign-language interpreter. He got his seat after the death of the party's secretary. Under parliamentary rules, the party was allowed to nominate a successor. It is not known how long Sr Bottini lasted as an MP.

VICENTE SANZ, a member of the Spanish centre-right Popular Party in the regional assembly of Valencia, was sacked by his party in June 1994 for his honesty. He had said in an interview that he was in politics 'to line my pockets'.

DEAD MAN WINS ELECTION

IN CONTRAST, Thomas Krüger campaigned as Social Democrat candidate for Berlin in the German federal elections in 1994 by plastering the city with posters of himself in the nude, accompanied by the slogan: 'An honest politician with nothing to hide.'

ELLEN SOERMELAND was 104 when she became the oldest Norwegian to be elected to public office when she won a seat on the local council of Osen, central Norway, in September 2003. She died before she could take her seat.

JACK CHASE, who reached 100 years old in October 2006, is believed to be the oldest and longest-serving elected councillor in Britain. Member of Caister-on-Sea Parish Council in Norfolk, he was first elected at the age of 21 in 1927. Other than the war years, he had continued to serve unbroken ever since. The last we heard, he was still going strong two years later, aged 102.

HAROLD GUNN, campaigning as a Republican candidate for the Texas House of Representatives in 2000, lost at the primary stage in March when it emerged that he had written and appeared in a pornographic film featuring naked women jogging through a Houston park and lathering themselves with motor oil. Gunn said this showed him to be 'a communicator', adding, 'It's as tasteful as it can get with naked women in it.' He was trounced by his opponent 78 per cent to 22.

IN SIMILAR VEIN, Teres Kirpikli, a female member of Sweden's conservative Christian Democrat Party, campaigned in the country's 2002 parliamentary elections on the platform that pornography should be broadcast on national television throughout Saturdays to encourage more people to have sex to help boost the country's population. 'I want erotica and porn on television every Saturday and all day,' she said, adding, 'I think most people like porn, even though they don't want to admit it.' She was quickly dropped by her party leadership.

THE MAYOR OF Guayaquil, Ecuador's biggest city, responded to local journalists' harassing style at press conferences in 2003 by hiring a parrot to speak for him. Jaime Nebot, who had been rankled by the press corps' criticisms of his policies, introduced the bird saying, 'Some people only approach me with nonsense talk, so the parrot will answer back in the same way. I need to use my time to work.'

THREE WEEKS AFTER she won election to Maidstone Borough Council in May 2003, Annabelle Blackmore announced she was leaving Kent to accompany her financial consultant husband, who had been posted to Bermuda for two years. She rejected suggestions that she should resign as councillor, maintaining she could 'do an OK job' representing her constituents in the village of Marden just as effectively from the island, 3,500 miles away. 'If I resigned, I feel I would be relinquishing my responsibility and letting down those who voted for me.' Blackmore survived a complaint to the English Standards Board, which oversees conduct of elected officials. It found that she had not brought her office or council into disrepute, or broken any code of conduct. She appears to have completed the long-distance service adequately enough to continue to be re-elected to the council where, by 2009 and back in Marden, she had become chair of the Environment and Leisure Committee. According to the council's log of meeting attendances, it was September 2007, four and a half years after her election, before she actually attended her first meeting.

THE MAYORS OF two Paris suburbs engaged in a skirmish on traffic congestion in 2009 by declaring the same stretch of road a one-way street, but in opposite directions. Patrick Balkany, conservative Mayor of Levallois-Perret, decided to improve flows in his area by designating a key through road a one-way route. His neighbour, socialist Mayor of Clichy-la-Garenne, Gilles Catoire, complained that the decision increased congestion in his area and declared the stretch of the road under his control one-way, but in the other direction. The stalemate was referred up the lengthy administrative chain to the Prefect of Paris for a ruling. Balkany eventually won out.

No excuses

Philadelphia City Councillor Angel Ortiz was discovered in 2001 to have been driving for the last 25 years without a licence, including 17 years when he was a municipal employee or council member. 'I kept trying to make time to get a new licence,' he claimed, 'but it seemed that something pressing always took precedence.' When police delved further, they found he also had 53 outstanding parking tickets.

WHILE CHAIRMAN OF a 1982 New Zealand parliamentary committee examining a toughening of the country's drink-drive laws, Junior Minister of Trade and Industry Keith Allen was convicted and fined NZ$145 – for drink-driving.

LIBERAL POLITICIAN BARONESS Seear failed to fulfil her engagement as a guest speaker at a British Institute of Management conference in 1979. A spokesman tactfully put it down to 'an unfortunate slip in transport'. The conference was entitled 'Can Women Manage?'

DATUK LEO MOGGIE, Malaysia's Telecommunications Minister, laid on an elaborate publicity event in 1986 to herald the country's advances in telephone technology and mark the signing up of the millionth subscriber. In front of the press corps, he dialled the lucky customer – and got a wrong number.

THE LEADER OF the Swedish Conservative Party, Ulf Adelsohn, was charged with illegally importing a cordless telephone in 1985. His claim not to know it was against the law rang a little hollow. The Act banning such phones had been passed and signed by him when Communications Minister.

BRITISH ENVIRONMENT MINISTER Alan Meale attended a conference in Peterborough in April 1999 to press the government's green credentials and speak about the environmental damage caused by excessive car travel. He turned up at the venue having been driven the two miles from the railway station in a stretch limo that did 17 miles to the gallon. Meale was soon lecturing the audience that 'the way we travel is damaging our towns, harming our countryside and already changing the climate of the planet'.

LABOUR DEPUTY PRIME Minister John Prescott got into the same hot water at the party conference in Bournemouth that September by using a three-car convoy to take him and wife Pauline the 300 yards from their hotel to the conference hall. He was due to deliver a speech on increasing the use of public transport. He initially, and in the media's eyes unchivalrously, blamed the journey on his wife's dislike of having her hair blown around by the sea breeze. He then cited security. The next day, he walked.

AN ISRAELI MOTORING magazine campaigning for a rise in the national speed limit exposed the driving practices of cabinet ministers to illustrate their 'do as we say, not as we do' habits. Reporters using a radar gun revealed that every minister using the main motorway between Tel Aviv and Jerusalem one morning in 1986 was travelling at least 11 mph over the 56 mph speed limit. Fastest, perhaps appropriately, was Moshe Shahal, Energy Minister, who clocked 86 mph, more than 50 per cent over the limit. Police Minister Haim Bar Lev was only slightly slower at 79 mph. The slowest, again perhaps appropriately, was Health Minister Mordechai Gur, who breezed along at 67 mph. On average, the cabinet travelled at 76 mph. It may have paid off. In 1993, Israel raised the limits on main freeways to 69 mph.

A SIMILAR ENDEAVOUR by French car magazine *Auto Plus* in October 2003 caught two French ministers speeding on their way to the official inauguration ceremony of the country's first speed cameras.

Transport Minister Gilles de Robien was clocked by a journalist's radar gun going 61 mph in the suburbs of Paris where the limit was 43 mph. Future President Nicolas Sarkozy, then Interior Minister, sped past at 64 mph. De Robien's office later did not contest the evidence, explaining that the minister was running late, and had to be present as he was presiding at the ceremony. In contrast, and perhaps indicative of his future trajectory, Sarkozy yielded no ground, getting his spokesman to tell the media that they were 'verifying the conditions under which the speeds were recorded'.

TWO YEARS AFTER its creation, Argentina's Ethics Office, established to set standards for integrity and honesty in government, was voted by a survey of electors as one of the most corrupt institutions in the country. Of 40 public institutions covered in the poll, the graft-busting office was seen as the fourth most corrupt body, after the country's trade unions, customs service and the judicial system.

Ignorance in motion

A satirical magazine in Washington, DC, shed an alarming light on the lack of worldly knowledge of newly elected members of the 1993 Congress. During apparently serious interviews, the reporter threw in a question about an entirely non-existent country. To the question, 'What should we be doing about the ethnic cleansing in Freedonia?' a large number of politicians rolled out very serious answers. Corrine Brown, a freshly elected Florida member, called the situation 'very, very sad', adding, 'We need to take action to assist the people.' James Talent (Missouri) opined, 'Anything we can do to use the good offices of the US Government to assist stopping the killing over there, we should do.' Jay Dickey from Arkansas took the easy route and blamed then-President Clinton for the debacle. Jan Inslee, a Washington state representative, confessed not to be familiar with Freedonia, but urged action nevertheless as, 'It's coming to the point now that turning a blind eye to it for the next ten years is not the answer.' Steve Buyer (Indiana) acknowledged, 'It's a different situation than the Middle East.' The magazine commented that politicians 'are asked a lot of dumb questions, and they are all used to supplying answers'.

IN MARCH 1993, Bucharest television conducted a similar survey of Romania's legislators. Reporters asked several members for their reactions to the high levels of hydrogen being found in drinking water. Most expressed themselves appalled and concerned. An opposition spokesman described the 'problem' as 'yet another proof of the government's incompetence'.

IN SEPTEMBER 2007, a New Zealand MP fell for a long-running hoax exposing the gullibility of MPs who jump on political bandwagons. She wrote to the country's health department demanding immediate action to curb use of the drug dihydrogen monoxide. Jacqui Dean, opposition National Party member for Otago, urged Health Minister Jim Anderton, in charge of government drug policy, to have his advisory committee on drugs take a view. He wrote back pointing out that the substance was…water.

ITALIAN POLITICIAN Tommaso Coletti provoked fury in 2006 when he used the infamous Auschwitz slogan 'Work makes you free' to promote local job centres in his area. The President of Chieti province in the south of the country, Coletti wrote, 'I don't remember where I read this phrase but it was one of those quotes that have an instant impact on you because they tell an immense truth.' His regional governor quickly apologised to the local Jewish community.

THE ART OF THE parliamentary question is ostensibly to elicit information one did not previously know. Jenny Tonge, Liberal Democrat MP and the party's spokesperson on international development, twice got more than she bargained for within the space of three weeks in 2001. On 15 November, she asked the International Development Minister, 'how many students from southern Sudan have been awarded Commonwealth scholarships in 2000–01?' She received the answer: 'Sudan is not a member of the Commonwealth and is not eligible for such awards.' On 5 December, she asked the Foreign Secretary 'what action the Government are taking to make the EU embargo on arms exports to the Great Lakes Region [in central Africa] legally binding' and received the answer, 'There is no EU arms embargo for the Great Lakes Region.'

WHEN THE HOUSE of Commons editors of *Hansard*, the daily verbatim record of parliamentary debates, analysed a week's worth of proceedings in July 1989 to discover what size of dictionary base they needed for new computerised shorthand machines, they discovered that MPs used only 12,000 words. The average vocabulary of an educated native English speaker is estimated to be about 24,000 to 30,000.

Desperate measures

In September 1994 Japhet Ekidor, Assistant Minister for Lands and Settlement in the Kenyan Government, bit off the ear of a political rival in a brawl during a public meeting in the rural district of Turkana. The pair were locked in a dispute over who should be the head of a local charity. Ekidor severed the ear of Danson Ekuam, the local MP, after Ekuam had bitten him on the arm. Despite calls for the minister's dismissal for embarrassing the government, it was the MP who ended up being charged with assault.

FRENCH TOURISM MINISTER Olivier Stirn resigned in disgrace in July 1990 after he used a novel way to ensure a high-profile policy summit he was organising was a successful event in the eyes of the media. The three-day *Dialogue* 2000, a centrepiece of the socialist government's programme, attracted a stream of government ministers on the first morning, but the audience dwindled dramatically in the afternoon. With two days still to go, and thinking to spare blushes, Stirn's aides hastily contacted an employment agency and secured 200 out-of-work actors to fill the seats. For the rest of the conference, the press witnessed a rapturous and intense audience hanging on every word of the party spokesmen. The ruse was only discovered at the end when a departing journalist was mistakenly handed an envelope with the agreed day's fee.

AS THE 2000 US Presidential election approached, Vice-President Al Gore established his future campaign credentials around concern for the environment. Even before the campaign officially opened, observers noted his visits to key states had taken on a suspiciously election-style feel. In July 1999, he went to New Hampshire, which happened to hold the crucial first primary election. His aides suggested he do a press call paddling a canoe on the picturesque waters of the Connecticut River that runs through the state. It later emerged that US Secret Service agents had insisted the local authorities release four billion gallons of water from an upriver dam to ensure that the VP's canoe did not get stuck on the riverbed. Water was at unprecedentedly low levels as the whole of New England was suffering its worst ever drought. By the time Gore performed his sail-past in front of the assembled press corps, the Connecticut was 10 inches higher, ensuring a safe passage. Within minutes of his departure, the water was shut off and the river sank back to a trickle.

SUSTAINING FAITH IN the country's leadership knows fewer bounds than in China, where gerontocracy is something of a tradition. The most memorable recent showing was the 1982 National People's Congress, where the chairman was a frail 85-year-old. Marshal Ye Jian-ying had to be helped to his seat by a group of nurses, one of whom stayed to guide him through his speech, prompting him several times by pointing out which words to read. Even less reassuring, another member of the leadership was reported as having been brought in in a wheelchair and given oxygen through nose-pipes throughout the session.

THE INDIAN GOVERNMENT tried unsuccessfully in 1992 to introduce a law that would prevent anyone being elected as an MP if they had more than two children. The move was aimed at promoting the country's birth-control programme, at a time when the population was approaching 900 million and growing at 17 million each year. 'Elected representatives must set an example,' the bill said. It failed to pass.

PERHAPS THE EPITOME of the concept of incapable politicians was French councillor André Isoardo, who committed suicide in October 1997. A member of the Provence Regional Council, he shot himself, having left a note to his family citing depression. According to the coroner's verdict, however, it took him five attempts to complete the task. The first four shots would not have caused unconsciousness, the coroner ruled. One bullet scraped his stomach and three others entered his wrist, groin and throat. The fatal shot was the fifth, fired into his mouth, which entered his brain.

Odd ideas

Conservative MP Jim Lester proposed after a bout of football hooliganism in 1982 that those convicted of offences should be branded for public humiliation by having their heads shaved Mohican-style and their hair painted red or blue.

INSTEAD OF CONCENTRATING on his constituents' more worldly concerns, maverick Nebraska State Senator Ernie Chambers embarked on a quixotic mission in September 2007 to sue God. Claiming he was doing so to reinforce the right under the US Constitution to bring any issue to court, however frivolous, Chambers lodged a claim in the state courts seeking an injunction preventing God – whom he cited as causing 'calamitous catastrophes resulting in the widespread death, destruction and terrorisation of millions upon millions of Earth's inhabitants' – from inflicting further 'grave harm' to his constituents. He lost the first hearing in the district court and his appeal was thrown out a year later on a technicality – that God having an address could not be served papers to be notified of the proceedings as required by the Constitution. Chambers announced that he disagreed with the ruling on the grounds that since the court acknowledged God's existence, and hence His omniscience, 'as God knows everything, God has notice of this lawsuit'. However, by the time the verdict came, Chambers had had to retire from the Senate in compliance with term-limits laws Nebraskans had – they might now think wisely – introduced a few years earlier.

The ultimate insult

A survey by *Paris Match* magazine in 1991 discovered that more than eight of out ten French people could not spell the name of their leader, François Mitterrand, almost ten years into his presidency.

PERHAPS THE MOST humbling discovery for the egocentric politician is the realisation that people do not take much notice of them. A 1982 experiment by West Germany's reputable Emnid Institute tested the knowledge of the electorate with spectacular results. Asking respondents to rank the popularity of a list of current cabinet ministers, an entirely fictitious minister whom the survey had invented for the exercise came in sixth. 'Minister Meyers' beat a number of German heavyweights including both the Ministers of Defence and Interior.

IT IS ONE thing not to be recognised by the common people; another when it is one's own staff. Hungary's new Defence Minister, Janos Szabo, suffered that indignity in 1998 when he arrived to preside over an officers' inauguration ceremony. Guards on the gate of the army base refused to allow him in as no one recognised him. Szabo later issued photographs of himself to every military base in the country, with orders to put them up at gates and in duty officers' rooms.

From the history books

The most durable elected politician of all time is believed to be József Madarász, who has the longest span of service, sitting across 83 years. He was a member of the Hungarian Parliament, initially between 1832 and 1836 and again between 1848 and 1850, but then continuously after 1861 until his death in 1915.

THE LONGEST CONTINUOUSLY SERVING elected national politician is believed to be Charles Pelham Villiers, who sat in the British House of Commons for 63 years and 6 days until his death in January 1898, aged 96.

LORD PALMERSTON HOLDS the all-time record in British politics for ministerial service – 48 years, including War Secretary for an unbroken 18 years, three times as Foreign Secretary (16 years), once as Home Secretary (2 years) and twice as Prime Minister (over 9 years). He combined unparalleled energy for work with a fearsome temper that was always on the point of boiling over into a rupture with his cabinet colleagues. He was renowned for regularly threatening to leave the government by firing off a resignation letter to the Prime Minister of the day. He did so by employing a lame war veteran as messenger, who would be despatched across the quadrangle of the Ministry towards Downing Street. Invariably, his temper cooled as soon as the messenger had left, so he retained the services of a second (able-bodied) valet, among whose duties was to head off in pursuit of the first and overtake the letter-bearer before he had chance to leave the precincts.

FOR ALL THAT was to come, Palmerston's entry into politics was distinctly unusual. He secured his place in the House of Commons in 1807 at the fourth attempt after twice failing to get elected for Cambridge University while studying for his MA and, in between, at Horsham. Despite his failure, he had obtained, through contacts, a government appointment as a Junior Lord of the Admiralty. It was imperative he got a seat, and a deal was stitched up with the landowner who controlled his father's old seat at Newport on the Isle of Wight. Sir Leonard Holmes agreed to let Palmerston stand on the condition – thought to be unique in British political history – that in order to avoid him building up a local following which might threaten Holmes' power base, Palmerston was forbidden from ever setting foot in the constituency he represented.

CONSERVATIVE MEMBER Christopher Sykes represented three Yorkshire constituencies in his 27-year parliamentary career dating from 1865 to 1892. In all that time, he spoke only six times, and asked three questions.

DESPITE BEING BORN with atrophied arms and legs, Arthur Kavanagh, the 'Limbless Wonder', was elected MP for County Wexford in 1866 and served in the House of Commons for 14 years until 1880. Unique among Members; he is the only MP to have been permitted to vote without getting up from his seat to process through the division lobby.

LORD STANHOPE, the last-but-one holder of the office of First Lord of the Treasury before it became recognised as Prime Minister, died after making a vehement speech in the House of Lords in 1721 defending himself against allegations surrounding the handling of the South Sea Bubble financial scandal. He apparently burst a blood vessel in his head, retired home and died the next day.

ROBERT WALPOLE, who is regarded as our first Prime Minister, was also implicated in the South Sea Bubble scandal. He is thought to have indulged in insider-trading, selling his shares (having made a 1,000 per cent profit) just before the bubble burst in 1720. Walpole had a track record for skulduggery. He had been convicted of corruption while Secretary at War a decade before and even while Chancellor of the Exchequer he traded in contraband goods from the Continent. He became famed for his observation that 'every man has his price'. He claimed to one parliamentary colleague during a debate, 'I know the price of every man in this House except three.' It was with some irony that he became Prime Minister as a result of the Bubble affair, with the task of sorting out the national mess from which he had so handsomely profited.

THE MARQUESS OF SALISBURY was so unconcerned about his appearance that when he was in Monaco recovering from illness in the summer of 1886, he was turned away from the casino at Monte Carlo for being too scruffy. He had just ceased being Prime Minister at the time.

GEORGES CLEMENCEAU, one of France's greatest politicians, who had a 40 year career in Parliament and served twice as Prime Minister – between 1906 and 1909 and again during the crisis of the First World War – was paranoid about being caught unprepared. He took to the habit over decades of sleeping fully dressed, replete with shoes and sometimes even gloves. On waking each morning, he would promptly change.

WITH SHADES OF modern PR concerns (see Nicolas Sarkozy's image issues in Chapter 6), Italian dictator Mussolini compensated for his short stature by standing on hidden stools to make speeches, and sitting in a specially created higher chair at meetings to bring him up to the same level as others. Photographers were strictly forbidden from disclosing the aids. When first in power, he had taken to wearing a bowler hat, until his advisers told him that the Anglo-Saxon press was remarking on the image's similarities with 'the fat one' of the comic duo Laurel and Hardy.

IN SEPTEMBER 1942, as the tide of the Second World War turned against the Fascist powers in Europe, with Italian troops facing acute shortages of ammunition, uniforms and supplies, and the country 10 months away from being invaded by the Allies, Mussolini approved the expenditure of several million pounds to improve the winter sports facilities at Cortina, in the hope that he might win the right to host the first post-war Winter Olympics.

BEING THE VANGUARD of the Marxist revolution, champion of workers' power and proponent of social equality did not stop Lenin from accumulating nine Rolls-Royces. According to the company, Lenin ordered and received a unique model – one fitted with tank-like tracks at the rear and skis at the front which allowed him to get about in the frozen Russian winters. The explanation given at the time that he was simply using vehicles that had been requisitioned from the Tsar was entirely untrue. Lenin employed a buyer in London to purchase all his cars new.

THE FAMOUS NASAL tone that helped political rabble-rouser and traitor William Joyce ('Lord Haw-Haw') establish the instantly recognisable sneer which became the hallmark of his wartime broadcasts of Nazi propaganda came from a childhood fight at his school that landed him with a broken nose. He did not report the injury and delay in treatment left him with permanent damage, and the tone. According to his biographer, his experience at the same school provided prophetic insights into his future treachery. He was once sent off in a rugby match for not knowing which side he was on.

TRIALS AND ERRORS – ELECTIONS

The democratic process requires regular elections. Attention usually focuses on judging the extent to which they are free and fair. Our interest here lies a step or two beyond the norm. Even in free and fair contests, the startlingly unusual is more common than you would think. An election is the warlike moment when the human ambition for elected office is forced to place itself at the mercy of the vagaries of the common people, all armed with their fragment of the decision – their vote. How those two forces play off each other is the subject of this chapter. We must begin, however, where any review of electoral oddity must start – with the bizarre lengths to which autocrats have gone to mangle the process in order to show outwardly that they are playing the democratic game.

Free and fair?

The greatest effort to try to look proper was made by communist Albania. In its 1982 general election, official results claimed that every one of the country's 1,627,968 eligible voters had cast their ballots. Support for the ruling regime was not universal, however. A spokesman told news agencies that 'eight ballots were found invalid and one elector voted against'.

Things had clearly improved five years later. The official returns for the February 1987 election showed that only one invalid vote had been counted out of more than 1,800,000 ballots. There were no negative votes.

AS THE WEST MOBILISED itself for invasion in the autumn of 2002, Iraq's Saddam Hussein held a referendum on his leadership. On 15 October, in an atmosphere of hysteria across the country, 11 million voters were encouraged to exceed the vote of support they had given him in the last plebiscite seven years earlier when 99.96 per cent approved of him continuing in office.

Amid the nationalist fervour being whipped up by the impending hostilities with the West, there were few observances of normal electoral niceties. The absence of polling booths – voters marked their ballots openly in front of the watchful eyes of the security forces – was portrayed by state media as symbolic of the transparency of the vote. Other regulations appeared relaxed. A British journalist witnessed a six-year-old boy cast his vote in Saddam's home town of Tikrit 'amid much acclaim'.

When the government announced the result later the next day, Vice-President Izzat Ibrahim declared that every single one of the 11,445,638 Iraqis on the electoral roll had cast their vote, and every single one had voted in favour of Saddam Hussein's continued rule.

Observers noted that the victory was the first unanimous vote in electoral history. North Korea's Kim Il-sung had claimed a 100 per cent vote in 1962, but even he had not claimed a 100 per cent turnout. Ibrahim told Western reporters the referendum 'was a unique manifestation of democracy…superior to all other forms of democracy, even [that of] countries which are besieging Iraq and trying to suffocate it'.

SIMILAR PROBLEMS AFFLICTED Philippines President Ferdinand Marcos' last election in February 1986. Reports before polling day indicated massive fraud in the registration of voters. One small suburban house in the capital, Manila, was recorded as having 204 people living in it. Observers mused on the apparent overcrowding, suggesting that some ought to move next door where only 147 appeared to live. A remote jungle town returned a voting list that was two and a half times the size of its last known population. Not surprisingly, Marcos officially won the election, but the corruption was so transparent that even he was forced to admit 'irregularities'. He left the country within a week of the results for exile in the United States.

EXAGGERATING THE LEVEL of support at political rallies during election campaigns is a tried-and-tested tactic. When the Mexican National Action Party claimed a turnout of 100,000 for a rally in the national elections in 1988, an opposition newspaper contested the estimate, reporting that barely 20,000 had taken part. To prove his point, the editor of El Norte blew up a photograph of the rally and, under the watchful eye of a lawyer, got his staff to stick a pin into the head of every attendee. At the end of the exercise, the issue was resolved with 11,153 pins. The paper published its result the following day – adding to the effect by sarcastically presenting the findings as being a correction to its own original overestimate.

The dead are returned

State Senator John Wilson was re-elected in Austin, Texas, in 1982 despite having died 44 days before polling day. He won 66 per cent of the vote.

POPULAR PATSY MINK won her seat for the 14th consecutive time in the House of Representatives in Hawaii in 2002, even though she had died five weeks before the election. She won an impressive 56 per cent of the vote against three other candidates.

THE PRESTIGIOUS New York Times urged voters in primary elections for Congress in 1992 to vote for a dead candidate. Ted Weiss, a long-serving Democratic politician in Manhattan's West Side, had died the day before the poll. The paper urged the electorate not to allow that to let in his only opponent, a right-wing extremist. The locals dutifully and overwhelmingly did so, giving the dead man 54,168 votes to his rival's measly 7,560.

VILLAGERS IN THE Romanian hamlet of Voinesti re-elected Neculai Ivascu as their mayor in June 2008 even though he had died just after voting began. Leader since 1990, he prevailed over the living candidate by 23 votes. One elector told reporters, 'I know he died, but I don't want change.' The elections authority later awarded the post to his rival by default.

HARRY STONEBRAKER WAS re-elected for his fourth term as mayor of the small community of Winfield, Missouri, in April 2009 having died a month before polling day. Astonishingly, he won by a landslide with 90 per cent of the vote.

CARL GEARY WAS elected Mayor of Tracy City, a community of 1,600 near Chattanooga, Tennessee, in April 2010 having died of a heart attack at the start of the campaign. He trounced his only rival, winning over three-quarters of the vote. Barbara Brock, who had campaigned on a platform of beautifying the city, showed less than fulsome grace in defeat, bewailing the fact that the council would be run by someone 'pushing up the daisies instead of planting them'. A local restaurateur offered a confirmatory insight into the electorate's view of her: 'I knew he was deceased, but we wanted someone other than her.'

SUCH EVENTS DO not just happen for minor office in out of the way places. Even at a national level, dead candidates can succeed. In the 2000 national election, former Missouri Governor Mel Carnahan won his campaign to sit in the US Senate for his state despite having been killed in an air crash three weeks before election day. He won by a 2 per cent margin. His wife temporarily took the seat, before losing a year later.

SHERMAN BLOCK SECURED more than a third of the vote in the election for Los Angeles County Sheriff in 1998 even though he had died five days before polling day. He had held the post for 17 years and had been expected to win again comfortably, despite his chronic illness that required him to undergo dialysis three times a week. He even managed to vote for himself by sending in a postal ballot before his death. Block supporters continued his campaign despite his death in the closing days of the election, reasoning that if the dead man was elected the Sheriff Office's Board of Supervisors would have to chose the new sheriff rather than the post going to his opponent. An incredible 629,289 Los Angeles residents turned out to vote for the dead candidate, Block winning 39 per cent of the poll.

'I want to be elected'

Ilona Staller, a 35-year-old Hungarian-born porn actress, made headlines in Italy's 1987 general election when she was elected as a Radical Party MP. She became notorious for stripping off in public, once leading a demonstration topless to persuade sailors about to be despatched on a controversial NATO mission to the Arabian Gulf to mutiny and make love instead. One account sonorously described her election campaign: 'Her main argument has been to take off her clothes and occasionally to let voters fondle her breasts. This seems to have restored the Italian faith in politics, and gained her a respectable number of votes.'

After her election success, she became an active member of the Defence Committee, but missed a crucial debate on the Gulf deployment because she was making a pornographic film. She also offered to have sex with Saddam Hussein in 1991 if he agreed to release Western hostages he was holding as Allied forces readied for the Gulf War. 'I would do it holding my nose and closing my eyes,' she said, 'but I would do it for peace.' She completed a full term and retired from politics in 1992. She attempted a revival in 2002 when she stood for mayor in the northern town of Monza, but won only 1.5 per cent of the vote.

HER MANTLE WAS temporarily taken up by 31-year-old fellow porn star Moana Pozzi for the 1992 campaign. She founded the Party of Love, one of 116 parties competing (others included the Bird Shooting Hunters' Party, the Fast Lane Drivers' Party, the Housewives' Party and three campaigning for pensioners' rights). Pozzi's merits were described by Italy's leading journalist. 'At the end of the day, Moana is a lot less obscene when naked than many gentlemen who are well-dressed.' Her party HQ in Rome collected funds by charging £5 to any voter who wanted to watch their leader remove all her clothes. Regrettably for many, the party failed to win any seats, and won less than 1 per cent of the vote.

SO MANY CELEBRITIES from the world of arts and sports became candidates in the 1992 election that national broadcaster RAI was forced to cancel the airing of dozens of events and popular shows to comply with Italy's electoral law that forbade candidates from appearing on state television except during strictly allotted party political broadcasts. A marathon was pulled because an Olympic gold medal winner who was standing was taking part. Thousands complained at the last-minute cancellation of a boxing match featuring national hero Francesco Damiani, a former world heavyweight champion and a candidate for the opposition Republican Party. An Italian tennis star, Paolo Cane, had his Davis Cup tie blacked out, and films starring the popular actor Gian-Maria Volonte had the plug pulled without warning when he announced his candidature for the former Communist Party. Commentators described the strict interpretation of the rules as 'grotesque'.

SILVIO BERLUSCONI, ITALY'S Prime Minister between 2001 and 2006 and again since 2008, became a byword for scandal and sexual sleaze. The long-standing national passion for turning elections into beauty contests reached its apogee under the septuagenarian leader. Forming his government on re-taking power in 2008, he attracted publicity for appointing Mara Carfagna, a former topless model, as his Minister for Equal Opportunities. She quickly became dubbed 'the world's sexiest minister'. For the 2009 elections to the European Parliament, he nominated a bevy of attractive young women as candidates for his centre-right People of Freedom Party. They included a TV weather girl and nightclub hostess and an actress, but his plans were scotched when Berlusconi's long-suffering wife publicly derided them as 'shameless trash for the entertainment of the emperor'.

A year later, with Berlusconi separated and facing divorce proceedings amid a prostitute scandal, the showgirls resurfaced as candidates for the party's regional election campaign in March 2010. By then he had added Nicole Minetti, a 25-year-old dental hygienist whom he had met when having his teeth repaired after an assault during a rally, Graziana Capone, a sultry model nicknamed the 'Angelina Jolie of Puglia', and Francesca Provetti, a Miss Italy finalist. Despite the controversies, Berlusconi's party surprised pundits by improving its standings on polling day.

TAIWANESE ELECTIONS HAVE acquired a reputation for wackiness and unorthodox campaign methods since repressive one-party government ended on the island in 1987. Chen Shui-bian, the opposition victor in the 2000 Presidential election, used his nationwide chain of clothes stores to promote his image during the campaign. Every item he sold bore his nickname. He also sold small plastic dolls of himself dressed in a range of characters. The most popular were said to be Chen dressed as a long-haired, bandana-wearing Rambo muscleman and as a punk rocker with spiky green hair.

The trend had been set by the ruling party, which in local polls the previous year had dressed 75-year-old President Lee Teng-hui in various outfits as he campaigned around the country. At one rally he appeared in a *Star Trek* uniform; at others as King Arthur, a tribal chieftain and as a farmer, complete with live water buffaloes.

In 1992, the newly founded Labour Party tried to win hearts and minds by employing the talents of Hsu Hsiao-tan, a 30-year-old nude model, for the seat in the southern city of Kaoshiung. Her talents were bountifully expressed. Cited in an academic review of political development in Taiwan as 'a rather unorthodox strategy', Hsu spent most of her campaign baring her breasts, jumping naked into polluted rivers and streaking through municipal rubbish dumps. 'My body is a political weapon. My breasts are nuclear warheads,' she declared. She amassed over 32,000 votes and fell only 108 short of getting elected.

THE BEER LOVERS' Party won nearly 3 per cent of the vote in the Polish general election of 1991, and captured 16 seats in the 460-seat national Parliament. They remained there until the 1993 elections, when they all lost their seats.

TO COUNTER PERCEIVED right-wing, male chauvinism in Polish politics, a group of liberal females formed the Women's Party to fight the October 2007 general election. As part of their campaign to confront typical male attitudes to women, they chose the curious tactic of announcing their formation by having seven of their members pose naked behind a placard reading 'Everything for the future...and nothing to hide' that also covered their modesties. Not only did the poster cause outrage among the deeply conservative Catholic establishment, most observers concluded that it only reinforced Polish men's attitudes to the position of women. The party won just 0.28 per cent of the vote and failed to secure a single seat.

IN IRELAND'S 1989 general election, the opposition Fine Gael party campaigned on a platform of not making irresponsible high-spending promises. One high-profile environmental pledge was to make all the country's buses run on lead-free fuel. It was later pointed out that, as they ran on diesel, they already did.

TO OVERCOME NEW campaign spending limits introduced for India's 1996 general election, the People's Party in Bihar released thousands of native green parrots across the state each of which had been trained to chant the party's election slogan.

IN 1994, DANES elected Jacob Haugaard, a comedian styling himself the head of the Union of Conscientiously Work-Shy Elements. Although his campaign pledges included promises of better weather, shorter queues in supermarkets and increased tailwind for bicycle lanes, he garnered over 23,000 votes, enough for a seat in the national Parliament. He served his full four-year term.

FINNISH MP Jyrki Kasvi, campaigning for re-election for the Green League in 2007, translated his website into Klingon, the fictional *Star Trek* language, apparently as a means of showing his connections to the interests of young people. He successfully retained his seat.

IN MAY 1998, electors in Ashburton, Devon, elected Alan Hope, representing the Official Monster Raving Loony Party, as chairman of the town council and their mayor.

ASPIRING TO BE as successful in politics as he had been in the television business, Los Angeles game show producer Howard Felsher launched his campaign for a seat in Congress in 1982 by outlining his views on juvenile crime. He proposed that all teenagers should be jailed before they have a chance to commit a crime. His scheme would introduce a three-day mandatory jail sentence for all high-school students to show them 'the realities of modern living'. The evidence base for his idea was unapologetically simple: 'Nothing has worked in 2,000 years, so we should try something new.' He lost in the first round of voting, and disappeared back into political oblivion.

WHEN A CONTROVERSIAL hypnotist and faith healer, Anatoly Kashpirovsky, who had become a national sensation for his televised mass-healing events, stood in Russia's December 1993 election, he was forbidden by officials from canvassing in his constituency for fear he would use his powers to unduly influence electors. He had to run his campaign entirely from abroad. He based himself in the United States and, astonishingly, won. He sat in Parliament for two years until leaving permanently for America in 1995.

MUSIKARI KOMBO, a Kenyan opposition MP, was unseated by the country's High Court in November 1994 for having used witchcraft to win votes in his victory in the 1992 general election. Kombo, who won the Webuye constituency in the west of the country, had paid 70,000 shillings (about £1,000) to a local witchdoctor to conduct a ceremony four days before the election, involving the killing of a ram and the aspiring candidate sitting in its intestines dressed only in underpants.

The ejection turned out to be only a temporary setback. He was back in the seat in 1997 and eventually became a minister during another ten years in Parliament.

THE NARROW LOSER in Romania's Presidential election in December 2009 blamed the malignant effect of a government-sponsored mind controller as the cause of his defeat. Opposition candidate Mircea Geoana, who lost by just 70,000 votes in a 10 million turnout, called for the result to be nullified after television footage showed a shadowy character dogging him at various campaign visits. Identifying him as Aliodor Manolea, a well-known parapsychologist, journalists then turned up multiple examples of his presence at key Geoana rallies, lurking unobtrusively in the background and fixing the candidate with a menacing stare. They also noticed that Manolea was almost permanently in the entourage of the incumbent President, Traian Basescu, and was with him when he celebrated his narrow victory. Geoana's wife publicly claimed that her husband had been hexed by the mystic, who had launched 'negative energy attacks' on him. The President's office issued official statements denying the parapsychologist had been part of the official campaign, but – a point seized on by conspiracy theorists – was unable to explain why he had appeared so often in the strictly controlled crowds around the President.

LOCAL ELECTIONS IN Italy in 2006 produced a bizarre campaign for mayor and council in the Piedmontese village of Bergolo. The population of just 63 registered voters had 40 candidates to choose from.

DEAD MAN WINS ELECTION

SOMERSET MAN Chris Byrne was elected to nine different councils in May 2007 without having a single vote cast for him. As the only candidate in each of the nine seats, he did not require any voter actually to cast a ballot in his favour. He was nominated for positions on Axbridge Town Council, parish councils for Cheddar, Rooksbridge, Compton Bishop, Weare, Banwell and Draycott, as well as two more on Sedgmoor District Council. He claimed he would not be overstretched in his duties, saying, 'I am very organised.'

So far...so near

An Indian businessmen, named only as K. Padmarajan, secured the unenviable title of the world's least successful politician in April 2001 when he stood for a seat in the southern state of Tamil Nadu, having failed in 44 previous attempts at election. He lost. Recognised by the Indian edition of the *Guinness Book of Records*, he has continued his efforts unrelentingly. When last heard of, in November 2009, he had just registered for a state by-election, his 103rd election contest. He is not thought to have won.

OLEH PERKOV, WHO failed in his bid to become mayor of the Ukrainian city of Zaporizhia in June 2003, castrated himself after receiving fewer than a hundred votes in the election. The head of a local research institute, Perkov told local press that he had cut off his testicles because of the 'humiliating defeat'. He was reported to be in a stable condition after doctors had operated to repair the damage.

HERBERT CONNOLLY CAMPAIGNED to the last moment in his 1988 effort to retain his seat on the Massachusetts Governor's Council. He lost track of time and arrived to cast his own vote 15 minutes after his polling station had closed. He polled 14,715 votes to his opponent's 14,716, and thus lost by his own single uncast vote.

TRIALS AND ERRORS -- ELECTIONS

DOMINIC VOLPE, CAMPAIGNING in 2007 to be a legislator for Westchester County, Virginia, lost critical ground a few days before polling day when his team inadvertently dialled automated telephone calls to thousands of residents soliciting their vote – at 2am. It may have cost him dear indeed. He lost the election by 4,394 votes to 4,302, a margin of just 92.

IN JUNE 2004, Noel Carino was formally declared the winner of a tightly contested 2001 general election seat in the Philippines' lower house, the House of Representatives. Legal challenges on questionable ballots had taken nearly three years to settle, including his opponent appealing all the way to the country's Supreme Court. The court finally pronounced Carino the winner two days before Parliament ended its session. He was sworn in the next day, to serve a solitary day as elected representative before the House was dissolved for the next elections. 'Better late than never,' the House Speaker was reported to have told him.

BRIAN DONOHOE, LABOUR MP for the Ayrshire constituency of Cunninghame South, set an unenviable record in the wake of Tony Blair's landslide election victory in Britain in 1997 by being appointed a minister for all of eight seconds. He received what every backbencher dreams of, the telephone call from No. 10 informing him that he had been appointed as Minister of State for Agriculture. He was asked to hold the line in readiness for the Prime Minister. He recounted shortly after: 'They put me through to the Prime Minister. He then obviously recognised that there was a mistake and somebody pulled the plug.' Donohoe rang back, to be told that it had been a wrong number. No. 10 later announced the appointment of Bernard Donoughue to the post. As a Scot, Brian Donohoe reflected that it had been his accent that had most likely given away instantly to the PM that his team had rung the wrong man.

Scary contests

ONE OF THE MOST entertaining elections of recent years was the battle in 2000 for the Berkeley County seat in the South Carolina House of Representatives. It pitched sitting member Mrs Shirley Hinson against her husband of 32 years, James. The couple were gripped in a bitter divorce battle, and the campaign descended into little more than a public marital row. Mr Hinson used the campaign to pour out his divorce case. He accused his wife of having an affair with another state politician. He had earlier been charged by police with making death threats to the person cited. Mrs H. vehemently denied any romantic involvement. The couple's divorce papers were widely, and anonymously, faxed to the local press and radio stations. Campaign broadcasts ostensibly to the electorate turned into personal vendettas. Mrs Hinson accused her opponent of being 'a self-serving, mean, vindictive individual who will do anything to get a result'. He retaliated by warning the voters, 'You have to be very careful of a pretty face.'

Mrs Hinson won the contest with a 42 per cent vote to his 32 per cent. Four years later she married the politician with whom she had denied having the affair.

WILLIAM LEVINGER, RUNNING as the Republican nominee for election to the US House of Representatives in Idaho in 1996, spent most of the final six weeks of his campaign holed up in a state mental institution after spectacularly imploding during a television interview. For reasons only he himself could know, halfway through the interview he propositioned the female reporter, offering her $5,000 if she would kiss him on camera. He then began stripping off his clothes. The station cut the broadcast when he was down to his underpants. Despite the restrictive circumstances of his last weeks of electioneering, he still managed to win 32 per cent of the vote on polling day.

IN TAIWAN'S 2001 general election, Yen Ching-piao, a former council head from the central city of Tai-chung, won a seat despite being in jail for the entire campaign. Yen was in the middle of an appeal against his conviction for corruption, attempted murder and illegal possession of firearms, for which he had been sentenced to 20 years behind bars. He would have to vacate his seat if the sentence was upheld. He need not have worried about the pace of Taiwanese justice. Eight years later, it was reported that the appeal was still before the courts.

IN APRIL 2010, Andrew Romanoff, the Democratic candidate campaigning for a Senate seat in Colorado, admitted having doctored a photograph of one of his rallies posted on his website by adding black and Latino supporters to the crowd to appear prominently alongside him. Romanoff, who is white, claimed that the image was modified 'to improve the illustration', calling any other interpretation – like deceiving voters about the level of support he had from minorities – 'outrageous and reprehensible'. He initially stuck to this defence. Within 48 hours he had pulled the picture.

ED MATTS, the Conservative candidate for Dorset South in the 2005 general election, was found to have doctored an old photograph of himself with leading Tory Ann Widdecombe, and reversed the messages to make him look tough on migrants and appeal to the current anti-immigration sentiment of his party's campaign. The original shot showed Matts and Widdecombe campaigning on behalf of a Malawian asylum-seeking family. Looking concerned and not a little pious, the pair carried placards with a photograph of the woman and her four children along with a plea to 'let them stay'. The new photograph showed the pair still as concerned, but with placards reading 'Controlled Immigration' and 'Not Chaos and Inhumanity'. Matts apologised for the deception. He failed to win the seat.

JACOB REES-MOGG, the Conservative prospective candidate for North East Somerset, was revealed to have run a publicity campaign calling for 'more honesty' in politics in 2009 by using a leaflet with a faked photograph. The handout which purported to show him talking with 'a woman in the village of Midsomer Norton', turned out to show him with a member of staff from his own finance company posing as the concerned citizen. The leaflet piously told readers how 'Jacob Rees-Mogg believes it is time to be honest with North Somerset residents.' Despite the exposé, Rees-Mogg increased his party's majority when he won the constituency in the 2010 general election.

IN JULY 2003, Norway repealed its law that had banned intoxicated persons from voting in elections.

All for nothing

After months of energetic campaigning in the 2000 election to the city council of Southwest Ranches, a suburb of Fort Lauderdale, Florida, a candidate spent his last week begging the electorate not to vote for him. Doug Couvertier, a fire chief in nearby Miami-Dade County, signed up for the election unaware that the rules of Miami-Dade forbade County employees from running for public office unless they took leave of absence and resigned if they won. 'If I win, I'll be fired from my job,' he told reporters. 'In three more years, I can retire.' When he realised his dilemma, and was also told that it was too late to take his name off the ballot paper, the election took on a bizarre hue as friends rallied round to dissuade electors from voting for him. Vince Falletta, running for mayor, promised, 'I'll make every effort to see that he's not elected, so his job and pension won't be jeopardised.' In the event, Couvertier lost by a landslide. He got just 74 votes of the 1,700 cast.

PAUL HEROLD HAD a narrower escape in the city council election for the Minneapolis suburb of Blain in 2006. After he had put himself forward for election, and after the deadline had passed for withdrawals, he had got a new job which would leave him too busy for councillor duties. He spent the final weeks of the campaign urging people not to vote for him. In the event he succeeded in losing, but despite his pleas he still secured 35 per cent of the vote in the two-horse race.

ORGANISERS OF THE 2010 election for County Court Judge in Galveston, Texas, created a bureaucratic nightmare for candidates when they mistakenly set the deadline for nominations to come after the state's legal deadline for withdrawing them. When Trey Dibrell, a judge for 16 years, changed his mind about wanting to stand again and decided to retract his name from the ballot in early January, he was told that the deadline for being able to do so had already passed, even though there were still six days to go before the closing date for nominations. He began a 'don't vote for me' campaign before taking his case to the courts. A judge granted him his wish to have his name deleted.

JOE SELLE, RUNNING unopposed in April 2007 for re-election to his seat on the city council of Missouri City, Missouri (which despite its grand name is a small hamlet of 300), failed to get any votes at all. He did not even vote for himself as he had forgotten when election day was. So apparently had all the other 34 people registered to vote in his district. The potential awkwardness of a 'no result' was solved by the city's legal adviser confirming that under the city's charter, incumbents kept their seats unless another person was elected in their place. The thrill of small-town politics was clearly stronger in Selle's neighbouring district: the turnout there was two.

SIMILAR PROBLEMS AFFECTED the race for mayor and council in the North Dakota community of Pillsbury (population: 11) in 2008 when the whole town either forgot or was too busy to vote. It could have been because current mayor Darrel Brudevold was standing unopposed, and his wife and another councillor also had no opponents for their two alderman seats, but not one single elector managed to cast their ballot. 'We usually get half a dozen making it to the polls,' said Brudevold. He had planned to vote but he had crops to tend. His wife, who doubled as postmistress and local beauty salon owner, was also too busy to get to the polling station. Under the rules, incumbents could stay in post until the next election.

STATE LAW IN Mississippi was different back in 1991. Denny James was the only candidate in one ward in elections for the town council of Centerville. At counting time it emerged that not a single person had voted, not even the candidate himself. As the law required a candidate to obtain at least one vote before they could be elected, a re-run had to be called. He got 45 the next time.

A BY-ELECTION for a seat on the Oxfordshire Parish Council for Shenington with Alkerton proceeded in March 2008 at the cost of £800 even though there was only one candidate standing. The local district council responsible for organising the election said it had no legal power to declare the election a victory for Emma Jane Philcox, the solitary nominee after her only rival had pulled out at the last minute. So the polling station opened as normal, replete with tellers and a returning officer. Ms Philcox duly romped home, with all legal niceties duly observed.

MUNICIPAL ELECTIONS FOR mayor and a five-seat council for the small town of Littleton, West Virginia, proceeded according to the rule book in June 2004 even though there were no candidates for any of the positions. Not one of the 217 residents was willing to be considered for mayor or councillor. For the 'vote' to be technically legal, the polls had nevertheless to be open all day.

The incumbent mayor, elected by just 20 people in 2002, was reported to be planning to file for the town's charter to be wound up.

SIMILAR PROBLEMS CONFRONTED the parish council by-election in Bulford, Wiltshire, in July 1997. Setting what was believed to be an unprecedented UK record for apathy, not a single vote was cast at one of the two polling stations set up for the vote. Designed to serve a 2,800-strong military barracks, no one cast a ballot, despite the station being open for 13 hours. Fortunately, 163 of the other 2,300 voters in Bulford village proper did make it to the other one.

BERNIE WALSH, A LEFT-WING candidate standing in the Dovecote ward for Liverpool City Council in 1999, suffered the indignity of not receiving a single vote. He appears to have forgotten to cast his own vote in his favour, and even failed to get the votes of any of the 10 supporters who had been required to nominate him.

Animated contests

The 400 residents of the Californian town of Sunol elected Bosco, an eight-year-old Rottweiler-Labrador cross, as their mayor in 1981. He beat two human candidates for the post. He remained mayor unbeaten for 13 years until he died. In 2008, a bronze statue of the dog was unveiled and dedicated in the main street. It was a rather more fitting memorial than the one that had been installed when a new restaurant named *Bosco's Bones and Brew* opened in 1999. Its owner chose to memorialise the former mayor with a specially engineered life-size model of the dog planted on the bar. To draw a pint, the bartender lifted the dog's left rear leg and the beer came out from…you can guess where.

THE REMOTE WESTERN Texas border town of Lajitas (population 100) elected a goat as their mayor in 1986. Clay Henry started off a veritable dynasty as, when he died in 1992, one of his offspring succeeded him in the post, to be followed by Clay Henry III. All became icons locally for their beer-drinking exploits, mainly exhibited for tourists. Clay Henry Snr lived to 23, and then spent years on display at the local store, stuffed and with a beer bottle in his mouth. By the time it came to the third incumbent, rivalry had developed. Clay Henry III only won in 2000 after a battle against a dog called Buster and a wooden Indian statue.

Unusual outcomes

Angela Tuttle found herself elected Constable in Hancock County, Tennessee, in 2008 merely because she turned up to vote. There were no candidates on the ballot, and thus her write-in vote for herself carried the election.

ROSAMUND ROCYN-JONES, a candidate for a seat on the Grosmont Village Council in local elections in Wales in 1983, found herself elected even though she lost the contest. After a night of four recounts and 'two double-checks' showed she and her opponent were tied, the returning officer got them to draw lots. Rocyn-Jones' opponent, Trevor Sayce-Davies, picked the winning slip of paper, but the returning officer, who later blamed lack of sleep, then announced the wrong victor. No one else at the count apparently noticed the mistake. Lawyers advised that technically the losing Mrs Rocyn-Jones was the lawful councillor. It took a court case in front of two senior judges two months later to correct the mistake.

CONFUSION REIGNED IN the 1994 European Parliament election for Devon and East Plymouth when maverick Richard Huggett stood as a 'Literal Democrat'. Although he issued no election literature and did not campaign, he managed to poll 10,203 votes. The mainstream Liberal Democrats, who were beaten by the Conservatives by just 700 votes, claimed that thousands of their voters had been confused by the name into voting for Huggett by mistake. Six months later, an election court upheld the result, ruling there was nothing unlawful in the practice. It declared that there was no requirement that the descriptions of political parties 'be true, fair or not confusing'.

Changes to Britain's electoral law in 1998 now prevent candidates from assuming potentially confusing party names.

THE CONCERN FOR accuracy over party identification came back to bite the Liberal Democrats in the 2002 local elections when an error over naming blew their chances of capturing Harrow Council. Of the 63 Lib Dem candidates for the borough, 60 put down the wrong party name on their nomination papers. They called themselves the 'Liberal Democrat Focus Team' instead of the 'Liberal Democrats', the name registered with the council. In accordance with the 1998 Act that they had fought to get on to the statute books, they were all duly disqualified.

AN OBSCURE NEW party managed to win a seat in Paraguay's national elections in May 1998 by calling itself the 'Partido Blanco' (White Party). It achieved most of its 35,000 votes because of alleged confusion among those in the electorate who intended to cast 'blank' votes, a peculiar provision of Paraguayan procedure allowing electors to register a 'none-of-the above' choice. Analysts feared that many had stamped the White Party's box instead of the 'blank vote' option. The ruse appeared to have capitalised on a country where 60 per cent of the population were classified as functionally illiterate.

FOR 24 HOURS AFTER the count in Britain's general election in 2005, it was believed that Catherine Taylor-Dawson had scored a British election record by recording just one vote when standing in Cardiff North for the 'Vote For Yourself Rain Dream Ticket'. The solitary ballot was not hers, as she was not registered in the constituency. The honour was short-lived. As officials at the count cleared up the ballots the next day they discovered more than 200 votes for her had been mixed in with the Liberal Democrat pile by mistake. The national all-time low remained at five.

SINGAPORE WAS ABLE to announce the outcome of its general election in October 2001 nine days before polling day – without any hint of malpractice. So few of the opposition bothered to challenge the ruling People's Action Party, which had been in power in the city state since independence in 1965, that fewer than half the seats faced contested elections when nominations closed just over a week before polling was due. With 55 members already returned unopposed out of the 84-strong assembly, Prime Minister Goh Chok Tong sailed into a further six years of office before even the first ballot was cast.

ISRAELI ELECTION LAW preventing political candidates being shown on television within a month of polling day led to bizarre coverage of Prime Minister Menachem Begin's vital summit meeting with Egyptian President Sadat in June 1981. While viewers could see all of Sadat, the only evidence of Begin's presence was a dismembered hand, or Sadat talking studiously to a shoulder or an elbow. Broadcasting chiefs branded the rule 'ludicrous'. Perversely, viewers could switch channels to neighbouring Jordanian television and see unrestricted coverage.

IN 1996, JAPAN'S electoral laws forbidding the alteration of approved election material meant that TV adverts for former Health Minister Saburo Toida, who had died during the campaign, had to continue to appear until the end of the election, even though his son had succeeded him as candidate.

THAILAND SET THE extreme record for electoral neutrality in March 2000 when it held the first elections for the country's Senate (members had previously been appointed by the government). To combat the country's notorious record for vote-buying and corruption, the Electoral Commission banned all forms of campaigning, all political broadcasts and all political debates. The law, which only allowed candidates to introduce themselves to the public, forbade them from expressing any political affiliation or viewpoint, or from using a microphone in public.

It still produced chaos. Amid accusations of widespread cheating, more than a third of the results were nullified by the Commission in the days after the election. Only 122 were declared to have been settled cleanly. Re-runs had to be held the following month, and for 12 seats a second re-run was ordered. Finally, on 27 July, the Commission was able to announce the confirmation of the 200th, and final, Senator.

The experiment was widely seen as a farce and was destined not to be repeated. By 2007, a military coup had thrown out the old order and re-established more traditional arrangements. The Senate was now smaller (175) and only half of the seats were to be elected.

Close calls

The 1998 election for the mayor of the small New Mexico town of Estancia was settled in local fashion when incumbent James Farrington and his challenger JoAnn Carlson tied on 68 votes each. Under the state's rules, the election was decided by a game of chance – a five-card draw from a pack of cards. Farrington won with ace high.

ONE OF THE closest elections on record was the 1994 contest for a seat on the city council in Rice, Minnesota. Virgil Nelson and Mitch Fiedler tied at 90 votes each, so went into the tie-breaker of drawing cards. The first attempt produced a pair of eights. Astonishingly, in the re-draw, both produced aces. At the third attempt, Nelson drew a seven to be pipped by Fiedler who drew...an eight. Fiedler later went on to become mayor and, at the time of writing, is still at the helm.

ADAM TRENK BECAME the youngest candidate ever to win a council seat in the small Arizona community of Cave Creek in June 2009 – on a draw of cards. The 25-year-old had tied with former Councilman Thomas McGuire with 660 votes each the previous month for the seventh and final seat on the council. The pair were summoned to the council chamber for the draw. Trenk prevailed with a king of hearts to his opponent's six of hearts. The state's law on deciding tied elections 'by lot' was not unknown for producing strange methods of tie-breaking. In 2008, tied candidates for a school board position rolled dice, and in 1992 a game of poker settled the issue in a deadlocked race for a seat in the state legislature.

CONSERVATIVE CANDIDATE Richard Blunt was awarded his seat on Leicestershire County Council three months and a court case after the election in November 1991 had ended in a tie. The returning officer had initially resolved the impasse by drawing lots and Blunt's Labour Party opponent, Derek Wintle, won out. A single ballot paper was at issue. It had been rejected as invalid because the voter had marked their choice not with a cross but with a tick, a smiley face and the words 'yes, please'. Under electoral law, any ballot was disqualified if written on as it might lead to the possible identification of the voter. A court hearing the following February, dismissing the fears on this occasion, ruled the ballot to be legal, one official commenting, 'It's obvious it's no Gainsborough. It bears a passing resemblance to Dennis the Menace.'

ADHERENCE TO THE rules reached extreme lengths in 2006 when the tied election for a seat on the school board in Adak, Alaska, was settled by the toss of a coin – even though one of the two candidates was dead. Katherine Dunton won, even though she had died on polling day. State law did not allow her rival to win by default.

Getting the vote out

To address voting apathy among its community, representatives on the municipal council in Lierne, near Trondheim in Norway, decided in August 1995 to make everyone who voted in the following month's local election eligible for an all-expenses-paid holiday to a Mediterranean resort.

TRIALS AND ERRORS — ELECTIONS

VOTERS IN SIBERIA were encouraged to cast their ballots in elections to the Yakutia Regional Council in the depths of winter in January 2002 by having all votes entered into a lottery with the chance to win a car or a television set. Turnout was boosted to an unusually high 70 per cent.

TO TRY TO REPAIR Arizona's notoriously low voter turnout – usually just above 50 per cent, one of the lowest in America – voters considered a proposal in 2006 for giving a $1 million prize to a random elector in each two-yearly election as an incentive to increase participation. The brainchild of Mark Osterloh, a past runner (unsuccessfully) for State Governor, the idea obtained 185,000 signatures, well past the required level to get on to the ballot in the November elections, where it was, perhaps surprisingly, defeated by a two-to-one majority by Arizonans. Critics worried that it would encourage people to think even less about who they voted for.

CAMPAIGNING IN THE 1979 British general election, Swindon Conservative candidate Nigel Hammond discovered the long memories of voters. A 94-year-old woman in an old people's home told him she would not be voting for his party because after the First World War they had campaigned to hang the German Kaiser but had not kept their promise.

THE FIRST DIRECT elections to the European Parliament in June 1979 struggled to attract public interest, achieving an average turnout across the UK of a mere 33 per cent. The Birmingham Evening Mail reported the extremely slow start at one polling station in the Birmingham South constituency where by lunchtime only one ballot had been cast. An 83-year-old woman was responsible, but there were doubts whether she really knew what she was doing. An official reported that she had declared that her vote was unlikely to help England win as 'Israel has already won'. It transpired she thought she was voting for the Eurovision Song Contest, and had arrived at the polling station clutching a copy of the Radio Times open at the voting page. The song contest had been held three months earlier.

ROY JENKINS, WHO famously returned to British politics as leader of the breakaway Social Democratic Party by fighting (unsuccessfully) a by-election in Warrington, returned to the town two years later during the 1983 General Election campaign claiming still to have 'fond memories' of the place. Fond, but clearly inaccurate – he turned up to canvass on a Thursday afternoon, when the town had half-day closing.

He had meanwhile secured a seat the previous year in the equally unlikely location of Glasgow Hillhead. During the campaign, the fish-out-of-water syndrome was never far away. At the university, he was asked by a professor about a locally pressing social question, the plight of Gaels in the Lowlands. Jenkins confidently replied that he thought 'the weather is much better at the moment'.

GEOFFREY FINSBERG, STANDING as the Conservative candidate in Hampstead and Highgate in the 1983 general election, is believed to have set a record when he addressed a campaign meeting attended by just one member of the public.

JOHN HORAM, CONSERVATIVE candidate in Orpington in 1992, extolled his experience in his campaign leaflet, telling potential voters that 'as a former MP and Minister' he had 'inside knowledge of Government and would bring that understanding to representing the interests of Orpington.' He did not mention that his ministerial service had been as a Transport Minister in the last Labour Government, having defected to the Conservatives in 1987 after a detour through the Social Democratic Party. He still won.

Organisational hiccups

Broward County in Florida, the centre of the storm in the disputed 2000 US Presidential election, encountered fresh mishaps in Congressional elections in 2002. Despite spending $2.5 million over the summer to correct faulty electronic voting machines which had delayed primary election results in March by a week, in the November election over 103,000 ballots — nearly a quarter of the entire vote — were misplaced and not counted. They were discovered almost a week after polling day. Officials claimed the extra ballots did not change the outcome of the election, which had already been declared.

ELECTIONS IN THE Kurdish region of northern Iraq in 1992 had to be postponed when German-gifted supplies of indelible ink designed to prevent voter fraud were found to be easily soluble in water. The ink was a donation from the German state of North Rhine-Westphalia, and part of the West's post-Gulf War effort to restore political life in the breakaway area. The problem was only noticed when a trial run, held the day before voting was due, revealed that instead of setting hard in minutes the ink was removable 'with a bit of spit and scrubbing'. 'We all trusted German efficiency,' said Hoshyar Zebari, an election official.

TO ENSURE NO ONE was impeded from participating in its second all-race general election in 1999, South African election authorities built a special polling station for Lincolnshire Farm in the remote Drakensburg Mountains region of the Free State province to cater for the single registered voter in the area. The elector did not show up to vote.

INDIA'S ELECTIONS COMMISSIONER, G.V.G. Krishnamurthy, tasked with overseeing arrangements for the country's 1999 election, found himself barred from voting when he arrived at his own polling station as his name was missing from the electoral register that his office was responsible for compiling.

A CHILEAN MAN whom election officials had repeatedly denied the right to vote on the grounds that records showed he was dead announced to the press in December 1999 that he was tired of arguing his case and declared he would never try to vote again. At 61 years old, Ernesto Alvear had just been prevented from voting in the country's Presidential election in his home city of Valparaiso. It was the third election from which he had been barred. Officially, the state regarded him as having been dead for the past 10 years. The mix-up had originally been caused by the death of a man with an identical name, causing Alvear to spend a decade in a bureaucratic nightmare trying to prove to the authorities he was alive.

TO ENSURE IMPARTIALITY, a televised election debate in November 2000 for the presidency of the Philadelphia branch of the National Association for the Advancement of Colored People installed a cardboard cut-out of one of three candidates after he had phoned in saying he could not make the broadcast because of a family emergency. The channel, WTVE-TV, propped up a life-size figure of Thomas Logan in a chair to comply with national election rules on equal representation.

IN A 1990 STATE by-election in Queensland, Australia, the opposition Labour Party withdrew a planned advertising campaign which would ridicule the outgoing member's claims of innocence on corruption charges by a series of posters showing Don Lane with a progressively longer Pinocchio-type nose. It scrapped the campaign when it learned that Lane had entered hospital – for a nasal complaint.

THE SHORT-LIVED centre-right government on the Mediterranean island of Sardinia, which won an unexpected, and narrow, victory in June 1999, collapsed three months later after losing a confidence vote in the regional Parliament. Part of the loss of confidence lay in revelations that portions of the party's winning election manifesto had been lifted directly from the 1995 manifesto of a sister party in Lombardy, in northern Italy. Evidently not expecting to succeed, party elders had failed to vet the programme properly. The document still retained promises to tackle the problems of Alpine populations.

AN INFAMOUS CAMPAIGN issue in the British election of 1979 was an embarrassing letter sent by Conservative leader Margaret Thatcher to a council tenant in which the Iron Lady brutally told the hapless complainant that she was lucky to have a house at all. The governing Labour Party printed half a million copies of it for their candidates to spread around. The first consignment arrived at Labour's HQ, in the days when both parties had their offices opposite each other in London's Smith Square. The driver pitched up at the Labour front door but, when told it was a delivery of 'the Thatcher letter', the night watchman directed the delivery man to the other side of the square with a kindly, 'Thatcher's lot are over there.' The van driver dutifully offloaded the whole consignment to the enemy. The Conservatives chivalrously gave them back when they opened the boxes.

A CONSERVATIVE POSTER campaign in the 1992 election emblazoned the words 'You Can't Trust Labour' on 5,000 sites across the country. It backfired when thousands were disfigured by simply pasting over the apostrophe and 't' with white paper to leave the message 'You Can Trust Labour'. It gave struggling Labour an unexpected, and free, boost early in the contest. The poster was pulled shortly after.

CONSERVATIVE LEADER Michael Howard was embarrassed on his party's campaign 'battle bus' touring Cornwall in the 2005 campaign when journalists pointed out — and photographed prodigiously for the following day's papers — that the bus's tax disc was out of date and was therefore being driven illegally.

CHANNEL 4 TELEVISION was forced to apologise to the Green Party for transmitting its 2005 election broadcast while putting up the subtitles of a rival party. Instead of words supporting the Greens' case for an environmentally sensitive future, hard-of-hearing viewers were treated to the text of the right-wing UK Independence Party attacking Europe and immigration. A deflated Green Party spokesman said, 'It's pretty awful. It totally lost the message.' Like all small parties, it was entitled to only one television broadcast for the entire campaign.

WAKEFIELD COUNCIL HAD to reprint polling cards for half its 250,000 residents for the 2010 local elections, being held on the same day as the general election, after discovering that they gave a deadline for applying for postal votes of 27 May – three weeks after polling day. It cost the council £33,000.

Organisational headaches

In elections for the Indian state of Karnataka in February 1985, 301 candidates stood for one seat. The ballot paper, printed on both sides, was the size of a table top.

ELECTIONS FOR THE 55 seats on the city council in Prague in November 1994 were run as a single constituency vote. It required a ballot paper 40 inches by 28 inches to list all 1,187 candidates. The ballot had to be sent to each registered voter – all 1,018,527 of them.

A BALLOT PAPER 42 inches wide and 30 inches deep, nicknamed 'the 'tablecloth ballot', was required for the election to the New South Wales Senate in March 1999, when 264 people stood, representing 81 parties or groups, for the 21 seats available. The state electoral commission was forced to double the size of its voting booths, build bigger ballot boxes and contract a special printer to produce the forms. Tagged 'the ballot paper from Hell', some politicians feared that it had the effect of deterring people from actually making their own choices, opting for voting 'above the line', which allowed the parties to distribute preferences as they chose. After the election, New South Wales changed its electoral laws to make it more difficult for so many aspirants to stand in future.

THE INTRODUCTION OF proportional representation, and a concern for fairness, produced a ballot paper in Italy's 2006 election that was over five feet wide. The 48 parties contending were all listed horizontally instead of vertically after evidence that those at the top of lists running down the page tended to be favoured by most voters who could not be bothered to get to the end.

GERRYMANDERING — THE ARTIFICIAL drawing of constituency boundaries to gain electoral advantage — reached such extreme proportions in some parts of the United States that the Supreme Court eventually ruled in 1997 that a constituency in New York was so bizarrely drawn as to be unconstitutional. The 12th Congressional District in New York, which stretched from Brooklyn to Queens to the Lower East Side of Manhattan, was drawn specifically to collect sufficient ethnic Hispanic voters together to guarantee a victory for a Hispanic candidate. According to court testimony, the borders of the sinuous three-pronged district changed direction 813 times. The Supreme Court ruled that it breached the Constitution's guarantee of equal treatment.

It was not the only extreme example of the practice. In the 2002 mid-term elections, political analysts estimated that the boundaries had been so manipulated in America's House of Representatives districts that of the 435 seats only between 16 and 35 — less than 8 per cent — produced genuine competition between opposing parties. In the event, only four incumbents lost to challengers, producing a 99 per cent return rate for sitting members. Around 80 per cent of seats were won by a margin of more than 20 percentage points and some 200 seats, nearly half, were won by more than 40. Eighty seats were uncontested, producing a state of affairs where only around 10 per cent of American electors live in seats where their vote actually stands a chance of making a difference. By the 2004 elections, experts estimated that only 29 of the 435 seats were genuinely contestable between the parties, with 68 seats being uncontested.

In contrast to the salamander that spawned the original phrase for the practice adopted by Governor Gerry of Massachusetts in the early 19th century, drawers of modern constituencies could use computer-aided analysis and mapping to select areas of similar political hue. As a result, in the words of one report, districts resemble 'scorpions or amoeba – sprouting long tails and tentacles', to take in neighbourhoods of one's preferred political complexion. Two districts in Chicago – the 11th and 17th – both appeared to be several large blocks spread either the length or breadth of town, tenuously connected by thin corridors. Their narrow ends did indeed resemble scorpion pincers squaring up to each other.

One of the most notorious examples was North Carolina's 12th district, created in 1992 when the state was awarded an extra seat due to population increases. It was designed as a black majority seat and snakes for nearly 100 miles across the state north-eastwards from the city of Charlotte up to Winston-Salem, taking in portions of five other cities on the way. At some points it is no wider than a highway lane. On its creation, the *Wall Street Journal* labelled the district 'political pornography'. At the time of going to press, it had been represented in Congress by the same individual since its inaugural election in 1993.

Another extreme example is California's 23rd district, which hugs the coastline in the southern part of the state for over 200 miles from San Luis Obispo County and rarely intrudes more than five miles inland. All parts of the seat are only completely connected when the tide goes out.

Taking defeat gracefully

The bitter 2000 US Presidential election between George W. Bush and Al Gore, which eventually had to be settled by a Supreme Court ruling after five weeks of dispute over confusing ballot papers in Florida, left more physical marks as the Democratic regime vacated the White House. Republican staff arriving to take over offices in January 2001 found that their predecessors had removed the W keys from 'dozens, if not hundreds' of computer keyboards according to Ari Fleischer, the new White House spokesman, preventing the new President's name being typed fully. Other acts of vandalism were reported, including obscene messages left in photo-copiers and on answering machines, telephone cables cut and filing cabinets glued shut. Another trick was for departees to re-route their phones automatically and randomly to other government offices. Fleischer graciously rose above the fray, commenting, 'The President understands that transitions can be times of difficulty and strong emotions. And he's going to approach it in that vein.'

From the history books

In the annals of bizarre elections, few will ever match the notorious 1927 Presidential election in Liberia, which has gone down in the *Guinness Book of Records* as the most fraudulent in history. Charles Dunbar Burgess King retained his presidency by defeating Thomas Faulkner with an official majority of 234,000. The only trouble was that there were only 15,000 registered electors at the time.

PRIOR TO THE Great Reform Act of 1832 which abolished dozens of Britain's unrepresentative constituencies, 'rotten boroughs' returned Members often from electorates of under 10 voters. Old Sarum, in Wiltshire, famously returned two MPs while being officially uninhab-ited, the seven absentee voters being landowners living nearby. Cornwall sent 44 members to Westminster; the whole of Yorkshire just two. Growing cities such as Birmingham, Leeds and Manchester did not have a single member. One calculation has suggested that in 1831, out of the 405 seats where there were elections, 293 were returned by fewer than 500 voters each.

DEAD MAN WINS ELECTION

IT WAS MORE usual for elections to be uncontested. Warwickshire went only once to the polls in the 127 years between 1705 and 1832, Oxfordshire once in 125 years (1701–1826), Nottinghamshire once in 122 years (1710–1832), Wiltshire once in 119 years (1713–1832), Worcestershire once in 109 years (1722–1831), Dorset once in 105 years (1701–1806), Lancashire once in 98 years (1722–1820), Buckinghamshire once in 97 years (1734–1831) and Yorkshire once in 73 years (1734–1807).

There were no contested elections at all for Shropshire between 1722 and 1831 (109 years), Monmouthshire for 105 years (1727–1832), Northamptonshire for 101 years (1705–1806), Cheshire for 98 years (1734–1832), Lincolnshire for 97 years (1710–1807), Somerset for 92 years (1715–1807) and Devon for 89 years (1701–90).

From 1701 until the 1832 reforms, of the 35 counties in England, two-thirds (23) had at least one period of more than 50 years elapsing between a contested county election. At the lowest point, the 1761 general election is recorded as having only 57 contested seats out of the 558 comprising the Commons.

ROBERT TURTON WAS elected Conservative MP for Thirsk and Malton in 1929 during the Great Depression after taking over the campaign following the sudden death of his uncle, the sitting member, who died on nomination day. He went on to hold the seat until retirement in 1974 and his elevation to the House of Lords as Lord Tranmire. His rapid selection was fortuitous. It was said the party was worried about the extra costs of changing its candidate. Choosing the nephew saved them the cost of reprinting the 'Vote Turton' posters.

PETERBOROUGH MP Harmar Nicholls holds the record for enduring probably the least secure parliamentary career. Although he won the seat in 1950 and successfully defended it at seven general elections, he needed a total of 21 recounts along the way. His initial victory was by the slender majority of just 144 votes. In 1966, it took seven recounts before he was declared winner – by a mere three votes. In

February 1974, he needed four recounts to establish he had scraped through again, by 22. He finally lost out in the October election of that year, going down by a hefty 1,848.

SIR HENRY GRAYSON, elected in 1918 for the Conservatives in Birkenhead, and reported to have been considered the best-looking member of the House of Commons, is reputed to be the only MP returned in modern times without having made a single election speech in his campaign. He still won a 10,000 majority.

ON TWO OCCASIONS around the world, national elections have been won by the closest possible margin. In the January 1961 general election on Zanzibar, the Afro-Shirazi party secured a majority of one seat, having won the seat of Chake-Chake by a single vote. After elections in the Cook Islands in the Pacific in June 1999, the coalition government of the Cook Islands Party and the New Alliance Party enjoyed a 13–12 majority in the legislature. Its lead rested on the contested result in the seat of Pukapuka, which had been won by one vote. An election court ruled the result invalid in September, depriving the government of its short-lived majority.

THE *GUINNESS BOOK OF RECORDS* cites two recorded cases of dead people being elected in Britain. In 1747, Captain the Hon. Edward Legge was returned for Portsmouth before it was known that he had, in fact, died in the West Indies nearly three months before polling day. In 1780, John Kirkman died during the election for the City of London constituency, but voters still elected him. In addition, at the 1906 general election, Irish Nationalist candidate Thomas Higgins died on the evening of the election, after voting had taken place but before the count. He received more than twice the number of votes as his opponent, and was declared elected posthumously.

THE SHORTEST SPAN as an elected MP is probably the sad case of trade unionist Alfred James Dobbs, who was declared elected as MP for Smethwick in the post-war Labour landslide on 26 July 1945 and killed in a car crash in Doncaster the following day on the way to Westminster to take his seat. As he never took the oath of office, he technically never became a member of the House.

WHILE CAMPAIGNING FOR US President in 1912, Theodore Roosevelt was shot in an attempted assassination as he left his hotel in Milwaukee for a rally. Despite being wounded in the chest, he refused to abandon his planned speech. He appeared on stage with blood oozing from his shirt. Starting by saying he hoped his audience would excuse him for making a shorter speech than intended, he spoke for an hour and a half before being taken off to hospital. He still lost the election, and carried the bullet in him for the rest of his life.

ODDEST OF ALL candidates perhaps was Thaddeus Stevens, US congressman from Philadelphia, who died in 1868 and whose corpse was nominated by the Republican Party for re-election to the House of Representatives as a tribute to his Civil War service. He was elected eight weeks after being buried.

RADIO BROADCASTING IN elections began in earnest after the Second World War. In marked contrast to our modern sound-bite times, Prime Minister Winston Churchill was firm with the BBC in the 1945 election when it had asked him to keep his first election broadcast to only(!) 20 minutes: 'I insisted on at least half an hour.'

TELEVISION CAMPAIGNING BEGAN in Britain in the 1951 election. The first TV party political broadcast was bizarrely by the 80-year-old Liberal veteran Lord Samuel, sitting alone in a studio talking for 15 minutes but rarely glancing up from his script to look at the camera. It ended inauspiciously. He was cut off in mid-sentence when he inadvertently gave the producer the pre-arranged signal that he had finished.

The first Conservative one later the same day set the pattern for the future. Anthony Eden caused a storm by producing a graph showing the cost of living under Labour. Labour, which used the same figures the following night but with a graph showing the rise much less steeply, called Eden's graph 'a deliberate fake'. Christopher Mayhew, Labour's spokesman, said, 'Just as Crippen was the first criminal to be caught by the wireless, so Eden is the first political criminal to be exposed by television.'

A similar problem was narrowly avoided in 1955. The Conservatives planned a broadcast showing Harold Macmillan holding a small money box to demonstrate how little money people had been able to save under the previous Labour government; he was then to walk over and put it on top of a much larger money box built to scale to show how under the Conservatives personal savings had been 30 times greater. Unfortunately the carpenter who made the big box misunderstood and made the box 30 times larger in each dimension — 27,000 times the volume of the smaller one. The discrepancy was discovered only on the night of the broadcast. The error was concealed by using delicate long-shot camera angles.

The taciturn Clement Attlee proved a nightmare for broadcasters. Labour's first broadcast of the 1955 election had him and Mrs Attlee in a mock-up of their cottage living room, being interviewed by the journalist Percy Cudlipp. In the answer to his first question, Attlee responded with a respectable four-sentence answer. That was the longest of the night. For the next 15 minutes, his replies were monosyllabic. Cudlipp had been given 28 questions for the slot; he had used them all up in the first five minutes. The rest of the broadcast was an impressive display from the increasingly desperate interviewer to think up new questions.

Eden attempted to use an early teleprompter in the 1955 campaign. Unfortunately, anyone trying to read off it gave the appearance of having extraordinarily rolling eyes that made it look as if they were seasick. 'It was decided Eden should not use it because it made him look completely mad,' Winifred Crum-Ewing, the BBC producer, recalled.

Macmillan also had problems. 'First, being very short-sighted, I couldn't see it. Second, if I could just manage to read the words by screwing up my eyes, I presented the appearance of a corpse looking out of a window.'

When Harold Wilson made his first broadcasts, his habit of raising his fist to emphasise his point appeared threatening on the small screen. His advisers decided to give him his pipe to hold, and he always appeared with it after that. Wilson actually preferred large cigars and would often smoke one after lunch. It was a sight he carefully kept from the screen in favour of the classless pipe. Another refined tactic was his habit of resting his face on his left hand during interviews, showing his wedding ring to portray the image of a family man.

Early television campaigns would feature short live excerpts of rally speeches broadcast on the evening TV news. Wilson used these to the full. As soon as the red light on top of the camera went on, indicating he was on air, he would stop in mid-sentence and pick up a piece of paper containing a crisp, crafted paragraph for the people at home. The mystified audience in the hall would witness their potential leader veer suddenly from one subject to a completely unconnected one. But Wilson knew the bigger audience lay behind the camera.

The 1964 campaign produced one of the most intriguing rows between party and broadcaster. Wilson was worried that, with the polls neck and neck, the showing of the BBC's most popular programme *Steptoe and Son* at eight o'clock on election night, an hour before the polls closed, would adversely affect his chances, as the majority audience were Labour voters who would stay in rather than vote. He protested to the BBC, whose Director-General Sir Hugh Greene eventually agreed to postpone the show until nine. Wilson thanked Greene saying, 'That will be worth a dozen or more seats to me.' Labour won by a majority of just four. Greene late recalled, 'I've often wondered in view of the closeness of the eventual outcome whether I should have a bad conscience.'

In 1966, the BBC pulled an episode of the children's cartoon *Pinky and Perky* due for broadcast during the campaign because it featured the pigs taking part in an election campaign and getting elected as joint Prime Ministers.

TRIALS AND ERRORS — ELECTIONS

Sir Alec Douglas-Home — television's least-photogenic campaigner — came in for complaint in the campaign for his skeletal appearance. A TV make-up artist said that his face looked 'skull-like'. He replied, 'Doesn't every face look skull-like?' An oft-filmed banner appeared during the 1964 campaign, reading, 'Who Exhumed You?'

FRANKLIN ROOSEVELT, campaigning for re-election as President in 1936, engaged in a radio debate with Alf Landon, his Republican challenger. Each had ten minutes to make a speech. Roosevelt went first, spoke for three minutes and then fell silent for the rest of his allotted time. By the time it was Landon's turn to talk, most of the audience had switched off.

LIECHTENSTEIN ALLOWED WOMEN to vote in elections only as recently as 1984, the last country in Europe to grant suffrage to women. Switzerland granted it only in 1971 and Andorra in 1970. Four Middle East states have recently relented after centuries of exclusion — Qatar (1997), Oman (2003), Kuwait (2005) and the United Arab Emirates (2006). There remains no right of female suffrage in Saudi Arabia and the Vatican City.

THE (MIS)RULE OF LAW – PARLIAMENTS

Electors rightly expect their parliamentarians to be giving their full attention to the most important affairs of state. But even in the course of 'normal' business, the workings of a parliament can involve many strange practices.

Honourable members

Until its repeal in 2000, section 10(j) of the 1963 Electoral Act of Western Samoa contained the rule that any Member of Parliament who had sex with a person other than their spouse was to be disqualified from holding their seat. As recently as 1982 a member was expelled on these grounds.

PRESIDENT MARCOS ordered the title of members of the Philippine National Assembly be changed in 1984 from Assemblyman to Mambabatas Pambansa (MP) so that the abbreviation appearing on name plates was no longer 'Ass'.

IN THE PARLIAMENT OF the Central American state of Belize, agreed protocol is that supporters of the government wear ties. Members of the Opposition go open-necked.

The rule of law

The publication in 2008 of a new edition of the definitive collection of all legislation in force in England revealed the astronomical growth in lawmaking and led critics to complain that Britain was one of the most over-regulated countries in the world. In just 21 years since the last edition of *Halsbury's Laws of England* in 1987, the size of the country's statute book had almost doubled from 56 volumes to 102. Another 900 Acts of Parliament and 30,000 regulations had been added. Since just 1997 – a mere 11 years – there had been 21 new Acts regarding education, 10 relating to health and 23 to criminal justice. Legislation covering education had increased fourfold since 1987, as had employment law. Road traffic law had doubled while criminal law had quadrupled.

The publisher of the collection, Simon Hetherington, said that the new edition was 'unarguable' evidence that 'there is more written law than ever before, and the growth of it has accelerated over the last three decades'. Other research by law publishers estimated that law creation was running at the rate of eight new pieces each day in 2007. The Thatcher premiership between 1979 and 1990 had produced an average of 1,724 new laws each year while the Blair years generated 2,633.

Commentators drew parallels with the tax regime, which had shown an even greater explosion of complexity. The standard guide to understanding Britain's tax law grew in just six years, from 5,952 pages in two volumes in 2001 to 9,866 pages in the four volumes of the 2007 edition. It was expected to break the 10,000-page barrier in its next edition.

The clarity of law

Irish legislators passed the 1984 Road Traffic (Insurance) Disc Regulations, Section 4 of which stated, 'Every insurance disc shall be in the shape of a rectangle.'

AN EXPLANATORY NOTE to Section 56, sub-section 6 of the Shops Act 1950 (which among other provisions controlled the sale of goods on sea-going ships) contained the following clarification: '*Sea-going ship*: This expression is not defined. But it has been held under the Merchant Shipping Act, 1854, that a sea-going ship is a ship that goes to sea.'

SOUTH AUSTRALIA DISCOVERED in 2002 that the state was still officially at war when embarrassed parliamentary authorities found that successive state governments had forgotten to repeal the Emergency Powers Act introduced in 1941 to manage business during the Second World War. No one had issued the formal proclamation required under the law to end the war, and the Act remained in force. On 16 August, Premier Mike Rann proclaimed the end of the conflict, explaining that the legal quirk was due to the fact that the Act was to have expired automatically with the expected peace treaties at the end of the war but, with the onset of the Cold War, no such peace treaty was ever achieved. 'It seems we are the only state in Australia with wartime legislation like this still on the books.' The Act was formally, and hastily, repealed with immediate effect.

AN UNNOTICED MISTAKE in an Arkansas law on marriage age introduced in 2007 temporarily enabled anyone in the state – even babies – to marry. What was designed to set a minimum age for marriage without parental consent was given the opposite effect by the typo, which was only discovered after the provision had been signed into law. A key section, intended to require girls who were under 18 and pregnant to have to show parental consent for the marriage, was found to have a rogue 'not' in the clause, which effectively enabled anyone to marry with their parents' blessing. It read: 'In order for a person who is younger than eighteen (18) years of age and who is not pregnant to obtain a marriage license, the person must provide the county clerk with evidence of parental consent to the marriage.' The Arkansas legislature had to repeal the law in April 2008 and start all over again.

THE IRISH PARLIAMENT was required to pass a special law in December 1988 to resolve the problem of a judge who had forgotten his date of birth. Three years earlier, District Justice Seamus Mahon, who sat at Portlaoise in County Laois, had duly applied for dispensation from the retirement age of 65 believing that the age deadline had just fallen for him. In fact, he had been born a year earlier than he thought, meaning his exemption was a year too late and technically invalid, as were the 120,000-odd judgements he had continued to make in the years that followed. The special Act gave retrospective authority to all his decisions.

DURING THE PASSAGE of the 1990 Broadcasting Act, the House of Lords found itself having to pronounce on the tricky issue of a legal definition of 'pop music'. It was necessary because the proposed legislation aimed to ensure that only one of the three franchises being set up by the Act would be for pop, so their Lordships tackled the (to them) obscure subject in one of the more surreal debates ever held in the Lords.

Earl Ferrers, Minister of State at the Home Office in charge of steering the measure through, confessed that he had lost his own attempt to describe the matter at hand as 'thump, thump, thump'. This had been judged by legal draftsmen to 'not be statutorily or parliamentarily adequate'. Instead, he proposed – and peers agreed – that the formal 61-word legal definition would be: 'Pop music includes rock music and other kinds of modern popular music which are characterised by a strong rhythmic element and a reliance on electronic amplification for their performance, whether or not, in the case of any particular piece of rock or other such music, the music in question enjoys a current popularity as measured by the number of recordings sold.'

NOT EVERY PIECE of legislation in Parliament is controversial. On 17 January 1986, the Marriage (Wales) Bill passed through all its stages in the House of Commons without a word of debate. Concerned with removing a loophole about reading marriage banns in church, it was subjected to more considered treatment by the House of Lords: 13 minutes on Second Reading. It then zipped through all its remaining stages without debate, becoming one of the least talked-about Acts of Parliament in history.

Strange lawmaking

The US state of Louisiana made lack of respect of teachers from schoolchildren formally illegal in a controversial 1999 law that came into force at the start of the new school year in September. The measure made it a legal requirement for every child in school from the age of five to ten to call their teachers 'sir' or 'ma'am'. The state, already notorious for the severity of its laws on abortion and divorce, was the first in the country to adopt legislation in the area. Both houses of the state legislature passed the law with overwhelming support, despite teachers' objections that it ridiculed their authority.

THE FRENCH NATIONAL Assembly adopted similar legislation in the summer of 2002, making it possible for schoolchildren to be sent to prison for up to six months for insulting their teachers. Prosecutions could be started against children who 'attack the dignity or respect due' to their teachers. In addition to prison, a fine up to 7,500 euros could be imposed. The law notionally applied to children as young as 13, although officials said it would almost certainly be limited in practice to those in sixth forms. Teachers expressed concern at the apparently draconian nature of the law and described the move as 'window dressing'.

IN MARCH 2003, the New Mexico legislature approved Representative Dan Foley's proposal for a law to designate an official 'Extraterrestrial Culture Day', to be celebrated on the second Thursday of each February. Foley, from the New Mexico town of Roswell renowned in UFO folklore for a supposed alien landing in 1947, introduced the legislation to recognise, in the words of the statute, the 'many visitations, sightings, unexplained mysteries, attributed technological advances, experimentations, expeditions, explorations, intrigues, provision of story lines for Hollywood epics, and other accomplishments of alien beings throughout the universe that have contributed to New Mexico's worldwide recognition as a unique and dynamic mosaic of cultural anomalies'. The day would be observed 'to celebrate and honor all past, present and future extraterrestrial visitors in ways to enhance relationships among all the citizens of the cosmos, known and unknown'.

IN APRIL 2003, the Oregon House of Representatives passed a law the sole purpose of which was to define 'science' ('the systematic enterprise of gathering knowledge about the universe and organizing and condensing that knowledge into testable laws and theories'). The sponsor of the measure, Betsy Close, was understood to believe that establishing the particular formulation in state law would constrain local environmental activists who had become successful in lodging 'scientific' evidence to challenge government activities.

THE GEORGIA HOUSE of Representatives passed a measure in 2004 requiring all buildings owned by the state, counties or cities to have twice as many women's toilets as men's to even up one of life's perennial practical inequalities. The state Senate failed to concur and the legislation died.

GUN-TOTING TEXAS passed legislation, which was signed into law by Governor Rick Perry in June 2007, allowing blind people to hunt with guns. The proposal had passed both houses of the legislature unanimously. The only requirement to ensure wider public safety was that the sightless hunter had to be accompanied by someone who was not legally blind, who owned a hunting licence and was at least 13 years old.

TEXAS STATE REPRESENTATIVE James Kaster from the border town of El Paso introduced a proposed law into the State Assembly's 1974 session which would require all criminals to give their victims 24 hours' notice of their intended crime. The notice could be given orally (such as by telephone call) or in writing. It would also require the criminal to acknowledge their acceptance of the victims' right to exercise lethal force in their defence. The measure failed to win approval.

IN MARCH 1978, Oklahoma State Representative Cleta Deatherage introduced an amendment in protest at an anti-abortion bill in her state assembly. It would require men to seek written consent from a female before having sex, and that before granting permission the woman should receive a warning about the risks of pregnancy and the dangers of childbirth. Should the woman be illiterate, the warning would need to be read to her (in her native language). The proposal was unsurprisingly defeated but the result, 78–9, meant that nearly 12 per cent of the members taking part supported the idea.

GERMAN LEGISLATORS HAVE considered three times since 2003 proposals to give the vote to babies. A move in September 2003 to entitle parents to cast an extra vote on behalf of each child until they were 18 failed to win support in the Bundestag, the national Parliament. The measure would have legally obliged parents to explain political affairs to their offspring and to comply with their voting wishes. With under-18s accounting for 20 per cent of the population, sponsors extolled the virtues of widening the franchise.

Antje Vollmer, a Green Party parliamentarian, said, 'There are millions of little people living in our society today who often have more informed political views than adults, but who are currently being discriminated against simply on account of their age.' A similar resolution was introduced in 2005 and also failed. Proponents were last heard of still trying to get the measure passed in 2008.

NEW MEXICO STATE Senator Duncan Scott waged a campaign in 1995 in protest at the growing trend of defendants pleading insanity in courts to avoid criminal convictions. Evidently no admirer of the psychiatric profession that helped them do this, he proposed amending state law to require that:

> When a psychologist or psychiatrist testifies during a defendant's competency hearing, the psychologist or psychiatrist shall wear a cone-shaped hat that is not less than two feet tall. The surface of the hat shall be imprinted with stars and lightning bolts.
>
> Additionally, the psychologist or psychiatrist shall be required to don a white beard that is not less than eighteen inches in length, and shall punctuate crucial elements in his testimony by stabbing the air with a wand.
>
> Whenever a psychologist or psychiatrist provides expert testimony regarding the defendant's testimony, the bailiff shall dim the courtroom lights and administer two strikes to a Chinese gong.

In March of that year the amendment was agreed by the Senate without a vote, and passed by the House of Representatives 46–14. It took a veto by State Governor Gary Johnson to stop it becoming law.

IN 1976, STATE legislator Michael Connolly formally introduced into the Massachusetts House of Representatives a proposed law that would sell the state back to the Native Americans. The draft bill required Massachusetts to be auctioned off on 3 January 1977. His fellow lawmakers failed to back the measure.

Parliamentary decorum

Karlene Maywald, a South Australian MP, was reprimanded by the State Assembly Speaker in October 2003 for using the word 'please', ruling that it represented begging and claiming that it had been banned in parliamentary practice for 300 years. When she asked at Question Time whether the minister 'could please advise the House' on water restrictions, Speaker Peter Lewis ruled her language out of order. 'The word "please" is to beg, no honourable member in this place needs to beg any minister for anything, least of all an answer,' he told MPs. Maywald expressed astonishment at being upbraided. 'I was only being polite.'

A month later, Speaker Lewis invited more controversy by ruling that Energy Minister Pat Conlon's use of 'bloody' during a heated exchange was in order. '"Bloody" is an oath, "by our lady", arising from the ancient English of Chaucer,' he opined, and thus ruled it entirely acceptable.

THE CITY COUNCIL of Palo Alto, California, spent an evening in May 2003 debating a proposal from one of its committees that, if passed, would have banned 'body language or other nonverbal methods of expression, disagreement or disgust' during council meetings. Aimed at enhancing decorum in debates, the measure, which had taken a year to develop and had already been inconclusively considered in a five-hour session two months earlier, sought to stop councillors using disparaging gestures. These, according to the new rules, would have included frowning, rolling of the eyes, shaking of the head and sticking out the tongue.

The idea attracted such ridicule from the local community that in the event even the head of the committee that proposed the rules voted against the idea and they were thrown out unanimously.

Beyond understanding

An Early Day Motion in the British House of Commons in January 2008 calling for the disestablishment of the Church of England appeared on the Order Paper numbered 666 – the 'Number of the Beast'. The numbering of the motion was automatically generated and corresponded to the order in which it was tabled. The author, Liberal Democrat member Bob Russell, said: 'It's incredible [it] should have acquired this significant number.'

THE MISSOURI HOUSE of Representatives passed a 1,012-page law in 1995...designed to reduce paperwork in the state government.

MARYLAND LEGISLATORS DECIDED in 1962 to make jousting its official state sport. It remains so to this day.

THE OREGON SENATE voted in 1989 to make the hazelnut the official state nut, the first state in America to have one.

IN NEBRASKA, WHERE since 1996 state law has allowed the Governor to declare official state items without the legislature first considering them, Ben Nelson signed a proclamation in May 1998 declaring the state now had an official soft drink – Kool-Aid, a nationally celebrated powdered soft drink, invented in the state in 1927. Alongside the traditional state symbols of official bird, tree and flower, Nebraska enjoys an official state rock (the prairie agate), official state fossil (the mammoth), official state grass (the little bluestem) and official state insect (the honeybee).

WHILE WEST VIRGINIA endured an unenviable reputation as one of the poorest states of the Union, with falling jobs numbers, high social deprivation and low health and education standards, legislators in the State Senate spent much time and energy in

DEAD MAN WINS ELECTION

February 2000 debating the merits of the dulcimer as the preferred candidate for selection as their official state musical instrument. Senators passed a resolution in favour, causing intense controversy in the lower House of Representatives, which favoured the fiddle. Such is the level of dispute that, as of 2010, the issue remains unresolved.

A SIMILAR TIME-CONSUMING dispute broke out in 2002 when the historic Californian town of Bodie, a former gold-mining settlement, won the support of State Assemblyman Tim Leslie for designating the place California's official state ghost town. The proposal was overwhelmingly supported in the lower house in May, but when it advanced to the Senate it encountered opposition from a rival historic park, Calico, a former silver-mining town, also now a deserted ghost town and reliant on tourism for survival. Fearful that granting the official designation to Bodie would disadvantage it, Calico secured the support of its local Senator Jim Brulte, who was unrepentant about the basis for his loyalties. 'I've been to Calico, and I haven't been to the other place, so I'm going with what I know.'

Months of wrangling followed. Compromises were proposed. Calico would withdraw its opposition if Bodie was merely designated 'an' official state ghost town rather than 'the' official ghost town. As this broke all the traditions of settling on a single recipient, legislators applied themselves further. The 'Great Ghost Town Compromise of 2002' resulted. Bodie would be declared the official 'gold rush ghost town' of California, and Calico would be enthroned later as the state's official 'silver rush ghost town'. On 4 September, the Governor of California signed the legislation adopting Bodie's new status. In 2005, legislation was passed that made Calico the official state silver rush ghost town of California, and it was signed into effect by Governor Arnold Schwarzenegger in July.

THE HIGHLY CONTESTED question as to the appropriate candidate for designation as the official state cookie of Pennsylvania remains unresolved seven years after legislation was introduced into the

State Senate in 2003 naming the chocolate chip cookie. The lower house refused to agree and introduced its own legislation in favour of the (admittedly lesser known) Nazareth sugar cookie.

IN APRIL 2009, Oklahoma Governor Brad Henry signed into law recognition of 'Do You Realize?', by the Flaming Lips, as the state's official rock song. Oklahoma became only the second state in the Union to designate an official state rock song. (Ohio had chosen 'Hang on Sloopy' as long ago as 1985.)

OTHER BIZARRE SELECTIONS, which have occupied the time and attention of tax-paid elected representatives, include:

Official State Aircraft (New Mexico – hot-air balloon)

Official State Artifact (Nevada – Tule duck decoy)

Official State Bat (Virginia – Virginia big-eared bat)

Official State Bean (Massachusetts – baked navy bean)

Official State Bread (South Dakota – fry bread)

Official State Cantata (Connecticut – 'The Nutmeg, Homeland of Liberty' by S.L. Ralph)

Official State Carnivorous Plant (North Carolina – Venus flytrap)

Official State Cartoon Character (Oklahoma – Gusty)

Official State Christmas Tree (North Carolina – Fraser fir)

Official State Cookie (Massachusetts – chocolate chip cookie)

Official State Cooking Implement (Texas – Dutch oven)

Official State Cooking Pot (Utah – Dutch oven)

Official State Covered Bridge (Kentucky – Switzer covered bridge, Franklin County)

Official State Dessert (Maine – Smith Island cake; Missouri – ice cream cone)

Official State Dinosaur (Maryland – *Astrodon johnstoni*)

DEAD MAN WINS ELECTION

Official State Doughnut (Louisiana – beignet)

Official State Exercise (Maine – walking)

Official State Grape (Missouri – Norton / Cynthiana grape)

Official State Hospitality Beverage (South Carolina – tea)

Official State Lullaby (Montana – 'Montana Lullaby' by Overcast / Gustafson)

Official State Macroinvertebrate (Delaware – stonefly)

Official State Meal (Oklahoma – cornbread, barbecue pork, okra, squash)

Official State Meat Pie (Louisiana – Natchitoches meat pie)

Official State Molecule (proposed, 2010) (Texas – Buckyball)

Official State Muffin (Massachusetts – corn muffin)

Official State Mushroom (Minnesota – morel mushroom)

Official State Neckware (Arizona – bola tie)

Official State Pepper (Texas – jalapeno)

Official State Percussive Musical Instrument (Oklahoma – drum)

Official State Pie (Florida – key lime pie)

Official State Prepared Food (Georgia – grits)

Official State Quilt (Alabama – Pine Burr Quilt)

Official State Raptor (Idaho – peregrine falcon)

Official State Snack Food (Illinois – popcorn)

Official State Spider (South Carolina – Carolina wolf spider)

Official State Steam Locomotive (Kentucky – Old 152)

Official State Toy (Mississippi – teddy bear)

Official State Troubador (Connecticut – Lara Herscovitch, 2009 & 2010)

THE KENTUCKY ASSEMBLY failed to pass its budget on time in its 2004 session but did devote hours to debating and approving a law to prevent humans and animals being buried in the same cemetery.

From the history books

In contrast to our modern legislators revelling in frequent and extended breaks throughout the parliamentary year, spare a thought for the English Parliament of 1648 – it adjourned that year for Christmas Eve and Christmas Day only.

THE VERY FIRST meeting of the US Congress, due to take place in New York, the temporary capital, on 4 March 1789, had to be postponed because not enough legislators had turned up. Only eight out of the 22 Senators and 13 of the 59 Representatives had managed to make it. It took a further month, until 6 April, before a quorum had been mustered.

DESPITE THE CONTENTION of the opening sentiments of the American Declaration of Independence that 'all men are created equal', when it came to writing the Constitution 13 years later the Founding Fathers applied a bizarre numerical restriction on reality. In calculating the population of colonies for the purposes of assessing levels of representation in Congress, they wrote into Article I Section 3 that each 'unfree person' (that is, slave) counted as only three-fifths of a free person. The clause remained in the Constitution until the abolition of slavery in 1865.

LANGUAGE CAN BE vital for good understanding. During a House of Lords hearing in 1736 into riots in Edinburgh which had led to deaths when the town guard opened fire on the mob, the provost of the city was asked what kind of shot the guardsmen had loaded their weapons with. In broad Scots, the man answered, 'Och, just sic as ane shoots dukes and fools wi!' The reply was judged to be a contempt of the esteemed surroundings and the provost was about to be hauled off to incarceration when the Duke of Argyll explained that, when rendered into the Queen's English, the man had meant shot used for ducks and fowls.

THE PEACE OF PARIS in 1763, the treaty that ended Britain's Seven Years' War with France and Spain and opened up Canada for uncontested British settlement, was reputedly only approved by the House of Commons by bought votes. The government paid over £80,000 (some £10.3 million in modern values) in bribes for over 120 votes to secure passage of the treaty. Among them were 40 members who received either £1,000 (£130,000) or £500 (£65,000) each.

A CURIOUS EARLY Victorian trade development was the importation of ice from Norway, used for catering, food preservation and medical purposes. According to an undated tale in a 19th-century collection of political anecdotes, the first consignment into Britain came up against an administrative conundrum, there not being a classification in the Customs House schedule for ice. An application was made to the Treasury, which the Treasury referred on to the Board of Trade. After some delay, it was decided that ice should be entered as 'dry goods', but by the time this resolution of the dilemma had been reached and conveyed back to the docking agents, the whole cargo had melted.

Questions in the House

Parliamentary Questions in the British House of Commons have become one of the most used methods by which Members of Parliament raise issues. It is generally accepted that the first PQ is that recorded as being asked by Earl Cowper to the Earl of Sunderland, the First Lord of the Treasury and forerunner to the Prime Minister, on 9 February 1721. It concerned the South Sea Bubble scandal. According to the House authorities, by the mid-19th century, questions tabled averaged one a day; by 1900, 41 a day – more daily than in the whole session of 1830. By 1920, there were 13,000, crossing the 100-a-day threshold. Today, the number tabled for written answer is in the order of 80,000 – around 400 per sitting day – and over 5,000 are laid for the oral question sessions with which the business of the House starts most days.

The problem of the explosion of questions is by no means a modern concern. It has been around for decades. In August 1901, future Prime Minister Arthur Balfour, then Leader of the House, described Questions as 'a scandal', saying that they referred 'for the most part to very trifling subjects', gave rise to 'constant friction' which was 'very destructive of the dignity of Parliament' and were 'constantly made the vehicle for calumnious attacks on individuals'. He proposed that, other than questions asked by ex-ministers and Privy Councillors, the rest should be dealt with at midnight, after all other business had finished. This would, he said, 'relegate to an unimportant hour…the piles of rubbish with which, for purposes of self-advertisement, Members now crowd the order book'. He speculated that this would 'prodigiously diminish the curiosity of Members'. Unsurprisingly, his idea did not attract wide support. Modern business managers would be forgiven for having the greatest tinge of sympathy with the notion.

Lloyd George once got lost while driving in the North Wales mountains, and asked a passer-by where he was. 'You are in a motor car' was the reply. Lloyd George later described this as a perfect form of answer to a parliamentary question: it was true, it was brief and it told him absolutely nothing he did not already know.

THE MOST NOTORIOUS – and amusing – exponent of the parliamentary question in the 20th century was the eccentric Conservative Member for Kidderminster, Sir Gerald Nabarro. Described by a contemporary commentator as 'undoubtedly the greatest House of Commons character since the War', for half a decade from 1958 he waged a one-man campaign against the iniquities and absurdities of Purchase Tax, Britain's precursor to Value Added Tax. This imposed a sales tax on almost every item purchased by a consumer, but was varied in amount – there were seven rate levels from 90 per cent to 5 per cent when Nabarro began his campaign – depending on detailed categorisations set by the

Treasury. To Nabarro's mischievous mind, it was a mother-lode of fun and anomaly, which he pursued relentlessly with over 400 questions aimed at every hapless Chancellor, regularly delivered at the rate of three a day (at that time the maximum allowed). In the months before the 1958 Budget, he had his full allowance down for every Treasury Question Time (then every Tuesday and Thursday) from 23 January to 1 April. Some of his most celebrated examples follow:

TO ASK THE Chancellor of the Exchequer...

...FOR WHAT REASONS it has been decided that brushes used for cleaning shoes or teeth shall be free of Purchase Tax, but that brushes used for applying shaving soap or brushing the hair, clothes, or nails, are liable to Purchase Tax at substantial rates. (January 1958)

...WHETHER HE IS aware that a container for shoe-*polishing* materials, which consists of a case fastened by a stud and containing two shoe brushes, two tins of polish, and two dusters, is at present subjected to Purchase Tax, whereas a shoe-*cleaning* case, made in the shape of a binocular case in three separate pieces, the ends of which contain a brush and the centre of which contains the dusters and polish tins, is free of tax; and whether he will review this matter, with the object of freeing from Purchase Tax all cases used for containing shoe-cleaning materials. (January 1958)

...WHEN THE REGULATION was introduced laying down that door-knockers five inches or more in length shall be free of tax whereas doorknockers under that length carry 30 per cent Purchase Tax. (February 1958)

...WHETHER HE IS aware that, in view of the fact that a nutcracker is liable to Purchase Tax at 15 per cent, whereas a doorknocker over five inches in length is free of tax, there is an increasing practice of supplying nutcrackers with screw holes so that they could theoretically be used as doorknockers, with the result that with such modification these nutcrackers become free of tax; and what instructions have been issued to Customs and Excise staff with regard to this matter. (February 1958)

In reply, Jocelyn Simon, Financial Secretary to the Treasury, opined that 'I do not think Customs staff need instructions to help them distinguish a nutcracker from a doorknocker.'

Sir Gerald's usual riposte was then to heighten the absurdity. On this occasion, he asked: 'Why is there this invidious distinction between doorknocking nutcrackers and nutcracking doorknockers?'

...WHY BLINDS FITTED with three-inch circular peepholes were free of tax, while those without peepholes were not. (February 1958)

The Chancellor himself, Derick Heathcoat Amory, took this one on: 'The 15 per cent tax is charged on blinds for domestic and office use. I am advised by the trade that blinds with peepholes are only used in shops.'

To which Sir Gerald then offered a worrying implication: 'Does not this fiscal discrimination encourage the sale of blinds with peepholes, and as the presence of these peepholes is an incitement to offences under the Justices of the Peace Act, 1361 – that is the Peeping Tom Act – will you not remove Purchase Tax from all these blinds, so as to give a modicum of comfort to law-abiding citizens?'

...WHY A POTTERY piggy bank used for saving is subject to Purchase Tax at 30 per cent as a toy, but if painted with the words 'razor blades' it pays 15 per cent as a salvage receptacle. (March 1958)

...FOR WHAT REASON a preparation used to black out teeth for theatrical purposes is free of Purchase Tax whereas a similar preparation used to brighten and whiten teeth for stage purposes is taxed at 90 per cent. (April 1958)

...WHETHER HE WAS aware that a horn regarded as a wind musical instrument is subject to Purchase Tax at 30 per cent, whereas a musical motor car horn does not attract Purchase Tax even if used occasionally for theatrical performances...what particular considerations guided his decisions as to the rate of Purchase Tax applicable to particular horns; and to what extent he was influenced in his decision by the volume or by the melodious quality of the noise produced. (February 1959)

During the exchange in the House, he pressed the unfortunate Treasury spokesman, this time the Economic Secretary: 'Is it not a fact that a motor car horn makes a harsh and raucous and unmelodious noise; and having regard to the fact that a 30 per cent Purchase Tax is placed on musical instruments, including the French horn, which make melodious noises and music and contribute to the arts and culture, why should the Chancellor of the Exchequer be depressing the arts by this vicious impost?'

...WHETHER HE IS aware that a few feet of polythene tubing, with an appropriate dowel, may be sold free of Purchase Tax, whereas a hula hoop is subject to Purchase Tax; and, in view of the desirability of increasing the sale of hula hoops as an encouragement to personal fitness, whether he will now relieve factory-made hula hoops from Purchase Tax. (February 1959)

...WHETHER HE IS aware that wadded, or otherwise filled, tea cosies are tax free, whereas wadded, or otherwise filled, cushions are subject to Purchase Tax at 5 per cent, and wadded, or otherwise filled, nightdress cases, for boudoir use and not for travel purposes, are subject to Purchase Tax at 30 per cent; and why such articles, all made from the same wadded material, should be subject to different Purchase Tax treatment. (March 1959)

...WHETHER HE is aware that the stand upon which a saxophonist rests his saxophone is subject to Purchase Tax at 25 per cent as is the saxophone, whereas the stand upon which a saxophonist rests his musical score is not subject to tax; why this discrimination exists as between stands for the saxophones and stands for the musical scores; and whether he will redress the grievances of saxophonists in this regard by abolition of all Purchase Tax on all stands whether used for saxophone rests or for musical scores. (February 1960)

THE (MIS)RULE OF LAW — PARLIAMENTS

...WHY BABIES' PLAIN teething rings, consisting solely of a shaped piece of bone, plastic or rubber, are not chargeable to 25 per cent Purchase Tax...whereas babies' teething beads, which can alternatively be used by the child as a rattle, are subject to such tax. (March 1960)

...WHETHER HE IS aware that babies' white carrying shawls not less than 48 inches square, knitted or made from woven cloth or such cloth with a mixture of rayon, silk or cotton, and blue or pink shawls, knitted, are free of Purchase Tax, but identical articles of a smaller than usual babies' size of 36 inches square are subject to Purchase Tax; why lemon, peach, maize, cream and pale green shawls are all subject to Purchase Tax, whereas white, blue and pink shawls 48 inches square and over, are exempt; why he is differentiating between colours of infants' shawls and against under-sized babies. (February 1963)

...WHETHER HE IS aware that whereas both motor-cars and smoking pipes are subject to Purchase Tax at 25 per cent, cleaning polish for motor-cars and all domestic polishes are untaxed, but cleaning polish for smoking pipes is taxed at 25 per cent; and why this discrimination in favour of non-pipe-smoker motorists exists. (July 1964)

MEMBERS BEHAVING BADLY – PARLIAMENTARY ANTICS

We saw in the last chapter how normal parliamentary duties can nevertheless produce curious outcomes. These are as nothing compared with the occasions when elected members choose to flout expected standards, whether it is the exploiting of often quaint rules of procedure for political advantage or rather more crudely breaching the norms of behaviour.

Extremes of debate

The head of the Kwa-Zulu homeland, Chief Mangosuthu Buthelezi, set a world record for political loquacity when he opened his Parliament in 1993. His speech setting out the government's policy for the year ran to 427 pages. It took him 18 days' to deliver it. Starting on 12 March, he had reached the end of the 'introductory overview' after six days (and 145 pages). He spoke every weekday, giving legislators the weekend off. The undertaking was not helped by the need to translate parts rendered in Zulu into English and *vice versa*. He concluded on 30 March, when exhausted parliamentarians reportedly leapt to their feet in acclaim. Every member had been required to be present throughout, unless they had urgent business, in which case a deputy had to take their place.

THE SHORTEST SITTING of a parliamentary committee is believed to be the standing committee meeting in December 1990 to debate an Order amending drugs legislation. Conservative government members turned out in full, expecting a prolonged and heated confrontation. To their surprise, not one member of the Opposition arrived. The committee went through all its consideration in 24 seconds. Home Office Minister John Patten said it was 'a world, not to say inter-galactic, record'.

Go slows

The filibuster – the art of excessively prolonging a speech in order to disrupt the proceedings of a law-making body – has produced down the years some extreme examples both of political commitment and physical stamina.

THE LONGEST CONTINUOUS parliamentary speech on record was perpetrated in the United States Congress by crusty South Carolina Senator Strom Thurmond in 1957, when he spoke uninterrupted for 24 hours 18 minutes opposing civil rights legislation for Negroes. In doing so, he narrowly beat the existing record set by Wayne Morse, an Independent Senator from Oregon, who had held the floor for 22 hours and 26 minutes in 1953 protesting against plans to award states rights over their offshore waters for oil exploration.

NEXT IN THE line of honour for this dubious practice appears to be the speech delivered in Ontario's Legislative Assembly in Canada in 1990 by Peter Kormos. He had conducted an eccentric one-man campaign against reform of the car insurance laws. As the sitting on 26 April appeared to be drawing to a welcome 6pm close, he rose and launched into his usual speech – he did not sit down again until 11 o'clock the next morning, an uninterrupted 17 hours. He enlivened the marathon by giving out the Premier's home telephone number and urging people to call it, and offered prizes to those who phoned their support. Over 700 responded. The government hailed the exercise pointless – as indeed it was. Two weeks later, the new car insurance regulations passed unaltered.

RADICAL MP MASSIMO TEODORI set an Italian filibuster record in February 1981 when he spoke non-stop in the Chamber of Deputies for 16 hours and five minutes protesting against a proposed law giving police powers to detain terrorist suspects for 48 hours without their lawyers. As he made his attempt, the Speaker of the chamber was required to observe him through binoculars to ensure he kept within the rules. Teodori was not allowed to lean against his desk for support, and the only refreshment he was allowed was cold water. His party colleagues were suspected of managing to smuggle cups of cappuccino to him. At one point, supporters also provoked Communist deputies into making an intervention. During the interruption, Teodori was able to snaffle an orange.

BRITAIN'S LONGEST PARLIAMENTARY speech was made in 1983 by Labour MP John Golding, who spoke uninterrupted for 11 hours and 15 minutes in the committee scrutinising the legislation privatising British Telecom.

DURING A BITTER inter-party dispute that paralysed the Alabama Senate for nearly a month in the spring of 1999, Democrat members tried to strip powers from Steve Windom, the State's first Republican Lieutenant-Governor of the 20th century and Speaker of the Senate. Over one-third of the Senate's entire sitting days were lost by a Democrat boycott of proceedings which prevented any legislation passing.

They then opted for holding marathon sessions in an attempt to force Windom to leave his chair for a comfort break, at which point they planned to use his absence to vote through their reforms. Determined not to risk leaving his seat, Windom maintained his place uninterrupted for 29 hours. At one point, he was captured on film surreptitiously urinating into a jug hidden under his desk to avoid absenting himself. Commenting afterwards on his resistance, he said, 'It took guts — and a bladder of steel.' The local newspaper, the *Birmingham News*, took a more jaundiced view, editorialising on the politicians' antics that 'they have simply gone crazy'. Members of the House of Representatives, embarrassed by their upper house colleagues, wore lapel buttons declaring 'I'm in the House. I work.'

IRENE SMITH, A CITY councillor in St Louis, Missouri, was forced to relieve herself in a wastepaper bin in the middle of her filibuster in 2001 protesting at proposed changes to district electoral boundaries which would cost her her own seat. The Speaker refused to suspend the sitting to allow her a comfort break, so her colleagues gathered round, concealed her with a quilt and enabled her to 'alleviate' herself as she later described it. She was later threatened with prosecution for urinating in public but the charge was dropped.

CONTROVERSIAL PLANS IN June 1992 to commit troops overseas for the first time since the Second World War led to Japanese parliamentarians resorting to their own unique filibuster tactic. Members of the lower house, where votes are conducted by proceeding to a ballot box in the middle of the chamber, adopted the 'ox-walk' to prolong each vote on the proposals. Provided the member continues to advance towards the box, they remain within the rules. Those obstructing the government's plans shuffled infinitely slowly, fraction of an inch by fraction of an inch. They managed to stretch out the debate for three uninterrupted days.

The Texas House of Representatives was brought to a standstill for five days in May 2003 when nearly all the Democrat members mounted a novel ploy to thwart their governing Republican opponents from passing changes to the electoral boundaries. Described as 'brazen gerrymandering', the plans would have created seats which would join far-flung parts of the state together to benefit Republican representation in the US Congress. One seat was to be

500 miles long, with others narrowing in places to less than a mile wide before ballooning to take in Republican voters.

With 100 members of the 150-seat legislature required to be present for a quorum to conduct business and aware that, under Texas law, state troopers were empowered to compel attendance by force, 51 Democrat members sabotaged the session by fleeing out of the state just before the crucial vote and holing themselves up in a motel just over the border in Oklahoma. Beyond the reach of Texas Rangers, the House authorities were reduced to issuing arrest warrants for the missing legislators. In return, the Democrats vowed not to return until the controversial law was dropped.

They stayed away until a parliamentary deadline passed which killed the legislation. More than 300 other pieces of planned legislation were lost too as a result of the boycott.

The peace was short-lived, however. Two months later, when the proposals were re-launched, this time in the state's upper house, most of the Democrat Senators did a similar bunk, flying off to New Mexico to scupper the two-thirds majority needed to pass the law. They stayed away for six weeks before the protest lapsed. By mid-October, the measure had finally passed into law.

A Supreme Court ruling in 2006 later endorsed states' rights to 're-district' their boundaries how and whenever they liked.

With friends like these

For notoriety in political actions, the Texas legislature has a long track record. In 1971, Tom Moore Jr, a representative from Waco, set out to demonstrate his concern that few of his fellow members of the House of Representatives actually paid attention to the resolutions they were passing. He introduced a motion to honour Albert DeSalvo for his pioneering work in population control. DeSalvo was better known as the Boston Strangler, who had murdered 13 women in the Massachusetts city in the early 1960s.

The citation lauded DeSalvo's 'dedication and devotion to his work [that] has enabled the weak and lonely throughout the nation to achieve and maintain a new degree of concern for their future... He has been officially recognised by the state of Massachusetts for his noted activities and unconventional technique involving population control and applied psychology.' The motion passed unanimously.

Contributing in their own way

The shortest ever speech in the British Parliament is thought to be Lord Mishcon's contribution in May 1985, proposing a clause be added to a piece of environmental legislation that would require environment authorities to report annually on their performance. He simply rose and said, 'Why not?'

LORD ORANMORE AND BROWNE who, when hereditary peers ceased to be members of the House of Lords in 1999, held the record as the longest-serving peer, never made a speech throughout the 72 years he sat in the House after inheriting his title in 1927.

BARON TREVOR, a Conservative peer, made his first speech in the House of Lords in May 1993, 43 years after entering the House. His diffidence was by no means unique. Lord Cullen of Ashbourne, who succeeded to his title in 1932, waited 10 years before taking his seat in the Lords and another 30 before uttering his first speech. Lord Shaughnessy took his seat six weeks before taking part in the Normandy landings in 1944. He then did not make his maiden speech until 1986. The usual reason for these long silences was non-attendance. Perhaps the record for turning up and still not taking part is that of the Earl of Romney, who keenly attended debates but did not utter a single word from his inauguration in 1974 until the demise of the hereditary peers 25 years later.

DEAD MAN WINS ELECTION

FRANK MAGUIRE WAS MP for Fermanagh and South Tyrone for seven years between 1974 and his death in 1981. During that time, he visited Westminster infrequently, never actually spoke in the House and never asked a question. Known as 'the Invisible Man', his chief claim to fame was his abstention in the March 1979 no-confidence debate which the Labour government of James Callaghan lost – by one vote – precipitating the general election that brought Margaret Thatcher to power.

Parliamentary japes

During a late-night transport debate in the House of Lords in 1985, Lord Carmichael, an opposition peer, spoke unusually slowly. Afterwards he confessed that the whips had told him to string out his speech to keep the debate going until 10.40. At that point, according to House rules, the door keepers and other support staff qualified for free taxis home.

JIM WEST, US Senator from Washington State, proposed to his girlfriend in the middle of a 1990 speech in the Senate. The bride-to-be, sitting in the gallery, hurried down to the floor and the couple stood for several minutes in front of the podium while his colleagues applauded.

LORD HAILSHAM, who as Lord Chancellor in the 1970s and 80s presided over the House of Lords, revealed in 1992 how he kept awake during the more soporific debates. 'When close to nodding off, I whisper "Bollocks" at the bench of bishops.'

THE LOBBY CORRESPONDENT of *The Times* reported in 1990 on the means by which Harold Walker, a Deputy Speaker in the Commons, and thus tasked with overseeing the more tedious proceedings of the House, kept awake: *The Times* crossword. 'He cuts it out and sticks it behind his order paper. The only place from which you can see what he is doing is a certain section of the press gallery behind the Speaker's chair.'

KEEPING ORDER IN an often unruly House is one of the hallmarks of a Speaker's reputation. Bernard Weatherill, who occupied the chair from 1983 to 1992 and who oversaw the introduction of the televising of Parliament, lost through the coming of the cameras one of his signal tricks for keeping rowdy Members in order. In March 1987, during a heated Question Time, a Conservative member, John Heddle, mimicked the Speaker in shouting out the command 'briefly' to urge an Opposition member to end his speech. Overhearing it, the bewigged and stately Mr Speaker solemnly raised two fingers in a V-sign in Heddle's direction.

TAKING THE OATH of allegiance when retaking his seat after the 1992 election, notorious Derbyshire anti-establishment MP Dennis Skinner ('the Beast of Bolsover') refused to stick to the script. He offered, 'I swear allegiance to a taxpaying Queen but none of her heirs and successors.' The new Speaker, Betty Boothroyd, allowed him to get away with it.

EXTREMIST MP Filippo Berselli was ejected from the Italian Chamber of Deputies during a rowdy debate in the summer of 1989 on the problems facing the country's beaches after an invasion of slimy algae had devastated much of Italy's Adriatic coastline and ruined the season's tourism. He made his point by taking off his shoes and socks and standing in the middle of the chamber in a bowl of the polluted sea water, shouting accusations of government inaction.

TO ADDRESS FINLAND'S alarmingly worsening divorce rate, eccentric television star and Social Democrat Member of Parliament, Tommy Tabermann, introduced a bill in April 2008 that would require the Finnish state to provide a week's paid holiday annually to every worker for the sole use of shoring up their personal relationships. It has yet to be passed into law.

FOR THREE MONTHS in 2002, Labour MP Austin Mitchell, who represented the fishing port of Grimsby, legally changed his name to Austin Haddock to promote his constituency's industry. He adopted the new moniker as 'a fun way of getting some more publicity for the seafood cause', he said. His wife Linda was reported to be contemplating changing her name to Chips. In December, he announced his intention to revert to Mitchell, saying rather deflatedly that 'I didn't get a single letter of thanks' for the stunt.

THE MOST FEARED – by civil servants – parliamentary committee in the British Parliament, the Public Accounts Committee, grills public officials over their management of public funds. Few senior mandarins have managed to defuse the wrath of the cash scrutineers better than Sir Frank Cooper, Permanent Secretary at the Ministry of Defence from 1976 to 1982. Facing a particularly tricky PAC hearing, he invited the Committee, which usually meets in the Houses of Parliament, to hold its meeting on a nuclear submarine at Chatham. He later observed that the session had gone spectacularly smoothly, the Committee, according to Cooper's obituary, 'behaving like children in a sweet shop'.

Cocking a snook at the machine

On the birth of Prime Minister Margaret Thatcher's grandchild in 1989, Conservative MP Harry Greenway put down a sycophantic Early Day Motion, a favourite device members use to draw attention to matters of the day, expressing congratulations and delight at the event. The House authorities rejected an amendment by the aforesaid Dennis Skinner that expressed the hope that the baby would learn to crawl as quickly as Greenway.

OF THE THOUSANDS of parliamentary questions tabled each year by Members, the majority are anodyne and workmanlike searches for information. Just occasionally, the glimmer of a deeper humanity peers through a question (or answer):

John Cummings (Easington): To ask the Secretary of State for Transport if he will travel by car from London to Peterlee via the M1, M18, A1M, A1 and A19 and then make a statement. (November 1989)

Robert Atkins, a junior Minister at the Department for Transport, replied that he had no plans to do so.

Lord Tebbit: To ask whether when questions are capable of being answered by either yes or no, the Government will make it their practice to so answer them. (May 1998)
Lord McIntosh: No.

Tam Dalyell (Linlithgow): To ask the Secretary of State for Transport what assessment he has made of the implications for transport safety of the decision to withdraw the services of watchmen from the Forth rail bridge. (April 1989)
Michael Portillo, Minister of State: Whilst this is a management matter for British Rail, which considers that the decision does not endanger safety, I understand that watchmen's duties were to guard against risk of fire from steam trains and to deter trespassers when the only other means of crossing the Forth was by ferry.

Robert Adley (Christchurch): To ask the Secretary of State for Transport what information he has available on the average speed of traffic in (a) central London, (b) Paris, (c) Rome and (d) Madrid. (May 1989)
Peter Bottomley, Minister of State: I have been asserting for a year that traffic moves faster in London than in comparable cities. I do not know whether this is true. So far no one has contradicted the claim…

Joan Walley (Stoke-on-Trent): To ask the Secretary of State for the Environment why there has been no lighting on the stairs leading from the Committee Corridor for the last 14 days. (December 1989)
Christopher Chope, Minister of State: From the limited description it is

not possible to identify which of the five stairs to the Committee Corridor the Hon. Member has in mind. A check on 13 December identified only two bulbs, each on separate stairs, which needed replacing, plus three emergency lights. But I hope the Hon. Member understands that it is not necessary to use the formalities of a parliamentary question in order to have a light bulb replaced.

An undated reply from an unidentified Minister:
The fact that the Bill did not appear in the parliamentary timetable for this session did not mean that it had a low priority, but merely that the other measures had a higher priority.

The following answer perhaps most readily conjures up the scene of a tired and overworked minister coming to the end of his tether after a long day:

Dennis Skinner (*Bolsover*): To ask the Minister for the Civil Service how many civil servants in employment at the latest date are (a) men or (b) women. (February 1992)
Timothy Renton, Minister of State: All of them.

AFTER 18 MONTHS in the House as member for Nottingham North, Labour MP Graham Allen acquired a reputation for tabling floods of parliamentary questions seeking detailed statistics on a range of difficult subjects. Ministers became accustomed to batting these back with the standard parliamentary get-out clause that the information was not readily available in the form requested and could only be obtained at disproportionate cost. In the end it clearly got to him. In October 1993, he tabled the following question:

TO ASK THE Lord President of the Council how many parliamentary questions have been answered in the past 12 months with the statement that the required figures are not available.

TONY NEWTON REPLIED: This information is not in a readily available form and could only be provided at disproportionate cost.

AFTER INTRODUCING ELECTRONIC voting in 1994, the authorities in the Romanian Senate soon had to plant sensors under each Member's seat to ensure they were actually present when their votes were cast. It had emerged that Senators had rapidly developed a deception scheme so that those who could not be bothered to turn up to proceedings would give their voting cards to colleagues, who cast the votes on their behalf.

NEIGHBOURING BULGARIA ENCOUNTERED an identical problem when its Parliament introduced electronic voting. In January 2002, the authorities announced that weighing scales were to be fitted to every MP's seat in the assembly to defeat the cheating members who were suspected of multiple voting on behalf of absent colleagues. The security devices would only register a valid vote if a person of the same weight as the MP who usually occupied the seat inserted the card.

THREE YEARS ON, matters seemed not to have improved. More than a third of Bulgarian MPs ducked out of a debate in August 2005 by asking a colleague to vote on their behalf. The debate was on truancy. A later debate on how to improve attendance in the chamber had to be postponed – due to the MPs' poor turnout.

SPANISH SENATORS DEMANDED a re-vote on a controversial income tax law in May 1991 because 177 votes were cast when only 156 members were present. Press reports cited video evidence of Joaquin Galan voting on his own button while activating another on a vacant desk by his foot.

EVEN AN EVENT as solemn as the election of a national President became mired in trickery when Italian Members of Parliament voted in 1992. A ballot of the MPs had to be re-run when officials discovered that some Members had taken more than a single voting paper and cast multiple votes for their candidate. Builders had to construct a voting booth in the chamber overnight, and the politicians had to process individually through to cast their vote, being handed a single voting slip as they went.

When the wheels come off

Otto Arosomena Gomez, an Ecuadorian Congressman and former President of the country, shot and wounded two colleagues when a debate in the national assembly turned heated in October 1980.

THE SITUATION WHICH every government minister dreads happened to Arts Minister William Waldegrave in July 1983. During Question Time, he had the rare experience for a Member of the House of admitting that he did not know the answer to a question. The briefing pack prepared for him by civil servants ran up to Question No. 28, usually far and away sufficient for the amount of time available. However, on this occasion, absences and shorter follow-up debate than usual found the House at Question 29 a minute or so before the session expired. The minister merely rose to inform the House that 'The Hon. Member will have noticed that my brief runs only up to question twenty-eight –' before being drowned out by mocking laughter. He volunteered to answer whatever the follow-up question would have been instead.

IN JUNE 1982, proceedings of the French National Assembly descended into chaos when a controversial bill on immigration was sabotaged by opponents. The measure would allow trade unions to carry on negotiations in the languages of the immigrant workforce (mainly Portuguese, Arabic and Serbo-Croat). Members opposed to the legislation began to conduct the debate in a range of languages to demonstrate the anarchy that would result. The short-hand recorders coped with German and Spanish but sent urgent messages to the Chair when one Member began speaking in an obscure language from Chad. The prospect of a string of further unfamiliar African and Caribbean tongues was too much. The Speaker announced that only those contributions made in French would be taken down for posterity. That was enough to call the protest off.

FRENCH MP Jean Lassalle interrupted proceedings of the National Assembly in June 2003 to protest about the relocation of a police station in his constituency by singing during Question Time. Lassalle, from the Pyrenees, performed a traditional folk song in local dialect and, despite repeated calls to order by the Assembly Chair, managed to get to the end. He said it had been the only way to draw attention to his complaint.

COLOMBIAN MP Luis Eduardo Diaz was suspended by his national Parliament in September 2003 for bringing out a rubber dildo during a debate as part of his campaign for sterilisation of poor people to cut unwanted births. He left the dildo on the desk of the Health Minister after complaints about his 'disrespect' for Parliament. 'A rubber penis is not something that should be brought to Parliament,' said a fellow MP. Suspended for five sessions, his antics appeared to have backfired. Rather than take notice of his controversial ideas, most members seemed distracted by the sex toy. One said, 'I guess we got so focused on the rubber penis we didn't even pay attention to what he was saying.'

THE SWEDISH PARLIAMENT was interrupted in 1985 by women protestors in the public gallery who rained down copies of porno-graphic magazines on MPs who had approved the opening of a sex supermarket in Stockholm. Reporters remarked on the number of copies that were secreted away by members 'for research'.

Behaviour unbecoming

Taiwan's Parliament has earned a reputation over the last two decades as the world's rowdiest chamber. It started right at the beginning. The opening session of the first Taiwanese Parliament to have a majority of directly elected MPs ended in violence in 1990 after a filibuster by the opposition stopped the Prime Minister from making his inaugural address. The Speaker finally called proceedings to a halt when opposition member Wang Tzung-sung squirted him with a water pistol.

Two years later, the same Parliament suffered ten days of turmoil during a dispute over a controversial nuclear power plant. Trouble started when an opposition deputy began taking photographs of fellow deputies voting in favour, leading to scuffles and fist fights. Officials estimated the disruption had cost 50 million Taiwan dollars (about £1.2 million) in lost time. The cost of damage to furniture when deputies jumped on it and ripped out microphones had not been calculated.

In 2004, a food fight erupted during a contentious debate over rises in the defence budget. Chu Fong-chih, an opposition deputy, hurled her lunch box of chicken and rice at Chen Tsung-yi, a legislator from the ruling Democratic Progressive Party. Chen responded by flinging his own lunch box at her.

INDIA'S LOWER HOUSE, the Lok Sabha, runs Taiwan a close second for its ingrained unruliness and, in the favourite description of Indian journalists, its 'uproariness'. A re-write of the members' code of conduct manual in 1992 found it necessary to remind MPs that it was out of order to knit in the House, carry hats or walking sticks, or read any material unconnected with the business at hand. Carrying arms and ammunition was prohibited, neither could an MP 'take shelter within the precincts of Parliament House if he knows he is wanted by the police authorities outside'. The latter provision appeared entirely necessary, as estimates in 1996 were that of the 545-seat House returned in that year's election, 27 had criminal records; of the 2009 intake, 153 – nearly a third of the entire House – had criminal charges against them, including nine ministers. In the case of 15 MPs, it was for murder.

WHEN THE ISRAELI parliamentary committee on science held hearings on the new wonder drug for impotence, Viagra, in June 1998, four of the eight tablets exhibited by doctors giving evidence disappeared during a break in the meeting.

MEMBERS BEHAVING BADLY — PARLIAMENTARY ANTICS

THREE SPANISH MPs from the ruling Popular Party were fined by their party authorities when they were caught looking at a pornographic website on a laptop while sitting in the parliamentary chamber attending a debate…on the evils of domestic violence against women.

Miguel Perez-Huysmans, the owner of the laptop, was also forced to resign as leader of the party's youth wing. He was fined £600; his two colleagues, £300 each.

A bid to ban laptops in the chamber was said, however, to be unlikely to succeed, as most observers agreed that MPs had little else to do when attending formal debates. Party management of the business of the Spanish Parliament had become so strictly controlled that the expression of personal views was discouraged, with votes being cast by managers on behalf of the whole party rather than by individual members. Real debate had all but disappeared, leaving idle and under-occupied MPs to their own devices for much of the time.

A NUMBER OF Conservative Members of the European Parliament were censured in 2003 for distributing 'sexist' photographs among colleagues to enliven boring committee meetings. Running a mock 'Man of the Year' competition, the organisers invited fellow MEPs to judge pictures showing men demeaning their women-folk. They included a farmer transporting his wife in a cage attached to his tractor and a man walking alongside his partner who was carrying a huge parcel of firewood. The winner was allegedly a picture of a husband genteelly carrying a six-pack of beer while holding hands with a woman struggling with a full crate of bottles.

MEMBERS OF THE United States Congress cannily secured themselves a pay rise in 1987 while being able to tell their constituents that they had voted against it. The skilful manoeuvre was made possible because President Reagan had decided to agree to 15 per cent salary increases for both the Senate and House of Representatives, to come into force unless Congress voted against them within 30 days.

Congressmen allowed the deadline to pass, and then took a vote formally rejecting the pay rise once it was impossible to stop it coming into force. They thus achieved the best of both worlds.

Order, order!

As if human occupants are not troublesome enough, India's legislature suffers from a unique hardship – monkeys. Hundreds live in the precincts of the Parliament building, and are notorious for entering MPs' offices, including the Prime Minister's Secretariat, attacking staff and destroying official papers. Any attempt to eradicate the menace is routinely blocked by Hindu members for whom the religious connection to the god Hanuman, who won battles by leading an army of monkeys, is revered.

MORE SERENE PROBLEMS confronted the Swaziland Senate during the budget debate in 1991. A member pointed out to the Speaker that others in the chamber appeared to be asleep. The Speaker refused to intervene, officially ruling that they could be 'concentrating deeply on communicating with their ancestors'. If this was the case, and they were suddenly disturbed, they could die from shock.

FACING SIMILAR PROBLEMS, in 1996 the Thai Parliament found the solution to members dozing: the authorities installed uncomfortable, low-backed chairs which made it impossible to lounge.

THE SPEAKER OF the New Zealand Parliament, Jonathan Hunt, introduced in November 1999 a soccer-style yellow and red card system to maintain order in his House.

ATTEMPTS TO BAN knitting in the New Zealand Parliament failed in 2002. Opposition members were infuriated when the Junior Minister for Commerce, Judith Tizard, got out her knitting on the government bench during a debate involving her ministry. Citing arrogance and disrespect for the House, they sought to have the Speaker rule the practice out of order. But to their dismay, Speaker Jonathan Hunt ruled that knitting was not prohibited in the chamber, although it would not be allowed from the seats occupied by ministers.

THE INTRODUCTION OF television into debating chambers has, according to some observers, harmed the spontaneity of proceedings in many parliaments. For others, it gives a warts and all portrayal of the people's representatives. In 2007, as election fever was rising, Australian viewers were treated to images, thought to date from eight years earlier, of Kevin Rudd, their future Prime Minister, then a lowly opposition backbencher, being caught in the background as a member of his party's front bench droned on at the despatch box, cleaning out his ear with his finger and eating the resulting earwax.

From the history books

In 1584, a member of the public is recorded as having wandered into the chamber of the House of Commons and sat for two hours before being recognised as an intruder. On 27 February 1771, the *Parliamentary Journal* records that a member of the public was admonished by the Speaker after he had entered the division lobby and taken part in a vote. Thomas Hunt claimed he had taken part on several votes on previous occasions.

A DOG IS RECORDED as having found its way into the debating chamber during Lord North's premiership (1770–82) and interrupted his speech by its loud barking. The records also show that on 14 May 1605, 'a strange spaniel, of mouse-colour, came into the House'.

ESSAYIST AND PIONEER journalist Joseph Addison sat in the House of Commons representing Malmesbury for 11 years from 1708 until his death in 1719 but never uttered a word in debate because of shyness. Despite this, he served as Secretary to the Lord Lieutenant of Ireland, became a Commissioner of Trade, Chief Secretary for Ireland and finally, two years before he died, Secretary of State for the Southern Department, a forerunner of the Foreign Secretaryship – all without ever speaking in Parliament.

Future Prime Minister Lord Bute, who became Premier in 1762, sat in Parliament for two months short of 25 years without uttering a word in debate. He made his maiden speech just three months before becoming Prime Minister.

The Duke of Portland managed to become Prime Minister in 1783 without having spoken in the House at all. He made his first contribution six days after taking the top office. He had held ministerial office as early as 1765.

Despite penning a million and a half words in his magisterial six-volume *The History of the Decline and Fall of the Roman Empire*, Edward Gibbon sat for eight years as a Member of Parliament between 1774 and 1782 and did not utter a single word in debate.

MANY WOULD HAVE preferred it if the same affliction applied to 18th-century member David Hartley. So notorious was he for treating the House to long, turgid speeches that he became widely known as 'the dinner bell'. As soon as he rose, it was safe to leave the chamber and go to dinner. Charles Jenkinson, father of future Prime Minister Lord Liverpool, took advantage of this in 1779 when Hartley had risen at about five o'clock on a summer's evening. It being 'generally understood that he would continue a long time on his legs, [Jenkinson] profited by the occasion to breathe some country air. He walked, therefore, from the House to his residence in Parliament Street; from whence, mounting his horse, he rode to a place…some miles out of town. There he dined, he sent his servant to the House to inquire who had spoken…and when a division might be expected. The footman brought back the answer that Mr Hartley continued still speaking.' When Jenkinson returned to the chamber at about 9pm Hartley was still on his feet 'regardless of the general impatience or of the profound repose into which the majority of his hearers were sunk'.

AT THE FIRST sitting of the Arkansas House of Representatives in 1837, Speaker of the House John Wilson became enraged by an amendment moved by Representative J.J. Anthony which he deemed to be intended to cast a slight on his integrity. When Anthony refused to back down and return to his seat, Wilson descended from the Speaker's chair, drew his Bowie knife and stabbed Anthony on the floor of the House. He died within minutes. Although expelled from office pending trial, he was later acquitted by a jury, which ruled the murder was 'excusable homicide'. Wilson later won re-election back to the House. The Arkansas chamber is said to be haunted to this day.

THE UNITED STATES Senate famously failed to endorse the post-First World War Treaty of Versailles, which created the League of Nations, the brainchild of their own President, Woodrow Wilson. In opposing approval the chief antagonist, Massachusetts Senator Henry Cabot Lodge, who chaired the Foreign Relations Committee, read the entire 264-page treaty aloud as part of a filibuster to draw out the debate.

SIR JOHN TREVOR, Speaker of the House of Commons in 1685 and again from 1690 to 1695, had one of the most unfortunate afflictions for his office. He was severely cross-eyed. Parliamentary legend tells of many occasions when confusion reigned as more than one Member of Parliament thought he had received the Speaker's nod to address the House next. As a direct result of the problems caused, Speakers introduced the practice, still in use today, of calling out the name of the Member selected to speak next instead of relying on the silent nod.

THE SHORTCOMINGS OF Charles Wolfran Cornwall, elected Speaker in late 1780, were entirely self-inflicted. He had the habit, in the words of a contemporary observer, of keeping a large pot of beer 'constantly at hand, from which he imbibed large quantities' during debates which 'considerably detracted from the dignity of his office'. The drunk Speaker often fell asleep, which 'on more than one occasion is said to have caused considerable inconvenience to the House'. Remarkably, he remained Speaker for over eight years, dying in office in January 1789.

JOSEPH BROTHERTON, MP for Salford from 1832 until his sudden death in 1857, had a religious obsession that all good Christians should go to bed before midnight. That the House of Commons regularly sat into the early hours was deeply offensive to him and, for over twenty years, every night that the Commons was sitting he would rise in his place on the stroke of twelve and formally move that the House adjourn. He rarely succeeded, but he never stopped trying.

THE ONLY DECLARED member of the Communist Party to sit in the British Parliament in the past 50 years did so in the least likely surroundings – the House of Lords. Wogan Philipps inherited the baronetcy of Milford from his father in 1962 and decided to take his seat in the Lords. As Lord Milford, he used his maiden speech to reveal that he was a Communist, and called upon the upper house to abolish itself. He was heard in stony silence, the traditional way for their Lordships to show displeasure. He died in 1993 after three decades of solitude in the House.

WOMEN WERE BANNED from observing the House of Commons for over 60 years after attending debates became a society occasion in the later 18th century. It reached a notorious crescendo in February 1778 when, for a major debate on the state of the nation, a flock of society ladies occupied all the seats in the public gallery. When complaints were made to the Speaker and they were ordered to leave, the women created two hours of mayhem in their refusal. A formal ban was quickly introduced, and was lifted only in 1842 when, seven years after the matter was re-raised, a special Ladies Gallery was built. To guard against a concern that male MPs might be influenced by the sight of females while they spoke, women were delicately obscured behind an ornate grille so that their presence could not be seen from the chamber below. They were thrown out again in 1888 because of the rising female-suffrage campaign which had led to frequent interruptions of debates. When they were allowed back in 1909, all women visitors had to sign a written declaration promising to behave. The grilles were not removed until 1918.

DURING THE AGITATION for women's votes in the early part of the 20th century, Catherine Griffiths, a suffragette, stole into the chamber of the House of Commons and left drawing pins strewn over the seat where Lloyd George sat 'to make him sit up'. She was also later convicted of breaking into the House of Lords.

THERE HAS BEEN one occasion when, for five months, a Prime Minister of another country sat as a member of the House of Commons. Maltese-born Sir Gerald Strickland set up and led the Constitutional Party as the main opposition force in Malta from 1921 to 1927. At the same time, he occupied a seat at Westminster, having won Lancaster for the Conservatives in 1924. In August 1927, he became Prime Minister of Malta. He continued to sit in London too until the principle was questioned by other MPs. The delicate situation was resolved by Strickland being made a peer in the New Year's Honours List of 1928. He remained Prime Minister of Malta until 1932.

REGINALD ROBINSON, a legendary correspondent who spent 54 years in the House of Commons Press Gallery, holds the unique place in parliamentary history of being the only journalist to be reported by Hansard as having taken part in debate. Obituaries on his death in 1998 recorded the occasion when Robinson failed to catch the words of Foreign Secretary Anthony Eden, and asked in a loud voice to his fellow reporters, 'What was that?' To his – and the House's – astonishment, Eden looked up and repeated himself for Robinson's benefit. The exchange was duly set down in the official record.

OFFICE AND RESPONSIBILITY – GOVERNMENT

The responsibilities of office take governments down many strange avenues. Some are of their choosing and others are forced on them by events. Picking one's way through the minefield is not always straightforward. What's clear is that the machinery of government often runs far from smoothly.

Affairs of state

When re-writing its constitution in 1978 after four military coups in 10 years, Nigerian lawmakers inserted a clause formally making *coups d'état* illegal. In the 15 years that followed, there were three more.

AS PART OF its anti-poverty strategy in the 1980s, the Bangladesh government subsidised the cost of gas to householders by levying a flat charge of £1 per month. It later found that users were keeping their cookers alight all day because it saved on the cost of buying matches. The ill-fated policy was thought to have cost the cash-strapped economy millions of dollars in wasted gas.

THE CANADIAN PROVINCE OF Manitoba was plunged into chaos in June 1985 when the nation's Supreme Court ruled that all its laws passed over the previous 95 years were invalid, and 'of no force or effect'. Legislators had passed an Act in 1890 declaring English to be the only official language, in contravention of the Canadian constitution, which gave equal status to French. The issue had languished in the prairie province because of the lack of French influence. Politicians faced the task of translating an estimated 4,500 laws and up to 30,000 regulations. It took until 1990 to re-enact them all.

THE PHILIPPINES PARLIAMENT voted to re-introduce the death penalty in 1993, specifying in the law that execution had to be by electric chair until a gas chamber had been built. A year later, the Director of the Bureau of Corrections officially wrote to Senators complaining that he had accumulated 54 inmates on Death Row, none of which he could execute because the gas chamber had been stalled by a safety inspector who had discovered that the brickwork leaked gas and could be 'a public health hazard'. The country's only electric chair had been destroyed in an accident years earlier.

Clearly neither problem was solved: when the first execution eventually took place five years later in 1999, it was by lethal injection.

DURING A PARTICULARLY nervy stage of the Iran–Iraq war in 1982, Iraqi leader Saddam Hussein sought to strengthen morale by publicising examples of heroic devotion to the cause. The most outlandish claim reported was of a charge on the battlefield led by 27 men – all blind. And after a spate of surrenders in 1986, the Iraqi military command reportedly halted the supply of white underwear to frontline troops.

THE FRENCH GOVERNMENT agency set up in 2009 to police internet piracy, illegal downloading and copyright theft issues, had to apologise when it was discovered to be using a copyrighted logo without permission. The owner of the logo, which had been copied from France Telecom, was at the time of writing threatening legal action.

DEAD MAN WINS ELECTION

IN JULY 1982, the ruling Crown Prince of the tiny Alpine state of Liechtenstein had to bail out his government when it discovered it had no law against the sale of narcotic drugs. Prince Franz Josef used his emergency powers to declare that the laws of neighbouring Switzerland on the matter had immediate effect.

THE TASMANIAN GOVERNMENT found itself unable to publish its list of censored publications in 1977 because the State's Attorney-General advised that doing so would contravene the government's own obscenity laws.

IN 2006, THE UK Government inadvertently repealed its law that made it an offence to use a forged passport. Due to a mix-up over the timing of bringing into force the new Identity Cards Act, ministers found they had repealed the old law relating to passports without introducing the new provisions. Several courts around the country were forced to dismiss cases, as it was technically no longer illegal to use a false passport. The following month, the government hastily issued the necessary statutory instrument to re-establish the offence.

THE NEW MINORITY Conservative Canadian Government elected in January 2006 did not go out of its way to endear itself to a key segment of the populace when Prime Minister Stephen Harper appointed as Junior Minister for Francophone Affairs, the government post dedicated to maintaining the linguistic interests of French-speaking Canadians, an MP with a distinct disadvantage for the job: he could not speak French. Riling the perennially fragile Anglo-French cultural divide in the country, the appointment of Ted Menzies, an Albertan from the prairies of central Canada, caused an outrage when his lack of capacity in French was disclosed. He quickly committed himself to language lessons three times a week and to 'total immersion' in Quebec in his free time. Perhaps fortuitously for both parties, by October 2007 he had moved on.

In the public interest

In the 1970s, the Dutch Government required that all television adverts for sweets show a toothbrush at least one-tenth the height of the screen throughout the commercial.

AFTER THE ISLAMIC revolution in 1979, the new rulers of Iran imposed strict moral codes for the defence of the nation's females. All buses required segregation, with men travelling on the top deck and women on the bottom.

THE COW, a film produced by the Iranian Ministry of Culture and Arts, was promptly banned on completion – by the same Ministry of Culture and Arts.

In 1995, tighter regulations on mixed gatherings were introduced. The re-named Ministry of Culture and Islamic Guidance instructed that male and female guests at weddings must be in separate rooms at the reception and the groom was forbidden from visiting rooms occupied by women. Photographs would only be allowed of guests of the same sex. Music bands could not be hired and any singer invited had to be approved by the ministry. Later that year, *Kayhan*, a daily newspaper, reported that a bride had been sentenced to 85 lashes by an Islamic court for dancing with men at her wedding. Her father and 127 guests had also been sentenced to floggings or fines.

ACCORDING TO LOCAL press reports, 15 Saudi Arabian girls died in a fire at their school in Mecca in March 2002, some of the deaths being caused by their being forbidden to flee the burning building without their scarves and robes to cover themselves up in accordance with strict Islamic law. Witnesses told police that officials from the Commission for the Promotion of Virtue and Prevention of Vice, the body that enforced Saudi Arabia's strict religious laws, beat three children until they retreated back into the flaming classrooms to retrieve their shawls. Others died because their escape was barred by locked doors throughout the school, the normal practice for girls' schools in order to keep out males.

IN 2001, THE Turkish Ministry of Culture part-funded *Buyuk Adam, Kucuk Ask* ('Big Man, Small Love'), a film about the country's minority Kurd population which won a number of awards and had been put forward by the government as a nominee for the best foreign film at the Oscars. In 2002, the same Ministry banned the film after Turkish police complained about how the force was portrayed.

IN 1973, THE government of the West African state of Sierra Leone instituted the Medal of the Mosquito, a new award to mark civil and military gallantry. It was named after the insect, according to the announcement, to honour the effect the bug had had on making the country a 'white man's graveyard' and preventing Europeans from permanently settling.

IN THE FACE of an increase in crime, the city council in the small US town of Kennesaw, Georgia, enacted a municipal ordinance in May 1982 making ownership of a firearm compulsory for every head of household. Anyone not having a gun and ammunition faced a $200 fine and 60 days in jail. The law exempted the disabled, householders with religious objections and, perhaps wisely, convicted felons. The law is still in force.

CITY COUNCILLORS IN Santa Monica, California, passed a by-law in November 1991 allowing women to use men's public toilets if the queue for theirs was more than three strong, on the grounds that, as men rarely had to queue, doing so breached rights under sex discrimination legislation.

SAN FRANCISCO'S GOVERNING BODY, the Board of Supervisors, voted in May 2000 to outlaw discrimination on the grounds of size. A 'fat acceptance' ordinance was passed unanimously that added to a long list of anti-discrimination measures. City laws already banned discrimination on the grounds of race, colour, religion, age, ancestry, sex, sexual orientation, disability, place of birth and gender identity (to protect transsexuals).

President of the Board, Tom Ammiano, claimed the move was needed because 'people are being denied employment, housing, bank loans on the grounds that they are overweight'. The new legislation decreed that 'weight may not be used as a measure of health, fitness, endurance, flexibility, strength of character or self-control'. The only employers exempted from the law were the police, fire service and unionised strip clubs.

From now on, San Francisco's Human Rights Commission was empowered to investigate allegations of discrimination. Among those affected by the rules were cinemas and theatres who were required to install an adequate supply of extra-wide seats, although ticket clerks were not allowed to point out their existence to ticket buyers as that would be discriminatory.

The self-styled 'fat acceptance' movement began in the city in 1999 after a health club advertising for new members ran a billboard campaign depicting an alien with the slogan, 'When They Come, They'll Eat The Fat Ones First'.

THE US FEDERAL tax authority followed suit in 2002 by announcing that obese people could claim tax allowances in future on weight-loss expenses. The Internal Revenue Service ruled that those with medically diagnosed fat problems could deduct the costs of 'mitigation, treatment or prevention' of their condition. Observers foresaw definitional difficulties ahead, with questions over whether gym membership or purchases of slimming foods would qualify remaining to be clarified.

SINGAPORE, WHICH HAS become notorious for its authoritarian approach to social engineering, banned chewing gum in 1992, supposedly because of the cost of removing discarded gum from pavements. Suppiah Dhanabalan, Foreign Minister and Minister of Culture, gave a little more away when he complained that gum-chewing was 'obnoxious. All it does is exercise the jaw.' Lawmakers imposed a penalty of a year in jail, and a 10,000 Singapore dollar (£4,000) fine for smuggling gum into the country. The ban had to be partially relaxed in 2004 to comply with international trade rules. Citizens, however, were still required to register for permission to acquire gum.

It was not the first anti-social practice to feel the wrath of Singaporean legislators. In 1989, the city state passed regulations making it an offence not to flush a toilet after use.

THE EASTERN CANADIAN city of Halifax, Nova Scotia, introduced what was thought to be a world's first in February 2000 – a ban on wearing perfume or scented products in a public place. Intended to prevent illnesses caused by allergies, the by-law applied to all public locations, including schools, hospitals and the public transport system. It covered not only colognes and cosmetics but scented after-shaves, hairsprays and deodorants. Stung by nationwide ridicule, the city authorities later replaced the ban with a public relations campaign advocating a 'scent-free' environment. It still runs today.

DETROIT CITY COUNCIL introduced a similar ban for all its employees in March 2010 after a worker managed to win $100,000 damages in the local courts by complaining that her colleague's perfume affected her breathing. Council staff would be discouraged from wearing scented deodorants, aftershaves or body lotions. Even air fresheners were on the forbidden list. Observers speculated how long it would be until the city faced its first reverse complaint about a co-worker's unhygienic body odour.

FOLLOWING THE INTRODUCTION of new laws prohibiting smoking in public places in the Netherlands in 2008, Dutch police found themselves obliged to arrest a man smoking cannabis in a coffee shop because the joint contained tobacco.

THE OHIO STATE Department of Natural Resources outwitted two environmental protestors in 2001 who staged a week-long sit-in to obstruct the logging of trees in rural Vinton County. Having arrested the pair for trespassing, the department chopped down the two trees they had occupied on the grounds that they contained the fingerprints of the culprits and would be needed for evidence in court. It then billed the protesters $152 for the cost of cutting down the trees.

PENTAGON OFFICIALS REJECTED a Freedom of Information Act request in November 2003 from a press reporter asking to see the Defence Department's internal training video 'Freedom of Information Act – the People's Right to Know', a film used to teach bureaucrats how to comply with the Act. No reason was given for withholding the film.

TO MAINTAIN THE standards expected in the upmarket Providencia neighbourhood of Chile's capital, Santiago, local municipal councillors introduced a by-law requiring every resident of private property to keep a grass patch in the street immediately outside their front gate. In April 2002, Gloria Cisternas, a mother of four, was sentenced to seven days in jail for refusing to lay turf outside her house. She spent two days incarcerated before a public outcry over the case forced the country's President to get involved. The conviction was later quashed.

Dire straits

The Swedish Parliament's introduction of stringent budget cuts and a ban on overtime in May 2001 led to the head of the national navy announcing that it was cutting back on around-the-clock operations. In future, it would provide defence services only from 9am to 5pm, Monday to Friday.

DEAD MAN WINS ELECTION

THE STATE GOVERNMENT of Acre in Brazil's remote western Amazon region discovered in 2000 that it was paying for 156 schools which either did not exist or were in adjacent states or even neighbouring countries. The area's remoteness stopped education chiefs in the state capital from regularly visiting their charges, so they relied on local administrators. These, it seemed, had reported over the years the development of school buildings that had not in fact taken place, while the funds to run them had been diligently claimed. Eighty-six of the suspect locations were found to be part of another state's school system. Three more actually lay across the border in Bolivia or Peru. The deception was only discovered when the state authorities decided to use satellite photography to undertake an audit of its infrastructure.

DURING THE ECONOMIC meltdown of Russia, the government of the autonomous republic of Altai in the centre of the country was so strapped for cash in 1998 that it began paying its teachers' salaries in vodka. Eight thousand were paid 15 bottles each. The authorities had originally tried to pay part of the six months' pay arrears with toilet paper – but staff rejected the idea.

Continuing economic hardship in 2001 led to 400 staff in the hospital at Nizhni Novgorod in central Russia being offered bags of manure in lieu of wages. They refused. Senior doctors said they would have to have been given six tonnes of manure to equate to their monthly salary.

The most celebrated example of workers accepting goods in place of cash was a group of loggers in Archangel in Russia's Arctic north. They were paid in tampons for the whole of 1994.

THE HEAD OF COLOMBIA'S armed forces, General José Manuel Bonnet, announced desperate measures in October 1997 in the country's 40-year-old war against drugs cartels. He broadcast on national television and radio an appeal to all Colombian women to deny sex to drugs traffickers, guerrillas and paramilitaries until they lay down their arms. 'I propose a sexual strike until December to demand an end to violence… I see it as a last resort attempt to bring peace to our war-ravaged country.' The war is still going on.

INTERNATIONAL EYEBROWS WERE raised in February 2003 when China's National Bureau of Statistics released its annual economic growth figures for 2002. It was not the country's impressive 8 per cent national average growth rate – the second highest in the world – that caused the biggest surprise. It was the detail that all 31 provinces of China were listed as recording growth rates higher than the national average.

Taxing matters

A year after the Danish Parliament legalised prostitution, the national tax authority ruled in September 2000 that a massage parlour worker was entitled to claim tax relief on her £2,100 breast implants as they constituted a legitimate business investment to 'improve facilities'.

THE NORWEGIAN TAX authorities were required by their national courts in 2005 to allow striptease clubs to enjoy the same exemption from 25 per cent Value Added Tax on entry fees as opera, ballet and theatre, ruling that the performance constituted 'art'.

IN JANUARY 2005, the Dutch tax authorities, following legal precedents, allowed a convicted bank robber to claim the £1,400 cost of the gun used in the crime as a business expense. He was able to set off the cost against the £4,700 proceeds of the robbery and had his court-imposed fine reduced by that amount. He did have to serve four years in jail.

LEGISLATORS IN KANSAS introduced the bizarre requirement in 1987 for dealers in illegal drugs to pay tax on every packet of narcotics they sell. Under a law that 20 American states have since copied, the state revenue service sells drug tax stamps that are required to be affixed to every pack of drugs traded. Officials defended the scheme against criticism of double standards by stressing that the stamps did not legalise drug dealing, and any trader caught without duly stamped drugs faces not only the drug offences but tax evasion too. The penalty for not buying the tax stamps is itself five years, along with huge fines for evasion.

Surprisingly, by 2003 nearly $145,000 was being raised in a six-month period on marijuana sales and $305,000 on cocaine and amphetamines. State officials pointed to constitutional protections against self-incrimination that enabled dealers to have anonymity when buying the stamps, and information on stamp sales was protected from being passed on to other law enforcement bodies.

BURIED IN ITS 305-page official instructions that the US Internal Revenue Service issues to US taxpayers on how to complete their returns in 2010, a chapter for 'Other Income' has the requirement that 'if you receive a bribe, include it in your income' (page 92). For anyone uncertain, there are more details under 'Illegal Activities' on page 94: 'Income from illegal activities, such as money from dealing illegal drugs, must be included in your income on Form 1040, line 21, or on schedule C or Schedule C-EZ (Form 1040) if from your self-employment activity.' Under 'Kickbacks' (page 95): 'You must include kickbacks, side commissions, push money, or similar payments you receive in your income.' And for the diligent burglar, under 'Stolen Property': 'If you steal property, you must report its fair market value in your income in the year you steal it unless in the same year, you return it to its rightful owner.'

FACING A BACKLOG of 38 million rupees in unpaid municipal taxes, the Indian city of Hyderabad inaugurated a novel method of recovering payment in March 2005. The revenue agency hired ten-strong bands of drummers to set up camp outside the homes of non-payers with orders to maintain non-stop drumming until recalcitrants paid up. T.S.R. Anjaneyulu, the local tax commissioner, told state media: 'They make a damned racket. Even the neighbours approve, as they see who hasn't paid up.' Five teams were deployed around the city and after a month 25 million rupees of the unpaid taxes had been recovered. Anjaneyulu reported that the ploy had prompted others to ensure they got their taxes in on time. The city had achieved an all-time high collection rate for the current year of 96 per cent. The drive was expected to be repeated in subsequent years.

THE IDEA CAUGHT on. In 2006, the municipal corporation of Patna, the main city of Bihar state, the country's poorest and most backward state that was managing a collection rate of only 4 per cent, went one step further and hired groups of eunuchs, transsexuals and hermaphrodites to stand outside non-payers' homes and businesses to humiliate owners into paying up.

Exploiting local superstitions about eunuchs – they were believed to possess occult powers and their curses were particularly to be feared, leading them to be largely ostracised by society – the groups of gaudily made-up men dressed in saris, accompanied by the now obligatory drumming groups, attracted huge crowds wherever they descended. In one day during the first week, they more than doubled Patna's normal daily collection rate, taking in 400,000 rupees, of which they earned a 4 per cent cut, a vast improvement on their usual source of income – begging on the streets.

THE BIRTH PANGS of freedom were felt acutely by some in Zimbabwe when independence in 1980 meant an extension of the tax regime. The Income Tax Commission sent forms to all those recently returned from exile after the independence war. The most delightfully naïve reply came from one recipient who wrote back saying that he was 'not interested in this tax service' and asking for his name to be removed from the mailing list.

Bureaucracy rules

The US Department of Housing introduced a sophisticated new computer program in 1987 to revamp its methods for assessing entitlements for federal funding across American municipalities. The program evaluated a raft of socio-economic data to find the neediest places in the country. On the first list churned out of the computer was Beverly Hills, California, possibly the most glamorous and well-endowed community on the planet. Investigations showed that the program had worked correctly. The housing stock of sprawling mansions, built in the Hollywood boom years between the wars, was interpreted as 'pre-1940 housing'; the army of retired film stars showed up as a glut of elderly unemployed; and the city's enormous but static wealth was scored as slow growth. Despite the flaws, the department still offered the city $56 million in grants. Graciously, it declined.

NEW YORK CITY'S Bureau for At-Risk Children introduced an anti-drugs campaign in schools in 1998 using pencils bearing the slogan, 'Too Cool To Do Drugs'. No one appeared to have thought through the consequences of extended use. Teachers reported that after a few re-sharpenings, the pencils carried the message, 'Cool To Do Drugs', and later, simply 'Do Drugs'. The scheme was abandoned.

A UK HOME OFFICE report on police integrity published in June 1999 condemned leaks from the force, citing them as tantamount to police corruption. Details of the report came as no surprise to journalists. The conclusions had been leaked to a police magazine two weeks earlier.

THE NEW HEADQUARTERS building of Germany's Construction Ministry in Berlin was reported to be falling down in 2003, just four years after it was put up. A spokesman said that the building was riddled with faults, including cracks in walls, a damaged façade, ill-fitting windows and inefficient insulation and air conditioning. The cost of repairs was estimated at £25 million.

THE UK DRIVER and Vehicle Licensing Agency launched a television advertising campaign in 2003 as part of the Department of Transport's efforts to combat car tax evasion. It hired the eccentric car used in the film *Chitty Chitty Bang Bang* to promote its powerful message, 'No exceptions. No excuses, No escape.' Except, however, car and film experts pointed out that as the car had been built in 1967, being more than 30 years old it was exempt from car tax under the DVLA's own rules.

IN A SIMILAR twist, a Japanese Government campaign in 2004 to persuade citizens to pay their pension contributions used popular actress Maikiko Esumi to front television and poster advertising across the country. The authorities then discovered that Esumi herself had failed to keep up her own contributions and she was charged with a back bill of two years' worth of unpaid premiums.

TRADING STANDARDS OFFICERS in Crickhowell, Wales, warned the makers of Welsh Dragon Sausages in November 2006 that they risked prosecution as the labelling could be misleading for customers. The problem appeared to be that the sausages, which were made from pork and chilli, failed to mention pork in the title, although it was clearly in the small-print list of ingredients. 'I don't think any of our customers actually believe that we use dragon meat,' the owner of the business told the press. 'This is bureaucracy gone mad.' He was forced to include the word 'pork' more prominently on the label in future to escape further action.

MINISTRY OF AGRICULTURE, FISHERIES AND FOOD civil servants were discovered in 2002 to have paid out financial subsidies to a fraudulent Devon farmer for fields that did not exist. What the investigating House of Commons Public Accounts Committee found most disconcerting was that the officials scrutinising the claims had failed to spot that the map references supplied by the fraudster put the fields in the middle of the North Sea, in the mid-Atlantic and in Iceland and Greenland. The 'appallingly lax controls' had allowed Joseph Bowden, who had since been jailed for two and a half years, to receive £157,000 through the false claims, amounting to nearly a third of his total grant.

He also managed to claim under separate crop schemes for two harvests from the same field, as there was no cross-checking between different schemes. MPs worried whether the case was symptomatic of how the subsidy programme was managed overall, which would be a major concern for taxpayers as the total size of the pot paid out was an eye-watering £860 million annually.

A GOVERNMENT REGULATOR for the railways, the Rail Safety and Standards Board, took two years and spent £500,000 to produce a report that concluded that passengers preferred their trains to run on time and not be overcrowded. Published in May 2009, it found that passengers were likely to be in a 'positive emotional state' if trains were punctual and announcements were audible and understandable. In contrast, they were likely to have 'negative' attitudes if trains were late and there was no information telling them why.

DURING POWER SHORTAGES in the Australian state of New South Wales in 1982, the State Electricity Commission rejected a request from the firm Polly & Sons for exemption from power cuts. The company made the application because of heavy demands for their product. They made candles.

NORTH CAROLINA PASSED legislation regulating funeral services in July 2001, which included a prohibition against the use of 'profanity, indecent, or obscene language' in the presence of a corpse.

THE ENVIRONMENT DEPARTMENT of California conducted its 1990 survey of sources of pollution with the intention of it being the most comprehensive scrutiny yet compiled. Its final report included in its list of 'sources potentially harmful to health' San Quentin jail – on account of its gas chamber.

RESIDENTS OF HARTFORD, Connecticut, were spared serving on federal grand juries for three years in the mid-1980s because a state computer system had registered all citizens of the city as being dead. When administrators, noticing the curious absence of Hartford addresses appearing on juries, reviewed the system they discovered that data had been entered in the wrong column of the database, having the effect that the 'd' of the city's name slipped over into the next column. There, the letter was recognised by the computer system as signifying the nominee had died.

ANNOUNCING THE ARRIVAL into service in 1986 of its B-1 Lancer, the next generation of nuclear strategic bomber, which is capable of delivering enough nuclear weaponry to destroy half a dozen cities, the US Defense Department was at pains to highlight how the design had catered for environmental concerns. The current official USAF fact sheet states that:

Development of the B-1, from the programme's inception, has been in consonance with all Federal environmental laws, executive orders, regulations, and with criteria and standards published by the Environmental Protection Agency. Every effort is being made to minimize the effects of the aircraft on the environment.

The B-1's engines incorporate new technology that makes them among the cleanest and most efficient ever built. Tests indicate that the F101 engine has a combustion efficiency of 99.5 percent and is virtually smokeless....

While specific fuel consumption is classified, the B-1 will use about 25 percent less fuel than the B-52 for the same mission....

Noise levels of the B-1, when its afterburners are not in use, are considerably lower than those of other military aircraft; they compare favourably with the newest commercial aircraft.

BENT ON CLAMPING down on loss of income, Indian State Railways Minister Laloo Prasad Yadav, renowned for his publicity-seeking, launched a high-profile campaign in 2007 to try to recoup millions of rupees in lost revenue from fare dodgers. It backfired for him personally when two of the first catches were his elderly in-laws, who were both caught in a first-class carriage without tickets and fined 1,800 rupees each.

In safe hands?

New Jersey's Chief of Division of Alcohol Beverage Control resigned in 1999 after being pulled over by police for drunk-driving. John Holl had served in the post for six years, leading a crackdown on alcohol-related crime, including organising a conference on responsible drinking and increasing police patrols.

THE NEW YORK TIMES, reporting in 1992 on a new regulation from the Department of Agriculture, reflected that while the Lord's Prayer contained 56 words, the 23rd Psalm 118 words and the Ten Commandments 297 words, the Department's just-released directive on the pricing of cabbage needed no fewer than 15,629.

IN 1997, THE written test for learner drivers set by New York State's Department of Motor Vehicles included a multiple-choice question which read: 'A "No Parking" sign at a certain location means...'

CONCERNED BY AN increase in failures in their state tests, the California Motor Vehicles Department simplified its written exam to a reading age level of 11. Among the multiple-choice questions was 'What does a six-sided Stop sign mean?' The most frequent answer in Culver City, Los Angeles, was 'Slow down to 25mph'.

THE US DEPARTMENT of Justice advertised in 2010 for new attorneys to join its Civil Rights Division, the part of the office handling discrimination laws. True to its philosophy, it stressed that it welcomed applications from those with 'targeted disabilities'. As well as deafness, blindness and other physical impairments, the accepted disabilities also included 'mental retardation' and 'mental illness'.

THE GREENVILLE COUNTY Department of Social Services, South Carolina, sent notification to a resident who had died in 1992 terminating his financial support, as follows: 'Your food stamps will be stopped effective March 1992 because we received notice that you passed away. May God bless you. You may reapply if there is a change in your circumstances.'

AN ELEVEN-MONTH-OLD Chicago baby was granted a gun licence by the state authorities when they responded to a prank application sent in by his father. Howard 'Bubba' Ludwig, who had 'signed' the form with a squiggle guided by his father, also called Howard, received the licence despite the inclusion with the application of a genuine photograph of the baby and personal identification information recording that he was two feet three inches tall and weighed 20 pounds.

AN AUDIT BY the US Department of Justice released in January 2008 revealed that a number of telephone tapping operations against criminal and terrorist groups run by the Federal Bureau of Investigation had collapsed because the FBI had failed to pay its bills and had been cut off by the telecoms company. The review found that more than half of a thousand bills sampled had not been paid on time. At least one wiretap conducted under the Foreign Intelligence Surveillance Act, covering the most sensitive of the US Government's espionage operations, had had to be abandoned because of 'untimely payment'. The report added: 'We also found that late payments have resulted in telecommunications carriers actually disconnecting phone lines established to deliver surveillance results to the FBI, resulting in lost evidence.' In one unidentified field office, the outstanding bill had reached $66,000.

DEAD MAN WINS ELECTION

THE CENTRAL COMMAND of Russia's Strategic Rocket Force base at Odintsovo, near Moscow, had its electricity supply cut for an hour and a half in September 1995 because it had failed to pay its bills. Power was restored only when an emergency payment of $6.75 million was made.

TWO DOZEN US soldiers who were returned from service in Iraq in 2008 suffering from shell-shock were sent by Army officials for rehabilitation at Fort Benning on the Georgia–Alabama border, home to one of America's largest complex of firing ranges. The soldiers later complained that the almost constant gunfire from the base's 67 live firing ranges was not assisting their recovery. Brigadier Gary Cheek, director of the army's Warrior Care and Transition Officer responded to media enquiries by saying, 'I can see how that would be a problem. It's something we haven't considered.'

MOSCOW CITY AUTHORITIES launched a safe-driving campaign in early 2000 by mounting car wrecks on top of poles on some of the city's busiest routes to warn drivers of the perils of speeding. After a month of operation, they claimed the scheme had reduced accidents. It had caused a few too. The dramatic sight of cars suspended above the street had caused motorists to take their eyes off the road and resulted in multiple shunts.

A RUSSIAN GOVERNMENT amnesty of petty criminals in Moscow in 2000 was followed by a spate of thefts from private garages around the city. Dozens of cars were stolen without any apparent sign of break-in. Police were mystified until they delved into the national prison service's social re-integration programme. Designed to train inmates in useful trades, prisons had taken on contracts to manufacture a range of products, one of which was padlocks. 'It was pretty simple,' a spokesman said. 'They make the locks in jail and, when they come out, they open them.'

THE AUSTRIAN JUSTICE Ministry introduced a money-making scheme for its prisons service in 2008 by setting up telephone call centres run by inmates on behalf of large consumer service providers. Controversy erupted when it emerged that most of the prisoners employed turned out to be inside for fraud or other financial crime, and that their tasks included extracting customers' personal details to be used for marketing purposes. Consumer organisations attacked the programme, which had been set up against the opposition of prison administrators, for allowing information to get into the wrong hands. Customers were not aware they were speaking to convicted prisoners, who presented themselves as employees of the service provider, usually a telecoms company. Asked to explain the choice of prisoner recruited for the jobs, the Justice Ministry said that the scheme preferred convicted fraudsters because they were 'experienced sales geniuses'.

SECURITY IN MEXICO reached a new low in June 1999 when a detachment of the elite Presidential Guard were ambushed by six armed robbers, reported to be teenagers, two blocks from the President's palace. The escorts, whose main duty was to protect the Head of State, were relieved of £30,000 intended for the military payroll. The attack left two of the guards dead. The entire gang escaped.

A FIRE CREW despatched from the Niles fire department in Ohio in January 2004 refused to put out a blaze destroying a man's house because they found it was 200 yards outside their city boundary. They waited until another crew from the neighbouring Weathersfield fire department arrived just to ensure no one was injured. The distraught owner, Jason Radcliff, complained that his house could have been saved if the first crew had acted immediately they arrived. The Niles crew were backed up by their superiors, who told press that the unit should never have been despatched in the first place.

DEAD MAN WINS ELECTION

A SPELLING MISTAKE led the Danish air force to unwittingly hire a haulage company from communist East Germany to help build secret hangars designed for NATO aircraft. It should have been Austrian. The mistake was not noticed until an East German articulated lorry arrived at the Tirstrup air base in Jutland in November 1988. The driver produced papers proving his company had been contracted to transport material to the site. The slip-up appeared to stem from the Danish words for Austria – Østrigsk – and East Germany – Østtysk – being so similar. 'We thought we had got an Austrian firm to do the job, so we were somewhat shocked to find an East German lorry on the site,' said Lt Col Egon Beck, the commander of the base.

THE AUSTRALIAN GOVERNMENT police mission on peace-keeping duty in Cyprus shared its secrets with the Soviets for an unknown period in 1988 until the discovery that all its messages back home had been going to the Soviet mission in Canberra instead of the police HQ nearby. The telex numbers differed by one digit. The mistake was discovered when an officer arrived back claiming his leave had been approved. When the papers could not be found, the truth dawned. The Soviets had been responding to routine messages on leave and overtime in the hope of netting significant material later.

IN JANUARY 2010, the Israeli Government laid on an exhibition of stolen ancient artefacts that had been recovered from criminals to educate the public about the problem of black-marketeering in looted art. The display, in an Ashdod museum, was raided by thieves and several of the items were lost again.

TOURIST JOE ADKIN, from Chesterfield, Derbyshire, picked up his wife's passport by mistake when going on holiday in March 2002. He got through check-in, passport control and boarding at Gatwick Airport. He was only stopped, by the Spanish authorities, when he arrived at Lanzarote.

HAZEL ELLABY, a British tourist returning from Turkey in July 2008, was given another person's passport by her hotel which she unknowingly used to pass successfully through both airport security in the holiday resort of Bodrum and arrivals at Manchester. She only noticed the error when she went to pack the passport away.

Moving in mysterious ways

The Washington-based National Fish and Wildlife Service changed the identification markings on its bird-tracking tags in 1998 after receiving a letter from an aggrieved camper in Arkansas. The man wrote that he had caught a bird and noticed the tag, inscribed 'Wash.Biol.Surv.' 'I followed the cooking instructions on the leg and I want to tell you it was horrible.'

THE INDIAN STATE government of Madhya Pradesh approved a scheme in 2004 to pay police officers an extra 30 rupees a month (about 40 pence) if they grew moustaches to give them a more military bearing. Research claimed to show that local people respected officers with moustaches, a traditional sign of virility in India, more readily than those without. A senior official explained, 'These men would patrol sensitive pockets in the district employing psychological tactics against criminals... Though thick moustaches have been traditionally associated with bandits dwarfing their victims psychologically, this "warfare" will be employed against criminals here.'

ACCORDING TO THE BEELD newspaper in 1993, a farmer who had applied to the South African Directorate of Financial Assistance in 1944 for a grant had just received a response 49 years on asking him to provide more details — 'as a matter of urgency'. The farmer had been dead since 1964.

DEAD MAN WINS ELECTION

RAVINDRA HALDER, WHO applied for a job in a state employment exchange office in Calcutta, received an invitation to attend an interview – 34 years later, in March 2002. Now aged 52, and a grandfather, he was ruled out because of his age. 'I'd given up hope. I'd applied in 1968. I'm now too old for a government job.' Halder still held out hope for his son, who had put his name down for a post in the same office four years earlier but had not yet been called. Minister of Labour for West Bengal, Mohammad Amim, was quoted as acknowledging that it often took 'a long time' for a person to be called for interview.

SICILIAN GERLANDO PETRUCCI was offered a school caretaker's job 22 years after he had applied for it. By the time he received the notification inviting him to report ('immediately') to his new post in Brusasco in the north of Italy, Petrucci had accumulated a 20-year career as a customs officer, and had no desire now to move to the other end of the country. He declined the offer.

THE ROMANIAN STATE telephone company replied to customer Gheorghe Titianu in August 2004, 28 years after he had applied for a phone connection. The joy was short-lived for Titianu, living in the remote northern town of Suceava, who was informed that there was no phone line yet available.

THE INDIAN STATE of Karnataka settled a 34-year dispute with one of its doctors in 2004, which produced a £30,000 payment to compensate the medic for not having made him work for nearly two decades. R.M. Sardesai, who had once worked in a primary health centre in Bijapur district, had stayed at home in 1970 because, he claimed, he had not been notified of his next posting. He remained unoccupied for the next 19 years, later saying that it was the government's fault if he was not sent on duty. The case eventually came to light only because he lodged a claim for salary increases he would have been entitled to over the years had he been properly posted. A tribunal ruled that he was officially 'on leave' for the first two years but 'waiting for posting' for the next 17. The state could not explain why it had lost track of him in its posting system.

PARESH BARUAH, a terrorist who had waged a 30-year war against the Indian Government in the state of Assam in the east of the country, was formally sacked in 2010 after the government discovered he was still on the books of the state-run railway company and had been receiving his pay as a porter even though he had not turned up for work since 1979.

FIRE ENGINES HEADING towards a fire in the Massachusetts town of Westfield in June 1999 were held up by a state toll-booth operator who insisted on charging each appliance before letting the emergency vehicles proceed.

A GOVERNMENT EMPLOYMENT office in Thetford, Norfolk, banned a recruitment company in 2010 from displaying a job advert for a cleaner that expressed a requirement that the successful candidate should be 'very reliable and hard working'. The office told the company, headed by Nicole Mamo, that the ad could not be run in case unreliable people sued for discrimination.

AS POLITICAL AND military analysts disputed Western intentions in the spring of 1999 on whether the US would intervene in Kosovo, more astute observers were confident of the inevitability of war several weeks before the event. Three weeks before the invasion, an insignia-making factory in Texas openly announced that it had just received a rush order from the Pentagon...for 9,000 Purple Heart gallantry medals.

THE TURKISH STATE Statistical Institute, responsible for undertaking the country's 2000 national census, introduced an incentive scheme for the army of data collectors working throughout the country to compile local returns. They were paid according to the number of people they counted. The system backfired when large population increases began to appear in the returns. Sefik Yildizeli, the Chief Statistician, conceded that the incentive payments had distorted the count. Census-takers in some areas had inflated their figures by taking names of dead people from cemetery headstones.

THE SOUTH AFRICAN Government laid on a spectacular public-relations show in February 1988 to mark the 500th anniversary of the landing of Portuguese explorer Bartholomew Dias, the first European to discover the Cape of Good Hope and the southern sea route to the Indies. A re-enactment of the landing and the first encounter with Hottentot natives was held at the site of the landfall in Mossel Bay, attended by President Botha, his cabinet and 8,000 African and overseas dignitaries. The strictures of apartheid caused one small problem however. To portray the native reception committee, the organisers had to make do with six white actors dressed in loincloths, wearing fuzzy wigs and liberally doused with walnut juice. The beach they were on was officially designated as Whites-only. According to reports, few in the audience appeared to notice the deception.

AN OFFICIAL BRITISH Government guide to the country's history, published by the Home Office in 2006 for immigrants wanting to take the knowledge test required to become citizens, was found by the prestigious History Association to contain dozens of factual and elementary mistakes. It placed Northumberland's Hadrian's Wall in Scotland, had Harold Wilson as Prime Minister in 1978 (he had resigned two years earlier), claimed the European Community was founded by five states (there were six), and mis-dated famous events such as the Glencoe Massacre. The Association sent a seven-page list of corrections to the government, which acknowledged that the document had been 'done fairly quickly'. A corrected version had to be issued in 2007.

THE GOVERNOR OF the central Russian region of Ulyanovsk launched a campaign to boost the dwindling population in 2005 by declaring 12 September an official 'Day of Conception'. Sergei

Morozov encouraged couples to take the day off to procreate on behalf of the country's future, which had been witnessing alarming population declines since the fall of communism. Women who gave birth exactly nine months later stood a chance of winning prizes, including cash, televisions, a car or even a refrigerator. After three years, statistics showed that the birth rate in June was three times the normal daily average.

WITH 14 MONTHS to go before the arrival of the year 2000, the Kenyan Government set up in the autumn of 1998 a commission to investigate the potential threat of the Millennium Bug, the computer chip flaw that experts predicted would bring chaos to the world's electronics. The commission was given 18 months to deliver its report.

BELGIUM BECAME THE last country in Europe to legalise nude bathing in April 2001. Legislators decided to designate as the nudist beach a stretch of coast near the resort of Le Coq.

Waste not...

The US Office of Economic Opportunity launched a $100,000 contraceptive supply programme in deprived areas of Cleveland and Philadelphia in 1971 targeted at promiscuous young males. The scheme amassed a list of 43,000 specific individuals known to local social services, each of whom received letters with vouchers for 12 free condoms. Only 254 of the recipients redeemed their vouchers, putting the cost to the public purse of the condoms at $400 per dozen.

A NEW 16-PAGE citizens' guide on anti-terrorism preparation issued by agencies in New York City in November 2003 contained the instruction, 'Do not accept packages from strangers; if you find yourself holding a mysterious substance, put it down.' Among the other helpful guidance was, 'If you encounter radiation, go outside (if you are inside a building) or go inside (if you are outside a building).'

THE US NATIONAL Parks Service, which is responsible for America's National Historic Landmarks programme, conferred the much coveted landmark status on a municipal rubbish dump at Fresno, California, in August 2001. It cited the tip as worthy of recognition for being the oldest sanitary landfill in the country.

LOS ANGELES CITY Council was discovered in 2005 to have been spending thousands of dollars of taxpayers' money on bottled water for its staff while it was running a $1 million programme trying to persuade residents of the city to drink the tap supply provided by the municipality. The Department of Power and Water – the agency managing domestic water provision – was responsible for more than a third of the spending.

BETWEEN 1975 AND 1988, Wisconsin Senator William Proxmire occupied a legendary position in American politics through the monthly publishing of his 'Golden Fleece' awards to publicise the most outrageous examples of waste by agencies of the US Government. His first award, in March 1975, went to the National Science Foundation for spending $84,000 on finding out why people fall in love. Among the other bizarre uses of taxpayers' dollars, Proxmire rewarded:

- the Head of the Federal Energy Administration for spending $25,000 and 19,000 gallons of fuel in 10 months flying around the country urging businesses and civic groups to economise on energy resources (November 1975);
- the Law Enforcement Assistance Administration for a $27,000 study to determine why inmates want to escape from prison (February 1977);
- the National Endowment for the Humanities for making a

$25,000 grant to Arlington County, Virginia, to study why people are rude, cheat and lie on the local tennis courts (May 1977);

- the Law Enforcement Assistance Administration (again) for developing at a cost of $2 million, and then scrapping, a prototype police car. The vehicle included, among other gadgets, a visual indicator that showed whether or not the siren was on (January 1978);

- the Federal Highway Administration for commissioning a $222,000 study, 'Motorist Attitudes Toward Large Trucks' (June 1978);

- the Environmental Protection Agency for spending $1.2 million to preserve a New Jersey sewer as a historical monument, despite being 25 feet underground and having been visited by just two people in 23 years (February 1980);

- the US Coast Guard for wasting $500,000 in starting a computer conversion project that was later abandoned when, after three years, only 7 per cent of the work had been completed (April 1980);

- the US Army for spending $6,000 on a 17-page document to instruct military supply managers how to buy foodstuffs (July 1981);

- the Army Department for a 13-year, $35 million programme on developing a better gas mask, whose product was no better than existing gas masks (May 1982);

- the US Coast Guard (again) for spending $1.1 million on a North Carolina boatyard that then remained empty and unused for a year (July 1983);

- the National Institute of Dental Research for sponsoring a five-year, $465,000 study on the psychological effect on patients of going to the dentist (April 1984);

- the Federal Crop Insurance Corporation for its $12 million publicity campaign for farmers, a follow-up study of which showed that awareness levels were no higher after the campaign than before (July 1984).

DEAD MAN WINS ELECTION

AN AUDIT IN 1990 revealed that the US Defense Department spent $3.5m reviewing how many shirt sizes it needed for women's uniforms. It concluded that an additional 68 were needed, to add to the 58 already existing. New designs left $18 billion worth of unwanted stock.

THE BRITISH MINISTRY of Defence put up for sale the aircraft carrier *Hermes* in 1985. It received an early expression of interest from an eight-year-old schoolboy who offered £15 plus £7.50 in gift tokens. The MoD declined the bid, saying it couldn't accept tokens.

SHORTLY AFTER TAKING office in 1993, US Vice-President Al Gore published a 168-page policy document outlining how the new Administration would be more efficient than the last. It ended up costing three times as much to produce as it should have done because it was printed on expensive ('Grade 1') glossy paper, in colour and sent as a rush printing job over a public holiday. Instead of costing 90 cents a copy to print, the bill turned out at $4, bringing the total expense to over $165,000 instead of the budgeted $55,000. The title of the report was *Creating A Government That Works Better And Costs Less*.

UNDER A CITY ordinance that provides for up to 2 per cent of costs of new public buildings to be devoted to art furnishings, San Francisco's new $54 million city jail, which opened in 1994, spent $600,000 on decorative adornments, including a $22,000, 60-foot long, hand-carved jade couch in the reception area, computer-controlled skylights that track the sun at a cost of $64,000 and $70,000 'meditation atriums'. The jail, known locally as the 'Glamour Slammer', was so over-budget when it was finished that to begin with the authorities did not have enough funds left to fully staff the facility.

THE COURT OF ACCOUNTS, France's top spending watchdog, issued an unusually scathing review of the wastage of public money in 1996. It highlighted a 140 million franc (about £14 million) airstrip built in

Antarctica for French scientists which had been completed in 1993 after seven years' work. The Environment Ministry had immediately banned use of the runway for certain months of the year because it was a breeding ground for penguins and other rare birds. Scientists then discovered that at every other time of year, the weather conditions were too bad for landings. The airport has never been used.

A POLICE STATION in the Swedish town of Hagfors ordered its first roll of toilet paper for 20 years in 2006 having seen itself through the consequences of a clerical error in 1986 when it ordered 20 pallets of rolls instead of 20 packets. It had been diligently working through the consignment ever since. The downside of the achievement, according to police chief Bjorn Fredlund, was that the paper had all been single-ply. 'Double-ply would have been nice.'

SHORTLY AFTER BECOMING State Premier of Victoria, Australia, Steve Bracks ordered a study costing the equivalent of £10,500 for advice on how to make his office more efficient. According to press reports in April 2001, the major conclusion provided by the consultants was for him to keep a pad and pencil beside his telephone to take notes during calls.

From the history books

Historians can't quite agree on how many changes of government Bolivia has had since independence in 1825. Up until the restoration of civilian government in 1982, Bolivia suffered 193 (some say only 189) coups in 157 years, making it modern history's most systemically unstable country.

ALTHOUGH LATIN AMERICA features strongly in any review of political upheavals, the next most persistently volatile system of government is, surprisingly, that of the French. The Third Republic that ran for 70 years between 1870 and its demise in the Nazi invasion of 1940 enjoyed no fewer than 88 governments. On seven occasions (1877, 1913, 1917, 1930, 1932, 1933 and 1934) the country had four governments holding office within the year. At its most frenetic, France had nine different administrations in the 33 months between February 1932 and November 1934.

The Fourth Republic, which followed in 1946, was arguably more chaotic, albeit mercifully shorter-lived. It was the time when being French Prime Minister became a byword for uncertainty. In its 12-year duration, it saw 21 separate governments. Only two ruled longer than a year. Three lasted for less than a month. It was eventually abolished by Charles de Gaulle in 1958, bringing to an end an inglorious period in French governance which had seen, if we include the Occupation and Provisional governments during the Second World War, a grand total of 115 administrations in 88 years, a rate – which astonishingly the people put up with for nearly a century – of a change of government every nine months.

SEVENTEENTH-CENTURY POLAND probably has the dubious honour of creating history's worst method of parliamentary governance. Commencing in the early 1500s, Poland enjoyed her golden age, as the second-largest state in Europe, and the wealthiest in the East. The Polish nobility forcefully developed the authority of the national Parliament, the *Sejm*. The Polish Crown was entirely under its thrall, having to convene it every two years, and being forbidden to dismiss any government official or raise an army without Parliament's approval. It became the most powerful example in Europe of a legislative body controlling royal authority, long before the rest of the Continent's assemblies had even tried. The seeds of ruin were sown, however, in 1652 when the nobility bizarrely introduced a rule – intended to reflect the principle of legal equality among members – that every member of the *Sejm* had to agree to any measure for it to pass. A single voice objecting was sufficient to block business entirely, even to dissolve the assembly itself, which under Polish law also nullified all Acts passed during the session. Not unexpectedly, the working of the Parliament became paralysed, there were frequent dissolutions, and the veto powers were exploited by foreign influences, to the point when, just over a century later, Poland's three big neighbours – Russia, Prussia and Austria – moved in and partitioned her. Not until 1791 was the *liberum veto* abolished. And not until 1918 would Poland re-emerge as a sovereign state again.

ARGENTINA HAD FIVE different Presidents in 13 days during an economic crisis at the end of 2001. On 21 December Fernando de la Rúa, facing riots in the streets, resigned as President two years into his term of office. Constitutionally, Ramón Puerta, Senate leader, became temporary President. Congress elected Adolfo Rodríguez Saá two days later, but he lasted for a week before resigning himself and leaving the office to Eduardo Camaño, the leader of the lower House of Congress (because the Senate had not replaced its leader), who took over on New Year's Eve. Eventually, on 2 January, Congress found Eduardo Duhalde, a losing candidate in the last Presidential election, willing to take on the poisoned chalice.

HAITI HAD SIX governments in 1991 during a period of turbulence surrounding the election – and almost immediate overthrow by the army – of reformist civilian President Jean-Bertrand Aristide.

CHILE HAD SEVEN changes of presidency between July and December 1829 during the country's short-lived civil war.

IN AN UNSTABLE period immediately following its declaration of independence in 1838, Honduras had nine different occupants of its presidency between January and September 1839.

EL SALVADOR HAD 53 governments in its first 50 years after becoming independent in 1821. This included seven in the two and a half years between March 1832 and October 1834, thirteen in the decade of the 1840s and fourteen in the 1850s. To 2010, its 189-year history has seen 94 governments.

DEAD MAN WINS ELECTION

SHORTLY AFTER IT gained independence from France in 1946, Syria suffered 11 changes of Prime Minister between March 1949 and December 1951, an average of once every three months.

MEXICO HOLDS THE distinction of having three Presidents in a single day, and therefore the world's shortest-serving President. On 18 February 1913, a notorious day in the country's history, President Francisco Madero was overthrown by the army commander Victoriano Huerta. To give legal cover to his coup, Huerta allowed Foreign Minister Pedro Lascuráin, constitutionally next in line to be President, to take office and got him to instal Huerta as his Interior Minister, which under the constitution was the next office in line for the presidency. Lascuráin resigned within the hour. Accounts vary as to exactly how long he was in office – either 15 or 55 minutes – but Mexico had its third President of the day by sunset.

POST-WAR ITALY, often the example of instability that comes to the modern mind, has by these yardsticks a modest record for fluidity. It is on its 61st government in the 64 years since the foundation of the republic in 1946. Giulio Andreotti served as Prime Minister no fewer than seven times, all between 1972 and 1992. Giovanni Giolitti, who was Premier five times between 1892 and 1921, was once asked whether governing Italy was difficult. 'Not at all,' he replied, 'but it's useless.'

THE RECORD FOR most Prime Ministerships appears to be Belgian leader Wilfried Martens, who headed eight separate governments in his country between April 1979 and December 1987.

FOR A FULLY FLEDGED parliamentary democracy, Britain's recent record for lengthy office-holding is notable. The country had just three Prime Ministers in the 28 years between Margaret Thatcher taking office in 1979 and Tony Blair leaving office in 2007.

POWER AND THE GLORY –
HIGH OFFICE

Leadership brings its own demands. Some are born great, some achieve greatness…well, we're not interested here in those who made a success of it. We're turning the spotlight on those leaders for whom the burden of being at the top of the tree proved rather more than they could cope with and whose travails, often in the glare of the public eye, demonstrate that fame can be the most poisonous of chalices. Others, though, seemed to embrace high office for all it could give…and, it seemed, then some more.

I am their leader...

To recognise his country's oil shortage, Ugandan leader Idi Amin turned up at Entebbe international airport by bicycle in April 1976 for the arrival of the visiting President of neighbouring Rwanda.

TANZANIAN PRESIDENT Julius Nyerere issued instructions to his ministers in 1979 to ride bicycles to work to conserve fuel. He said it would also reduce 'the pot bellies carried around by some party and government leaders'. It is not known whether any minister complied.

THE PERSONALITY CULT that grew up around Chinese leader Mao Tse-tung may have held back the country's economic and military advance. According to the *Guizhou Daily* in 1994, the 4.8 billion metal lapel badges that China produced during the Cultural Revolution, which became mandatory adornments for loyal citizens to wear, used up aluminium that could have made 39,600 MiG jet fighters.

JAPANESE PRIME MINISTER Takeo Fukuda served his cabinet with a luncheon of watermelon and peaches from an area of the country stricken with cholera in the summer of 1977 to calm public fears about contaminated food. He then left without touching his portion.

IT WAS CLEARLY a sensible option. When Peru suffered a similar cholera outbreak in 1991, Fisheries Minister Félix Canal Torres mounted his own televised stunt to reassure the public. He had his President, Albert Fujimori, and the country's Agriculture Minister join him in a meal of raw fish to prove it was safe for human consumption. Local press noted somewhat sceptically that the nation's Health Minister had declined the invitation. The next day, Torres fell ill – with cholera.

THE EUROPEAN UNION Food and Farm Commissioner, Franz Fischler, missed the launch of the European Food Safety Authority in January 2002 due, it was believed, to him having been struck down with food poisoning. He was scheduled to preside over the inauguration of the Authority, whose purpose was to provide an EU-wide early warning system for food safety scares.

ANTÓNIO NUNES, head of the Portuguese Food Standards Agency, which was in charge of policing the country's new ban on smoking in public places that came into force at the start of 2008, was caught in the early hours of New Year's Day lighting up a cigar in a casino on the outskirts of Lisbon. Although the official enforcer of the legislation, he claimed to journalists that he thought the rules did not apply to casinos. His government colleagues helpfully told him they certainly did.

Five months later, his own Prime Minister was embarrassingly caught having a cigarette on a Portuguese aircraft covered by the ban. José Sócrates was flying on an official trip to Venezuela in May and lit up once the first class curtain had been drawn across the cabin that shielded him from regular passengers. He was forced to apologise and promised to stem his habit. So far as is known, no formal action was taken against either politician.

Grand schemes

To mark more than three decades in power, Felix Houphouet-Boigny, President of the West African state of Ivory Coast, one of the world's poorest nations with a $10 billion debt, diverted over $300 million of his country's scarce finances to building a near full-size replica of Rome's St Peter's Basilica in his remote home village of Yamoussoukro. Air-conditioned, and only slightly smaller than the real St Peter's after discreet Vatican pressure, it was capable of holding 18,000 people inside, and a further 300,000 in a colonnaded esplanade. Only 30,000 people then lived in Yamoussoukro. Taking four years to complete, It was inaugurated by Pope John Paul II in an elaborate ceremony in September 1989. The 80,000 square feet of stained-glass windows were nearly three times that of Chartres Cathedral. One window portrays Houphouet-Boigny as one of the Magi, presenting a gift to Jesus.

JOAQUIN BALAGUER, dictatorial President of the Dominican Republic, the small and poverty-stricken Caribbean nation claimed (only by the Dominicans) to be the first landfall of Christopher Columbus when he arrived in the New World, ploughed an estimated $70 million into building a 688-foot-tall, 10-storey monument in his capital Santo Domingo for the 500th anniversary celebrations of Columbus' arrival in 1992.

El Faron a Colón (the Columbus lighthouse) was both a lighthouse – shaped as a reclining cross with 149 powerful lights capable of beaming the shape of a cross into the night sky, and visible from

DEAD MAN WINS ELECTION

Puerto Rico 150 miles away – and a mausoleum to Columbus' supposed bones, even though historians doubt that the island was in fact the first landing place of the explorer.

The construction was almost as heroic an enterprise, given that half the population lived below the poverty line and the country regularly experienced eight-hour daily power cuts. Most of the fish at the national aquarium had died in 1990 because a power failure starved them of oxygen. The project required 50,000 shanty homes to be demolished.

Balaguer had asked the Pope to officially inaugurate it, as he had honoured the Ivory Coast spectacle. This time, John Paul diplomatically decided to arrive later in the week for his Mass. Amid huge public outcry at the folly, only 100,000 people turned up for the blessing. The Pope's previous visits had attracted crowds of a million or more. The light has rarely been switched on since. When it is, it drains most of the supply from the rest of the neighbourhood.

IN AN ECHO of Balaguer's largesse, Abdoulaye Wade, the 83-year-old President of poverty-wracked Senegal in West Africa, inaugurated his own monument to excess in April 2010 when he marked the 50th anniversary of the country's independence by spending $27 million on a massive 160-foot-tall bronze statue celebrating 'African Renaissance'. It stood taller than the Statue of Liberty, and being built on a hill in the capital, Dakar, made it, in all, taller than the Eiffel Tower.

Depicting a three-figure combination of a man holding up a child, with a semi-naked woman in tow, it sparked controversy in the deeply Muslim country, where the amount of flesh exposed was condemned by local religious leaders. Wade proudly claimed that the monument was designed to last a minimum of 1,200 years. Insiders told of the fraught architectural battles behind the construction. Senegal's original choice of builders, South Korea, concluded that the hill it is on would not support its weight. Wade turned to North Korea, who accepted the challenge. The elderly President, already entering his second decade as leader, and who had courted further controversy by announcing earlier in the year his intention to stand for re-election again in 2012, added fuel to the fire by declaring that he would take 35 per cent of the revenue the statue would generate from tourists because the monument had been all his idea.

THE SELF-ESTEEM of another African leader got the better of him in 2009. President Denis Sassou-Nguesso, dictatorial strongman of Congo-Brazzaville, published a book of political thoughts with a foreword claiming to be from Nelson Mandela. Except that Mandela denied all knowledge of having written anything for the notoriously autocratic despot. Under the ironic title *Straight Speaking for Africa*, the foreword had Mandela praising the Congolese leader as 'a man who is not only one of our great African leaders…but also one of those who…worked tirelessly to free oppressed peoples from their chains and help restore their dignity and hope'. Mandela's foundation was last heard of contemplating legal action.

PHILIPPINES STRONGMAN Ferdinand Marcos built a 99-foot-tall concrete bust of himself on the slopes of Mount Pugo in the north of the country at the height of his power in the early 1980s. It remained a landmark well after his removal from office in 1986 and his death in 1989. It was suddenly blown up in a night-time raid in 2002, supposedly by treasure hunters who believed a long-held legend in the Philippines that Marcos had found, and stored in the giant head, a haul of treasure left behind by the occupying Japanese in the Second World War.

IRAQ'S SADDAM HUSSEIN took delivery in September 2000 of a copy of the Koran that he had had written in his own blood. Iraqi media reported that it was the President's way of giving thanks to God for escaping unharmed (so far) in his long career. The 605-page book had taken three years to finish. It was later placed in the Mother of all Battles mosque in Baghdad, completed in 2001 to commemorate Saddam's 1990 invasion of Kuwait. The mosque, adorned with sayings of Saddam and a plaque of his signature 10 feet long, boasted eight minarets. Four were shaped like Kalashnikov rifle barrels and four resembled Scud missiles. Each was 43 metres tall, representing the '43 days of US aggression' in 1991. A reflecting pool ringed the building in the shape of the Arab world. In the middle lay a monument of Saddam's thumbprint with his initials in gold.

(In)dignities of office

At the other end of scale from the largesse of dictators, Bill Skate, Prime Minister of Papua New Guinea, arrived for an official visit to Indonesia in 1998 without his luggage. His national airline, Air Niugini, forgot to offload his baggage before leaving. It had, however, delivered his wife's. So the Premier donned his spouse's attire, which was reported to include flowing, silky slacks, for the official welcoming ceremony, while his own clothes were hurriedly laundered locally. The episode only emerged when Skate was asked questions about the sudden, and otherwise unexplained, dismissal of the head of Air Niugini a few weeks later.

FOUR MONTHS AFTER entering office, Bill Clinton caused a political storm in May 1993 by keeping the Presidential entourage waiting for nearly an hour at Los Angeles airport while a celebrity Beverly Hills stylist gave him a haircut on board Air Force One. The appointment caused a 56-minute closure of two runways, leading to dozens of planes coming into land having to circle overhead. Clinton's press spokesman fended off critics: 'The President has to get his hair cut like everybody else and this was a convenient time to do it.'

ITALY'S PRIME MINISTER Silvio Berlusconi, whose electoral antics with showgirls have already been covered in Chapter 2, showed no signs of retreating from his increasingly outlandish behaviour when he celebrated the birthday of one of his female MPs in January 2010.

He invited Michaela Biancofiore, who was almost half his age, to mark her 39th birthday at his villa outside Milan. The cake depicted the MP with outsized breasts and the Prime Minister with his arms around her. Biancofiore denied anything improper happened at the event, and even claimed she had ordered the cake. Only the previous month, Berlusconi had come in for ridicule from the Italian press for reportedly whiling away time during a crucial international meeting on climate change in Brussels by drawing a series of doodles of thongs, French knickers and bloomers and passing them to his fellow leaders under the title 'Women's Underwear Through the Ages'.

POLITICS IN ECUADOR were enlivened for six months between August 1996 and January 1997 after the bizarre election to the presidency of Abdalá Bucaram Ortiz, a self-styled prankster using the nickname El Loco ('the crazy one'). Swept to power on a programme championing the poor, Bucaram became an overnight cult figure in the region, renowned for his publicity-seeking antics. He boosted his popularity by launching mass social schemes named after himself – Abdalact, providing subsidised milk to the poor in cartons emblazoned with his picture; Abdalagua, which did the same with drinking water; and Abdalafono, which brought telephone connections to poor areas. Soon after his election, the President achieved a probable world first by being the first head of state to appear on national television alongside a suite of cavorting showgirls to launch his pop CD, 'A Madman in Love'. Opposition parties demanded he should be examined by a psychiatrist. He took to leaving cabinet meetings to dance in impromptu street events, and became mired in corruption allegations. Street protests erupted in January 1997 as his promised reforms failed to materialise, and in the first week of February he was thrown out of office by the National Congress on the grounds of mental incapacity, fleeing to Panama for sanctuary.

THE MOST EXTREME recent example of a personality disorder taking over a country has been Saparmurat Niyazov, President of the former Soviet republic of Turkmenistan in Central Asia. First as the local Communist boss and then as leader of the newly independent country, Niyazov led his people for 21 years until his death in 2006. Glorying in his title of Turkmenbashi ('Father of all the Turkomans'), he engineered a semi-religious style of leadership, was revered as a prophet, and had every significant facet of the nation named after him. Streets, schools, airports, cities, even yoghurt and a perfume took on his name. A dahlia was named after him, and planted all around the capital, which led to the banning of most pets in the city in order not to overpower their fragrance. The President decreed that residents could own only one cat, one dog or a decorative bird. His presence also reached beyond the borders of Turkmenistan. Officials named a star in the constellation of Taurus and a crater on the moon in his honour.

When he was not renaming places, he was recasting the very fabric of his people's lives. In 2002, he renamed the months of the year. January became Turkmenbashi after himself; he renamed other months after national poets and writers, and April after his mother. He also renamed the days of the week with inspirational titles: Monday he named after himself, Turkmenbashi Day; Tuesday became Young Day; Saturday, Spirituality Day. The President would regularly take to the nation's airwaves to read his latest poetry, and his 400-page book of philosophical writings – the *Rukhnama* ('Book of the Soul') – became required reading in schools. Children had to memorise it, and copies on display at places of worship had to be kissed by visitors. Every office of government was required to spend an hour a week discussing it. Motorists had to attend a 16-hour course on it in order to pass the driving test and get a licence. On his 63rd birthday in 2003, he was officially bestowed the title of Prophet by his fawning ministers.

He turned his downbeat capital of Ashgabat into what one observer called 'a temple of kitsch', with outlandishly large public monuments springing up, most lavishly topped off in gold. Dozens of statues of the President and his late and esteemed mother were strewn around. There were estimated to be 10,000 statues in the country by the time of his death. The most notorious folly was a £6 million, 250-foot-tall marble arch, topped with a gold statue of the President which rotated during the day so it always faced the sun. In 2003, he bizarrely had built the world's longest shoe as a symbol of the 'great strides' Turkmenistan had made under his leadership since independence from the Soviet Union. Using 100 feet of leather, it measured 20 feet long and 5 feet tall. Its laces were 30 feet long. Its maker proudly declared 'there are no limits to our gratitude to our leader for the unlimited opportunities' Niyazov had bestowed on the country. In 2004 there were reports that he had started the construction of an ice palace three miles outside the capital so his people could go ice skating in one of the hottest countries on Earth.

His eccentricities took on a morbid streak in 2003 when a plot to assassinate him was uncovered. Niyazov went on national television to announce the date of the trial of the 32 alleged conspirators, and helpfully also told viewers the sentences that would be handed down – 20 would be jailed and 12 exiled to remote parts of the country. He closed all hospitals outside the capital and doctors were only allowed to study his book of writings and the medical works of an ancient Persian hero. As a result, illness and mortality rates soared to some of the worst on the planet.

In 2004, he banned beards and car radios, following up on his earlier bans on ballet, opera and circuses, which he regarded as contrary to national traditions. The next year, he banned the playing of recorded music on national holidays, on television and at private weddings. This ban was intended to protect traditional musicians from the 'negative influences' of performers who mimed to records, Niyazov said. In 2006, a decree issued just weeks before new teachers' pay scales were to be introduced required all teachers to write newspaper articles praising the virtues of the leadership. Those failing to get into print faced lower salaries under the new scheme. Reports spoke of chaotic scenes – and the paying of huge bribes – in local newspaper offices across the country as teachers scrambled to get their articles submitted. Pages and pages of laudatory articles appeared over the following weeks. Teachers were also now required to sit exams to demonstrate their knowledge of the *Rukhnama* in order to keep their jobs.

He rubbed his former overlords' noses in it when Russian leader Vladimir Putin made his first visit. Niyazov reportedly stretched the official banquet past midnight – by insisting on 42 toasts during the evening – so that he could boast later that Putin's visit had lasted two days.

When he died in 2006, he was buried in a 180-foot-wide gold-domed mosque, adorned with scripts from the *Rukhnama* inlaid around the inside, and built at the cost of £50 million. Two years later, his successor abolished the Niyazov calendar, turned off the power on his revolving statue in the centre of Ashgabat and ordered its dismantling and removal to an outer suburb.

THE 'FATHER OF TUNISIA', Habib Bourguiba, who served as President for 30 years after independence from France, left obituarists with rich fare when he died, officially aged 96 (his family claimed he was nearer 100) in 2000. His mental decline during the 1980s had given rise to a welter of tales of his idiosyncratic behaviour and bizarre leadership style. He disciplined underperforming or unco-operative ministers by spitting in their face. He made state appointments which he promptly forgot, leading at one point to Tunisia having two Ambassadors to the United Nations. In the space of four days in October 1987, he appointed three different people to lead his political party. He once announced on live television, during a nationwide address, that he had only one testicle. He was eased aside in a bloodless coup in 1987 and lived out the rest of his life in seclusion.

In the public eye

Cuban leader Fidel Castro became famed – or notorious, depending on one's political proclivities – for treating his people to lengthy political speeches, always covered slavishly by the state-controlled broadcaster. The record was set in his New Year speech for 1998, when he regaled the nation for a full seven hours, transmitted in its entirety on national television. It narrowly beat his seven-hour 1986 address to the National Party Congress. In 1960, he made the (still) longest speech to the United Nations General Assembly, lasting 4 hours and 29 minutes.

FIREBRAND PRESIDENT OF Venezuela, Hugo Chávez, took over the reins of the voluble Latin American leader when he instituted a Sunday television broadcast that saw him speak to the nation every week, frequently for more than six hours at a time. In September 2007, he managed an eight-hour non-stop address, from 11am to 7pm. Knowing he had beaten Castro's record, his parting words as he signed off were: 'The first time in history.' To mark his decade in power in 2009, he planned to excel even this with a four-day marathon starting on a Thursday and ending on the Sunday. He managed two four-hour sessions on the first day and a lengthy slot the next, but the promised continuation into Saturday never materialised for unexplained 'technical difficulties', which also caused the cancellation of the regular Sunday edition.

GERMAN CHANCELLOR Gerhard Schröder was so stung by media stories that he dyed his hair that he went to court in April 2002 to have the allegations legally stopped. An image consultant had told the DDP news agency that he thought the Chancellor should stop tinting grey streaks in his dark–brown hair. Schröder, who faced a General Election later in the year, took the claim with unexpected sensitivity, claiming that to accuse him of colouring his hair – which he denied – amounted to accusing him of being 'an established liar'. The case necessitated Udo Walz, Berlin's star hairdresser who barbered the 58-year-old Chancellor, to submit a deposition to the court refuting the claim that the hair was dyed. 'It is indeed unusual for a man his age not to have grey hair,' he told the press, but said 'a hairdresser could tell' if there was artificial colouring. However, a former wife emerged to claim, in contrast, how he would use a toothbrush to apply cream to his eyebrows before press interviews. The affair gripped the usually stolid Germanic press for a month until, in May, the court ruled that the broadcaster had been wrong to air the claim without making an effort to verify it. Schröder's demand for a retraction was granted and DDP duly broadcast his denial. The case was thought to have cost thousands of euros of public money defending the Chancellor. In September, Schröder retained power in a narrow win in the election.

FRENCH PRESIDENT Nicolas Sarkozy was less successful in his battle against personal critique when he went to court in October 2008 to stop the selling of a 'voodoo' doll in his image. A hit among his countryfolk, the doll came complete with pins for the owner to stab into the figure and a manual on how to put a curse on him. It followed the success of a similar doll in the image of Sarkozy's election rival, Ségolène Royal, who had laughed off the stunt, saying, 'I have a sense of humour.' In contrast, Sarkozy, known for his pomposity and resorting to the courts – it was his sixth lawsuit since being elected only a year and a half earlier – claimed the doll ridiculed the office of the President and by extension France itself. A judge disagreed, ruling that the doll was 'within the authorised limits of free expression and the right to humour'. Not content to leave it there, Sarkozy appealed. A month later, he won a ruling that while the dolls could continue to be sold, they would have to carry a warning on the packaging that sticking pins into the figure was an affront to his dignity.

SARKOZY'S SENSITIVITY ABOUT his diminutive stature (five foot five) required special arrangements to be made for public appearances. Famed for wearing elevated heels to increase his height by a couple of inches, it also emerged that he had his aides ensure that people assembled for his set-piece events should be no taller than the President. The cat was let out of the bag in September 2009 when Sarkozy visited a factory in Normandy. Workers later told the media of the elaborate arrangements to ensure the President was not overshadowed. An appeal had gone out around the factory for short people no taller than the President to stand on the dais behind Sarkozy while he made a key televised speech. Pictures of him addressing the gathering on stage showed him confident amid 20 white-coated factory staff, all of whom remarkably looked shorter than the President.

POLITICAL, AS MUCH as physical, stature dominated the Sarkozy approach to image-making. Critics lambasted the relaunch of the President's official website in March 2010, the day after he had finally dined with Barack Obama, his US counterpart, in a prolonged effort to restore Franco-American relations after their breakdown over Iraq. The new site appeared to be a 'cut-and-paste' of the White House design, using almost identical layout, font style and colours. Even the 'stay connected' section at the end of the front page had been slavishly translated as *'restez connecté'*. Designed to also lift the President domestically after catastrophic local elections earlier in the month, it added to his stuttering image when English users discovered the sound translation of Sarkozy's biography contained what one UK newspaper correspondent termed language 'worthy of Inspector Clouseau', describing Sarkozy as the 'président of ze franche république'.

PAKISTAN LEADER Asif Zardari announced in July 2009 that he was banning political jokes that ridiculed his presidency. The country's Federal Investigation Agency had been instructed to investigate any quip sent by e-mail, text message or posted on an internet blog. Notoriously thin-skinned about his reputation, Zardari announced he would use the newly introduced Cyber Crimes Act to outlaw 'ill-motivated' comment about his leadership. The move came as the President's official e-mail account was reportedly being deluged with jokes and sarcastic comments as his popularity (as husband of the assassinated Benazir Bhutto) waned.

THE KING AND QUEEN of Sweden caused a diplomatic flap in April 2006 when returning from their Easter holiday in neighbouring Norway. Carl XVI Gustaf and Silvia stopped at a petrol station to re-fuel but drove off without paying. The 'wel-groomed couple' were only recognised when station attendants re-ran CCTV footage to identify the miscreants. The royal household later blamed their chauffeur.

BLAMING HIS late-night watching of Tiger Woods playing in the US Masters golf championship, President of the Philippines Fidel Ramos apologised in April 1997 for arriving late at a national launch event…the start of his government's Punctuality Week.

Styles of leadership

Newly crowned King Abdullah of Jordan carried on in the tradition of his father in 2000 when it was reported that he had slipped out of the royal palace one night in heavy disguise to observe how his people lived. He spent the night at a public hospital 20 miles outside the capital, Amman, to find out for himself the state of health care in his country. Having rarely been seen in public before his accession less than a year earlier, few of his countrymen recognised him (a problem that foiled his father by the end: having ruled for nearly 50 years, he was frequently recognised on his nightly visits). He returned to the palace to voice criticism of the quality of the service being provided.

It was not the first occasion. It emerged that the previous August, the King had posed as a taxi passenger in the centre of Amman to ask probing questions about his people's normal life. He was nearly discovered when the driver was pulled up by police for a driving offence. Earlier in the same week he had donned a false beard and dressed up as a television reporter to inspect Jordan's free trade zone.

PAVEL BÉM, Mayor of Prague since 2002, achieved notoriety in the Czech Republic for his novel ways of keeping a finger on the pulse of his city. After a run of complaints by foreign tourists in 2006 about overcharging by taxi drivers, Bém donned a fake goatee beard, false sideburns and dark glasses and passed himself off as a visiting

English rock star to test the integrity of his cabbies. He had indulged in a similar stunt the year before when he disguised himself as an Italian businessman. His experience then had led him to denounce the rampant overcharging by taxi drivers. On the latest occasion, he told local press that he was suitably encouraged by the progress. Only one driver had tried to double the officially set fare.

ANALYSTS NOTED IN 2000 possible signs of political reform in Morocco, a traditionally austere and conservative country. According to seasoned observers, one indicator that a warmer attitude to social integration might be emerging was the change of practice of the young King Mohammed VI, who had succeeded six months earlier: his motorcades were now reported to be stopping at red traffic lights.

ERNIE FLETCHER, Governor of Kentucky, applauded a campaign to improve the fitness in his state by signing into law a Wellness and Physical Activity Initiative in April 2006. Calling it a 'vital measure' that would 'bring greater focus on combating the lifestyle issues that are destroying the health of Kentuckians', Fletcher urged people to take up the opportunities afforded by the programme for a healthier life. These did not, it seem, apply to himself. He insisted on retaining use of his limousine to ride from his official mansion to the Governor's Office – a distance of 500 feet. A local newspaper added, 'There is not a river, swamp, or alligator between them.'

The test of office

William Clark, selected as second-in-command at the State Department in 1981, was one of the least auspicious appointments in Ronald Reagan's first Administration, causing a storm in his confirmation hearings before the Senate Foreign Relations Committee for his ignorance of the issues for which he would be responsible. A judge by background and one of the closest friends of the President, Clark astonished his audience by his apparent lack of awareness of current affairs. He said he had 'no opinion' on the spread of nuclear weapons (the world was in a distinctly chilly phase of the Cold War), could not name the leaders of South Africa or Zimbabwe and, when pressed on his thin knowledge, he said he was confident he would learn as he went along. Asked to define the Administration's foreign policy, he replied 'peace through strength'. Asked to be more specific, he responded, 'It would be presumptuous of me to give priorities...I'm not prepared to assess that.'

Appalled members of the Committee were unable to stop the appointment. He was voted into the post only through the Republican majority. He lasted less than a year in the role, but exited upwards – to become National Security Adviser for 18 months and then, in 1983, to become Secretary of the Interior.

AS TEMPORARY Prime Minister of Belgium in the summer of 2007 while leading complicated negotiations over forming a coalition government, Yves Leterme fatally failed to capture the confidence of his fractured Dutch–French speaking country when he wrongly sang the French national anthem when asked to recite his own. Asked by a journalist following up a poll showing that three-quarters of Belgians did not know the words of their national song, he began singing *La Marseillaise*, instantly losing the loyalty and confidence of the Dutch-speaking half of the nation. Ironically, he was already viewed with suspicions by the French-speaking population, as he hailed from Dutch-speaking Flanders and had established a reputation for looking out for regional interests (he was nicknamed 'Mr Flanders') above those of Belgium. Managing in one go to lose both sides, his attempts to shore up a coalition seemed increasingly heroic. He gave up the effort after a month. After another failed attempt in the autumn, Leterme did eventually become Prime Minister in early 2008 and lasted nine months. He was back again at the helm in late November 2009...and out again by April 2010.

THE DEFENCE MINISTER of the West African state of Ivory Coast performed one of the oddest of state functions in April 2002 when he was called in by the national football association to lead a forgiveness ceremony with witch doctors after the team had reportedly reneged on paying for their services ten years earlier. The country had won the 1992 African Championships, supposedly with the help of the witch doctors, but had never paid them after their success. There followed a decade of abysmal performances, and they had just failed to qualify for the 2002 World Cup. Summoning the heavy political guns, the national coach got Moisa Lida Kouassi to lead a meeting with the witch doctors to seek their forgiveness for the apparent curse. Presenting them with alcohol and an undisclosed amount of cash, he told the sorcerers, 'I ask pardon for the unkept promises.' The team successfully qualified for the next two World Cups (in 2006 and 2010) and since 2006 have been successively runners-up, fourth and quarter-finalists in the African Championships.

THE HEAD OF the Philippines Central Bank had to apologise to the country's President, Gloria Macapagal Arroyo, in 2005 when a new print run of 100-peso banknotes spelled her name wrong. Millions of notes flooded the country before the mistake was spotted. Worse, the misspelling – Arrovo – sounded in Spanish, the language of the Philippines, like 'robbery'. The poverty-afflicted country could not afford to recall and reprint the notes, so they stayed in circulation.

THE GENERAL MANAGER of the national mint in Chile was sacked in 2010 for allowing thousands of coins to be released which misspelled the name of the country. No one noticed the 2008 issue of 50-peso coins had 'Chiie' instead of 'Chile' until late in 2009.

EDWARD NATAPEI INADVERTENTLY sacked himself as Prime Minister of the South Pacific nation of Vanuatu in November 2009 because of an administrative oversight. Under the country's constitution, any Member of Parliament was automatically disqualified from their seat if they missed three consecutive sittings without informing the Speaker in advance. Natapei, who had left to attend the Commonwealth Heads of Government Meeting in the Caribbean, forgot to hand in his notification of absence and the Speaker was obliged to declare that the Prime Minister had given up his post. It took two weeks and a court battle to overturn the ruling on a technicality.

From the history books

If we know Zhao Zheng, China's first 'sovereign emperor' who unified the country in the third century BC, best today because of the terracotta army he left to guard his tomb in Xian, he had an even more bizarre way of making an impression on his people when alive. After managing to eliminate or annex the seven rival states into which China was then divided, and proclaim, in 221 BC, unification, he decided he wanted to emphasise how his dynasty was the starting point for China. In 213 BC, he ordered all books that were not concerned with agriculture, medicine or prognostication (he was an avid adherent of fortune-tellers) to be burned, thus creating a clean slate for history to begin again. Only the collection in the Imperial Library was spared. He also had 160 academics decapitated for good measure. He had little chance to recraft history himself. He died three years later, and within another four years the dynasty itself had collapsed into feudal in-fighting.

AFTER INHERITING THE mantle of the Russian crown from his mother, Catherine the Great, in 1796, Tsar Paul I exhibited bizarre ways of maintaining the security of the royal court. At a time of great uncertainty in Europe, with the French Revolution inspiring rebellion to authority all over the continent, Paul instituted a manic programme of self-protection. Any symbol of non-Russian influence was suspect. In 1797 he issued an edict imposing a rigid dress code for citizens, banning any styles that were associated with Western

Europe. The authorities enforced it vigorously, with people being stripped of offending articles in the street. Personal security concerns required that any occupant of a carriage had to stop and get out to be in full view of the royal police when the Tsar's entourage passed. Not surprisingly, the restrictions irked a society that had, under Catherine, flourished as a modernising country. Paul was strangled in a palace coup in March 1801, little over four years after he had taken the throne.

TURKISH SULTAN ABDUL Aziz reigned for just 15 years from 1861 until deposed and assassinated in a coup in April 1876, but in his short time in office his eccentricities and taste for largesse ruined the economy of the emerging Turkish state. He amassed an entourage of over 5,000 personal servants, including 400 musicians and 400 grooms. Among them was one man whose sole role in the household was to replace the royal backgammon board after use. Another was responsible for the task of cutting the royal fingernails, having no other function in between. He bought a collection of steam locomotives despite the fact that Turkey had no railway system – he developed the country's first network – and a fleet of modern iron ships, even though he did not have a navy that knew how to crew them. He mounted war games in his palace grounds for entertainment, using real soldiers from his army and live ammunition. For much of his reign, his annual personal expenditure ran at around £2 million, some £140 million in modern values. By the time he was ousted, Turkey had unsurprisingly slumped to a parlous state. Its overall debt amounted to £200 million (about £14 billion in today's values), costing over £12 million annually (£840 million today) – and half the national budget – just to meet interest payments. It would be the tipping point of the terminal decline of the Ottoman Empire.

HIS NEXT-BUT-ONE successor (Abdul's nephew Murad immediately followed but reigned for just 93 days before being deposed for insanity) took the burdens of high office equally bizarrely. Abdul Hamid II was a paranoiac *par excellence*. He built his own refuge palace at Yildiz a mile inland from the normal residences, which were all waterside locations next to the Bosporus, because he feared a waterborne attack. Yildiz was a surreal world in which the Sultan closeted himself away for 30 years, with his existence constantly constrained by fear of being murdered. Literally hundreds of loaded guns were placed around the palace for Abdul's ready use. Some rooms were booby-trapped, with firearms released from hidden panels at the flick of a switch. The palace was designed by a 12-strong team of architects, but none knew of each other's existence, so that no one had a complete knowledge of the layout of the building. Rooms were deliberately cluttered with furniture designed to ensure that visitors entering could only arrive in single file. Most were entirely mirrored so that Abdul could see every angle. All had secret passages enabling a quick getaway. Abdul had any food tasted twice before accepting it, had his clothes 'warmed' by an aide in case they had been laced with poison, and even had his documents baked and disinfected before being presented to him. He always wore chain mail under his clothes and a steel-lined fez. Even more bizarrely, certain language was barred in his presence or in papers to reduce the royal nervousness. 'Revolutionary', 'republic' and 'freedom' were all forbidden. A chef who produced a menu with *bombe glacée* was reputedly sacked on the spot. Notoriously, when the King and Queen of Serbia were assassinated in 1903 and their disembowelled bodies thrown out of a second-floor window, the Turkish press creatively reported that they had died of indigestion. Abdul endured his self-imposed isolation for decades, sending lookalikes to perform public functions in the city. He was eventually quietly deposed in 1909, and – after a lifetime of anxiety about a brutal death – died peacefully in his bed in 1918.

FÉLIX FAURE, PRESIDENT of France since 1895, died of a stroke in February 1899 while having sex with his 30-year-old mistress in his office in the Elysée Palace. Attila the Hun is also reputed to have died while having sex. He burst an artery while consummating his

12th marriage. At least one Pope – and possibly three others, but sources are not agreed – have died in similarly compromising circumstances. A history of the Papacy records that in the case of John XII, who ruled from 955 to 964, 'no Pope ever went to God in a more embarrassing position'. He was caught having sex with his latest mistress by the woman's husband, who beat the Pope with a hammer. Three days later he died.

GEORGES CLEMENCEAU, FRANCE'S Prime Minister at the end of the First World War, and renowned as 'the Tiger' for his forceful character, was shot and wounded by an anarchist gunman during the Versailles Peace Conference in 1919. The would-be assassin fired seven (some accounts say eight) shots at the Premier. One hit him near the heart, but he survived and was back at work after 10 days' rest. The bullet would remain lodged in his ribs for the rest of his life. When the death penalty was sought at the assailant's trial, Clemenceau intervened. 'We have just won the most terrible war in history, yet here is a Frenchman who misses his target six times out of seven... Of course the fellow must be punished – for careless use of a dangerous weapon and for poor marksmanship.' He recommended a sentence of eight years in jail 'with intensive training in a shooting gallery'.

ZAIRE'S KLEPTOCRAT DICTATOR, Mobutu Sese Seko, who ruled and plundered his country for over 30 years between 1965 and 1997, set the standard for turning one's home village into a palatial clearing in the jungle when he upgraded his birthplace of Gbadolite, conveniently just seven miles from the country's northern border. He constructed two vast palaces, one for official business and one for his personal use, gave the village an international airport and even built a nuclear bunker capable of holding 500 people, the only one in Central Africa. The bunker was connected by tunnel to the river that formed the border with neighbouring Central African Republic, and on which a military harbour provided the security of an escape route should it be needed.

DEAD MAN WINS ELECTION

HE WOULD CERTAINLY have felt secure in his neighbour's backyard. Jean Bedel Bokassa, who took over as President of the Central African Republic a year after Mobutu came to power south of the border, notoriously crowned himself Emperor in 1977 in what his *Times* obituary described as 'one of the most grotesquely lavish spectacles ever seen'. At a time when his people had an annual income of £100 each, he spent the equivalent of half the country's annual gross national product on his coronation. The total cost was thought to be in the region of $22 million. It was modelled on Napoleon's coronation, and saw a gold-plated throne in the shape of an eagle twelve feet high and weighing more than two tons, an imperial state coach drawn by a team of eight white horses imported from Belgium, 3,000 imperial guards all dressed in 19th-century style ceremonial uniforms, 20 tons of fresh flowers flown in from Europe, two specially written musical marches commissioned from a French composer, and 24,000 bottles of Moët et Chandon champagne. Sixty Mercedes limousines were shipped from Germany to coastal Cameroon and then airlifted over the jungle to Bokassa's capital, Bangui. His diamond-, ruby- and emerald-studded crown and robes alone were estimated to have cost £4 million. The day after his installation, he appeared dressed in the uniform of an 18th-century admiral to review a march past, a mixture of bare-breasted native girls, combat-clad assault troops and American-style majorette troupes with white busby hats. As Bokassa's behaviour became even more erratic once he began ruling as Emperor, he was deposed by French paratroopers less than two years later.

OMAR BONGO, PRESIDENT of the African equatorial republic of Gabon, is thought to have spent $350 million – half his country's annual wealth – in order to host the 10-day Organisation of African Unity conference in 1977 which brought all the continent's leaders together, the first time the country had attempted to get itself on the diplomatic map. Two replicas of the American President's armour-plated limo, six secret-service Cadillacs and 50 Mercedes limos were imported for the affair, as well as 300 BMW motorcycles for police outriders. Ten thousand hand-cut crystal wine glasses were also brought in for the top-class French wines on offer. Services were less well handled at the hotels in town. All backroom staff were withdrawn to act as cheering crowds lining the routes to the conference hall with instructions to break out in spontaneous applause whenever Bongo appeared. In consequence, none of the delegates apparently had laundry services for the entire 10 days.

KIM IL SUNG, the founder of the reclusive North Korean Communist dynasty, had every road in the country built with an extra lane for his own exclusive use. To mark his 65th birthday in April 1977, he was reported to have bought 40,000 gold Swiss watches bearing portraits of him and his son, Kim Jong Il – today's North Korean leader – for distribution to loyal party members. For his 70th birthday, the regime unveiled the 'Juche Tower', named after Kim's code of official thinking. It was built with precisely 25,550 blocks of granite, one for each day of Kim's life. In 1976, Kim launched a bizarre international operation to garner precious foreign exchange, which the North was finding increasingly hard to obtain given the country's limited economic production. He instructed all his overseas diplomatic missions to sell locally cigarettes and alcohol that they were entitled to import duty-free under diplomatic rules. The ruse even extended to smuggling hashish through the diplomatic channels for sale in Western countries. The scheme was quickly exposed. Suspicions were aroused in Denmark when the Korean mission lodged a request to import a consignment for the personal consumption of its staff – of 2.5 million cigarettes.

A TALE to show that however esteemed the leader or his office, human nature and fate can combine to reduce the aura of authority to some commonly recognisable basics. US Army leaders at Fort Bragg, North Carolina, laid on an elaborate dupe operation in February 1968 when President Lyndon Johnson made a sudden visit to their base at the height of the Vietnam War and declared he wanted to meet a troop of the 82nd Airborne Division just as they were about to embark for the war zone. Given about nine hours' notice, the commanders found the request problematic as the Vietnam-bound 3rd Brigade were by then fully engaged in an 'all-day beer bust and barbecue' and would be in no condition to parade before the President. So the deputy commander ingeniously borrowed a battalion from one of the Division's other brigades, which had only just returned from Vietnam, dressed them in battle fatigue without insignia and stood them in front of the 3rd Brigade's colours.

The plan had been for a straightforward inspection and Presidential departure. According to the account which made the affair public nearly a decade later, as he walked down the ranks, the President shook hands with each of them, glowing fulsomely with praise: 'God bless you, son... I'm proud of you, damned proud of you. I know you will serve the cause of freedom as your forefathers served it.' The men, unaware of the ruse, began to mutter with concern '... We're all going... We're going back to 'Nam.' Johnson was not apparently aware of the bewilderment growing on the faces of the soldiers.

Aiming to bring the episode to a conclusion, base commander Major-General Seitz sought to steer the President back to his car, diplomatically apologising for 'putting you way behind schedule'. To Seitz's horror, Johnson, overcome by emotion, declared, 'Schedule, Hell, forget the goddamned schedule, I came here to see those boys off, and I'm going to see them off.' Seitz's team had to continue the charade by marching the increasingly anxious stand-in troops off to an air transport plane, load them on board under the watchful and tear-stained eye of the President, and start the engines. The plane carried on through the motions of taking off, with Johnson standing to attention, hand over heart, paying tribute to his 'damned fine boys'.

As soon as Johnson left, the plane landed and the relieved troops disembarked. The President never knew of the deception. In his memoirs, he recorded the visit as one of the most memorable of his term of office, adding, 'It tore my heart out to send back to combat a man whose first son had just been born.'

POWER AND THE GLORY — HIGH OFFICE

We end with two examples of how high office is not always a guarantee of making one's mark.

KING FREDERICK OF Denmark, en route home after convalescing in the south of France, collapsed and died in a street in Hamburg, Germany, in May 1912 while taking a walk alone. No one recognised him as the monarch of their neighbour and his body was taken to a hospital and then a morgue before his identity was realised. It was five hours before his wife, Queen Louise, knew of his death.

STANLEY BALDWIN, who was Prime Minister three times (1923–24, 1924–29 and 1935–37), told an acquaintance in 1935 how during his previous premiership he had worn his old school tie while travelling in a train. A man opposite noticed and asked, 'You're Baldwin, aren't you? You were at Harrow in my time in '84.' Upon Baldwin's acknowledgement, a lengthy pause followed, and then the man asked, 'Tell me, what are you doing now?'

DARNED FOREIGNERS – DIPLOMACY

However much they are masters in their own backyard, all politicians eventually have to accept they need to deal with their opposite numbers in countries large and small. How they do it can often mean the difference between war and peace. Testing one's own demands against those of others is fraught with potential for dispute. Diplomacy has been described as the art of putting your foot down without stepping on anyone's toes. Here we survey the recent international scene.

The unique world of diplomacy

Officials in the Italian Foreign Ministry staged a novel industrial demonstration in 1981 when a national strike of civil servants took place during a pay dispute. They undertook a 'strike in reverse' and carried on working after the end of normal working hours. They refused to take meal breaks and continued their duties until 2am. Union representatives said they had decided against a traditional walk-out because 'professional habits' would lead most of the Ministry staff to turn up anyway. But they did not want to undermine their colleagues' strike elsewhere in the service.

THE MAYOR OF Rome headed a delegation to Tunis in 1985 to sign a treaty formally restoring peace with the city of Carthage, which the ancient Romans had destroyed in 146 BC.

THE DUTCH AMBASSADOR in Britain paid a long-overdue visit to the Scilly Isles off Cornwall in 1986 to sign a peace treaty between the Netherlands and the islands that brought to an end a state of war that had formally existed for 335 years. When Britain had settled its scores with the Dutch after war in 1651, no one had noticed that the Scillies had been left out. It was only in October 1985 that the chairman of the isles' council discovered the oversight.

FRANCE AND SPAIN reached an agreement in 1986 to exchange about an acre of territory each on their joint border because a statue of Luis Companys, the last Republican President of Spain before the Franco revolt, had been built by mistake on French soil.

IN 1992, AFTER 18 years of legal wrangling, diplomats for India and Bangladesh agreed a 999-year lease on the Tin Bigha corridor which links mainland Bangladesh with two enclaves in India, Dahagram and Angarpota. The size of the territory involved was the equivalent of a football pitch.

NEW MOORE ISLAND, a sandbar in the Bay of Bengal, was also the subject of protracted dispute between India and Bangladesh. For nearly 40 years, the two countries failed to settle ownership of the uninhabited island of 100,000 square feet – slightly smaller than London's Trafalgar square – after it had emerged from the sea in the wake of the 1970 cyclone that devastated the region. The problem solved itself in March 2010 when an oceanographer at Jadavpur University in Calcutta announced that global warming and rising sea levels had caused the entire landmass to disappear back under the sea.

RUSSIA AND CHINA edged closer to ending a 300-year-old border dispute with the announcement in April 1999 that they had made a breakthrough in talks to determine ownership of 2,444 islands in the Amur River that separates the two countries in the Far East. Diplomats reported that agreement had been reached allocating 1,281 of the islands to China and 1,163 to Russia. Only three further islands remained in dispute. All 2,447 in question are entirely uninhabited.

DEAD MAN WINS ELECTION

A GERMAN WATCHDOG of government waste revealed in 1992 that the authorities did not even know where Germany's borders were. It discovered that 100,000 marks (£35,000) had been spent on a small bridge across the river Blies in the Saarland to access land officials believed was German. It later turned out that the land was actually part of France.

JAPAN, IN 1988, 'dental-capped' two small rocklets 1,300 miles south-west of Tokyo to ensure that they did not disappear beneath the sea and deprive Japan of nearly 200,000 square miles of ocean. The tiny outcrop of Okino-torishima, the country's most southerly point, consisted of two barren rocks which, at high tide, were each the size of a double bed, and only four inches above sea level. No one had ever lived there, but their existence provided Japan with the fishing and mineral rights for several hundred miles in each direction. The operation involved placing $280 million worth of concrete and a $50 million titanium shield to keep the tips above sea level and guard against erosion. An observatory and a solar-powered lighthouse has now also been built to counter Chinese claims that the place is not land but a reef. In all, over the past two decades, some $600 million has been spent to preserve Japan's toehold.

Japan announced an intensification of its efforts in April 2006 with a programme to 'grow' the outcrops further by introducing fresh coral. After challenges from China which claimed the islets were 'rocks' not 'islands', and thus did not count under international law as conferring territorial water rights, Tokyo declared it would plant 300,000 'eggs' of three different types of coral, prepared in the warmer waters near Japan's southern coastline, on Okino-torishima the following year. Minister of Land, Infrastructure and Transport, Toru Noda, said this 'should help to preserve the islands'. There were also said to be plans to build an electricity power station on the reef to establish 'economic life', to further strengthen Japan's claim. The project duly transplanted the first young coral in June 2007. A further 50,000 shards were added in April 2008.

THE HEAD OF Thailand's Office of the Prime Minister, Somsak Thepsuthin, announced in December 2001 plans for a 27-hole golf course at the juncture of his country with Laos and Cambodia, with nine holes in each country, the first in the world to straddle three countries. Despite the possible downside of the area being littered with Khmer Rouge landmines from the wars of the 1970s, he was confident that golfers would fly in from around the world 'for the challenge'. To our knowledge, a decade on the course is still on the drawing board.

THE LANDLOCKED COUNTRY of Laos announced in 2007 that it was joining the International Whaling Commission. Diplomats suspected the sole motivation lay in pressure from Japan, a notorious and increasingly isolated proponent of continued whaling, which happened also to be Laos's largest aid donor. It duly joined on 22 May.

Disputed loyalties

In 1982 the Mayor of Key West and his council, frustrated by travel restrictions caused by US Border Patrol roadblocks set up to stem the flow of illegal Cuban refugees which had severely damaged the tourist trade, declared secession from the United States and the establishment of the Conch Republic. Declaring, 'We were once the richest town south of Savannah; now we're just the highest taxed,' Dennis Wardlow formally announced separation on 23 April in an elaborate ceremony in front of the roadblock at the entrance to the island chain, during which he was proclaimed Prime Minister and promptly declared war against America by ceremonially breaking a stale Cuban loaf over the head of an actor dressed in naval uniform. He rescinded the state of war after one minute and formally applied for $1 billion in aid from the US.

The 'republic' continues to this day, holding a celebratory week of events each year in April around 'independence day' on 23 April. The international airport at Key West is emblazoned with a banner welcoming arrivals to the Conch Republic, and sales of souvenir passports, ID cards and car bumper stickers have become a staple ingredient of the once ailing tourist trade.

A GROUP REPRESENTING residents of the District of Columbia, the federal territory that is home to the US capital, Washington, marked American Independence Day in 2002 by seeking re-accession to the United Kingdom in protest at the lack of representation in the US Congress that sits on their doorstep. Since DC is not a state, it does not send elected members to the House of Representatives or to the Senate. The 570,000 residents of the nation's capital have just a single, non-voting observer in the lower chamber. Despite years of lobbying, the other states, who need to approve the required constitutional amendment, have never summoned enough support to the cause. In 2000, the city authorities – elected local government has only existed since 1975 – formally adopted as its official motto for car licence plates the slogan 'Taxation without representation'. The protest group DC Vote presented a request to the British Embassy for the Queen to reassume sovereignty over the city. Paul Strauss, the movement's leader, said, 'We want Her Majesty to intercede on our behalf.' There were no immediate signs that the British Government was inclined to oblige.

IT WAS NOT the first time that suggestions had been made about the colonial cousins rejoining. Irked at Mrs Thatcher's leadership of Britain, which led to Malaysia deciding to stay away from the 1981 Commonwealth Heads of Government Meeting, the country's former Prime Minister Tunku Abdul Rahman called that September for the United States to join the Commonwealth and take over management of the organisation. The Queen would remain head of the Commonwealth, but the US President would take over as Chairman of the Commonwealth Conference. He conceded that his ideas were 'a dream' and not likely to succeed.

Testing relations

The personality cult surrounding Romanian strongman Nicolae Ceausescu reached its peak in 1988, the year before his downfall, when the country marked his 70th birthday. When insufficient tributes came in from leaders around the globe, anxious officials simply fabricated them, and also published them openly in the Foreign Ministry's international affairs magazine. To the surprise of the British Foreign Office, Her Majesty Queen Elizabeth had lauded Ceausescu's 'determination with which you affirm your independence' and described him as 'a statesman of world stature with widely recognised excellence, experience and influence'. The Romanian Ambassador in London was summoned to explain. It was not his first trip. The year before, he had had to explain how Prime Minister Margaret Thatcher had come to be reported by a Romanian Government press statement as having delivered an enthusiastic speech of support for the regime. That, too, had been faked.

MUSLIM PAKISTAN REFUSED permission for a delegation from the European Community to visit in 1982 because the team was headed by a man named Israel.

NEWLY ELECTED US President Barack Obama visited one of his arch opponents in the Americas in April 2009, Venezuela's firebrand leader Hugo Chávez. Obama graciously spoke at a news conference of the gift that Chávez had given him: 'Well, I think it was a nice gesture to give me a book. I'm a reader.' He had received Chávez's polemical study, *Open Veins of Latin America: Five Centuries of the Pillage of a Continent*.

IN NOVEMBER 2003, New Zealand Prime Minister Helen Clark was required by an airport guard to be frisked as a security risk as she went through metal detectors when changing planes in Sydney,

Australia. Reports of the incident outraged New Zealand opinion, which regarded it as an insult by their traditional arch rivals. The guard was said not to have recognised the Prime Minister, despite her travelling with a sizeable official entourage.

GERMAN DEFENCE MINISTER Volker Rühe ruffled feathers during a period of controversy in the summer of 1992 as the country faced growing demands from its European allies to contribute troops to the NATO peace-keeping effort in the civil wars in the Balkans involving Serbia, Croatia and Bosnia-Herzegovina. 'I am not willing to risk the lives of German soldiers for countries whose names we cannot even spell properly.'

NEGOTIATING AN AGREEMENT in 1986 on sharing state-of-the-art military and industrial technology, the United States was acutely concerned about the ability of West Germany to keep such secrets safe from being leaked to the Communist East. How do we know? Details of the negotiation and the secret treaty were leaked to the West German newspaper.

THE FORMAL WELCOMING ceremony for the new West German Ambassador to Honduras in 1989 was marred by a small but important oversight. The Honduran national military band had been unable to get the music for the German national anthem. They played the British one instead.

PROTOCOL SLIP-UPS are less uncommon than might be thought. In November 2009, Venezuela's Hugo Chávez entertained his equally erratic counterpart from Iran when President Mahmoud Ahmadinejad visited. Unfortunately, he was welcomed by the playing of Iran's old imperial national anthem of the previous, overthrown, Shah's regime.

In February 2000, Israel welcomed French Prime Minister Lionel Jospin to Jerusalem, and bedecked the city with what they thought were French flags. However, they had strung up the red, white and blue horizontal colours of the Netherlands, instead of the vertical stripes of France.

In October 2006, Russia's Foreign Minister Sergey Lavrov was greeted on his arrival in Poland with the Czech flag rather than Russia's. While both of the flags comprise sections of white, blue and red, they are very different in design.

The Royal Navy apologised to their Chinese guests in September 2001 when a senior Chinese Navy delegation being entertained in Portsmouth on board HMS *Ark Royal*, the navy's flagship, were greeted with the flag of Taiwan, the Communist republic's errant island off-shoot, instead of the mainland's red and yellow-starred emblem.

In October 1992, the US Marine Corps caused a diplomatic storm with its northern neighbour by flying the distinctive Canadian maple leaf flag upside down during the national anthems ceremony at the opening game of the baseball World Series between Atlanta and Toronto. As images of the debacle at one of the biggest sporting events in North America were beamed across the continent, President Bush had to be roped in to issue a formal apology to his Canadian counterpart.

The White House did not help President Bush's visit to southeast Asia in November 2006 by displaying on the President's official website the flags of the countries he was visiting. Included on the itinerary was Bush's first visit to Vietnam, always a sensitive affair for any American leader. The flag shown by the White House was the yellow and red emblem of the former US-backed South Vietnam, a country which had been extinguished more than 30 years earlier by America's withdrawal.

When Bush visited Bulgaria in June 2007, every other American flag flying on poles spread along the ceremonial route down the main boulevard in the capital Sofia was the wrong way round – flying the starred blue quadrant on the right-hand side.

In January 2010, during Bangladesh's hosting of the South Asian Games, officials managed to get the world's most unusual – and unique – flag in the world wrong: Nepal's dual-triangular flag – the only one on the planet not to be a four-sided flag – was nowhere to be seen. In its place was a four-sided depiction. The hosts also played Nepal's old royal national anthem, despite the abolition of the Nepali monarchy in 2008.

Saudi Arabia, playing host to Lebanon in a football international in Riyadh in June 2008, greeted the Lebanese team by playing the Syrian national anthem. Of all the possible mistakes, it was perhaps the one to most bite upon Lebanese sensitivities. For almost 30 years between 1976 and 2005, Syria had effectively occupied the country after the end of Lebanon's civil war and still retained a heavy and controversial influence on the country's affairs.

Australian officials caused a diplomatic incident with Spain in November 2003 at the opening ceremony in Melbourne of the two countries' match in the final of tennis's prestigious Davis Cup. Instead of playing the modern Spanish anthem, the tune that blared out across the stadium was the Communist Republican anthem used briefly in the 1930s during the Spanish Civil War. A version of the anthem includes a verse in which the Spanish Queen is beheaded and a man wipes his bottom on King Alfonso XIII, the grandfather of the present Spanish king, Juan Carlos. Unfortunately, the Spanish sports minister was present. He stormed out and the match only carried on after Australian diplomats had concocted a groveling apology for the slight.

It was not the first time Australia had slipped up. At a football World Cup qualifier match, also in Melbourne, with Israel in October 1985, the Australian hosts played, of all tunes, the West German national anthem for the Israelis.

BRITAIN COMMITTED AN own goal with its own flag at a high-profile ceremony in 10 Downing Street in February 2009. For the signing of a trade agreement with China, small flags of the two countries formed the centrepiece of the table where Trade Secretary Lord Mandelson and the Chinese Premier Wen Jiabao sat to exchange documents. Unfortunately, the Union Jack was flying upside down, traditionally a sign of distress. The Prime Minister's office had to issue a public apology regretting the mistake.

THE SECOND ISLAMIC Solidarity Games, an international sporting gathering designed to promote harmony and common understanding across the Muslim world, to be held in Iran in October 2009, were postponed by the hosts six months before the tournament was due to start because they could not agree on how to name the Gulf in the region. Iran, which while Muslim is not Arab, wanted the Games logo and medals to bear the ancient name of 'Persian Gulf'. The Saudi Arabia-based organising committee insisted on the Arab styling of the 'Arabian Gulf'. Even when the organisers allowed an extra six months to try to sort out the dispute by rescheduling the Games for April 2010, the two sides failed to break the logjam and the 57-country event was cancelled altogether in January.

AT THE 2010 Winter Olympic Games in Vancouver, Canada, Polish biathlon competitors revealed that they had been kitted out with uniforms bearing the wrong flag. Instead of the Polish colours on their sleeves and thighs, they wore those of Monaco. With both flags being effectively identical in colour and design – a combination of a red and white horizontal stripe – but with the colours reversed, the mix-up saw the biathletes emblazoned with Monaco's red over white patches instead of Poland's white over red. No one apparently noticed for the first 12 days of the Games.

IN JUNE 2001, a month before the International Olympic Committee was due to select its choice to host the 2008 Games, the mayor of one of the three strongest contender cities competing for the honour all but blew his home town's chances by publicly comparing Africans to cannibals in a newspaper interview. Mel Lastman, who headed the bid by the Canadian city of Toronto, was quoted telling a reporter that he had not wanted to go to a key meeting the previous month of African delegates who would vote on the decision because 'I and my wife hate snakes'. Had he stuck there, he might have got away with it, but he continued undiplomatically, 'What the hell would I want to go to a place like Mombasa for?… I just see myself in a pot of boiling water with all these natives dancing around.' Stung by the outrage of his civic colleagues witnessing the city's chances disappearing, he called a hasty press conference and apologised more than 20 times for the gaffe. A month later, Toronto lost out to Beijing on just the second round of voting.

Official visits

A three-day visit by Viktor Shushkov, a deputy Trade Minister, to London in 1981 at a deteriorating time in the Cold War was hailed as a breakthrough in Anglo-Soviet relations following the invasion of Afghanistan two years earlier. To mark the change, the Soviet Embassy obtained an interview for their man on the BBC's World Service to pronounce this success and demoralise those listening surreptitiously to the BBC back home. He was never heard. In common with all transmissions, Soviet controllers in Moscow routinely jammed it.

UK RELATIONS WITH the Gulf state of Qatar came within minutes of being derailed in the autumn of 1999 when British Department of Trade officials discovered an awkward inclusion in the dozen copies of a gift book that ministers were about to hand over to their Arab guests. Opting for a chic photography collection, *Britain: The Book of the Millennium*, they had neglected to notice one shot showing a model posing naked for art students. Civil servants were reported to have 'felt-tipped away like mad' to cover up the picture in all 12 copies. Told of the episode, the author of book acknowledged their problem: 'There are no two ways about it – she's completely nude,' adding, 'I only hope they did it tastefully.'

YOSHIRO MORI, WHO unexpectedly became Japanese Prime Minister in April 2000 after his predecessor suffered an incapacitating stroke, had a term of office which was both short – he lasted just a year and three weeks – and gaffe-laden. A poor speaker of English, his advisers gave him emergency lessons before he departed on a crucial visit in May to see President Clinton in Washington. According to accounts which have become legendary in diplomatic circles, he was taught that when shaking hands with Clinton he was to say, 'How are you?' Clinton would say, 'I am fine, and you?' and Mori was advised, 'Now you should say, "Me too". After that, the translators will do all the work for you.'

On the big day, when greeting Clinton, Mori mistakenly asked, 'Who are you?' Clinton, only slightly taken aback, responded jocularly, 'Well, I am Hillary's husband, ha ha...' Mori replied confidently, 'Me too, ha ha ha...'

BRITAIN WAS ON the receiving end of less than meticulous planning in March 2009 when Prime Minister Gordon Brown made his inaugural visit to the White House to meet newly elected President, Barack Obama. Aiming to shore up the 'Special Relationship', Brown went armed with a gift of a first edition of the multi-volume biography of Winston Churchill. Obama reciprocated with a DVD box set of 25 famous Hollywood movies. When the British party returned home and tried to play them, they discovered they were Region 1 format, playable only in North America.

IT WASN'T THE Administration's only blunder in its early days. Just three days after Brown's visit, Hillary Clinton, the new Secretary of State, (America's Foreign Minister), met her Russian counterpart Sergei Lavrov in Geneva. She gave him a joke gift of a small box the size of a television remote control with a single button on it. It was labelled, in Russian, a 're-set' button, and meant to be symbolic of President Obama's hope to recast US-Russian relations after a stormy period under the previous Bush regime. Unfortunately, linguistic expertise seemed to have been in short supply as a confused Lavrov quickly pointed out that the Americans had misspelled 're-set'. The word on the box translated as 'overload'. At least smiling, Lavrov told Clinton, who had spotted his quizzical expression when unwrapping the gift, 'You got it wrong.'

DEAD MAN WINS ELECTION

HILLARY CLINTON'S MONTH did not get any better. On a visit to Mexico in late March, she visited the Basilica of Our Lady in Guadalupe, the second most visited Catholic shrine in the world and home to Latin America's equivalent of the Turin Shroud – a 16th-century cloak with an image of the Virgin Mary. The image is said to have miraculously appeared, and the phenomenon is unexplained to this day. Its local fame had clearly not extended to Clinton. Her first question to her host was, 'Who painted it?' Rector Diego Monroy swiftly responded, 'God!'

VISITING ISRAEL'S SACRED Holocaust Museum in October 2000, German Chancellor Gerhard Schröder performed a ceremony alongside the Israeli Prime Minister that should have involved him turning up the Eternal Flame memorialising those killed in the extermination camps. Instead, he turned the switch the wrong way and extinguished the flame. Horrified officials were initially unable to reignite the flame, which had been burning since 1961. It was eventually relit with a cigarette lighter.

ANGLO-CANADIAN DIPLOMATIC feathers got ruffled in March 2010 when Nova Scotia planners of the Queen's visit that summer objected to Buckingham Palace's indication that the monarch wished to attend the provincial military tattoo in Halifax. The resistance centred on the necessity of the Queen having to climb 17 steps to a podium to address the audience, a feat the planners judged the 83-year-old was incapable of doing. Despite her aides' assurance that Elizabeth regularly managed the Grand Staircase at Buckingham Palace with three times as many steps, Nova Scotia was adamant. The show's artistic director was reported by UK media declaring the steps were 'very, very dangerous' and that 'the potential for disaster is very high'. Another spokesman for the tattoo added that the steps were not suitable 'for anyone who was not trained to use them'. The engagement was scrapped from the schedule.

BRAZILIAN PRESIDENT Luis Inacio Lula da Silva made few friends on his visit to Namibia in November 2003 when he tried to compliment his hosts on his departure from the capital, Windhoek, saying it was so clean, it did not seem like Africa. 'I'm surprised because…it doesn't seem like you're in an African country. Few cities of the world are so clean and beautiful as Windhoek.' So far as we know, he has not been asked back.

THE BODYGUARDS OF American Secretary of Defence William Perry were given a nasty surprise in January 1995 when he visited Pakistani tribesmen in the lawless hills near the Khyber Pass. As part of the reception ceremony, gun-toting elders danced in welcome, firing their automatic weapons in time to the music.

ALBANIA'S PUBLIC ORDER Minister had his official limousine confiscated by Greek customs when he arrived at the Christalopigi border crossing in December 1999 en route to an engagement in Athens. Spartak Poci's luxury Mercedes was subjected to a routine check that revealed the car to have been stolen in Italy. Embarrassed Greek officials said they had no option but to seize the vehicle, as Interpol had put out an order for its impounding. Stranded until his host sent up a Greek Government car, Poci continued his journey to the Greek capital…to sign an agreement combating cross-border crime. He returned home by air.

AN OFFICIAL VISIT to Washington in February 1996 by pomp-conscious French President Jacques Chirac – the first by a French leader for 12 years – nearly derailed when Congressional leaders intimated to Gallic planners that they were unenthusiastic about granting him a joint session of Congress, the privilege usually accorded to America's closest allies. At the time, France languished in bad odour in the US on account of its controversial nuclear testing programme in the Pacific. Chirac's threat to cancel the whole visit resulted in an elaborate subterfuge. According to diplomatic sources, while television cameras – and Chirac – witnessed a full chamber to listen to his speech, only 50 of the 535 seats were actually filled with Congressmen. The rest were ushers and pages dragooned in to spare the President the humiliation of having no audience.

THE US SECRET SERVICE mistakenly bombarded an Auckland chicken processing plant with top-secret security details of President Clinton's arrival plans for the September 1999 Asia-Pacific Summit. Despite reporting the errant faxes, the head of the plant told local press that the messages kept arriving for several weeks. One detailed the installation of the White House secure communications equipment at Auckland airport ahead of the arrival of Air Force One, the President's plane. Another had the names of military officers involved in the advance party, replete with code names and security badge numbers. US officials were reported to be 'looking into the situation'.

Anger management

Cadbury India, an offshoot of the global confectionary company, caused diplomatic tensions to rise between India and Pakistan in August 2002 when it ran adverts to launch its *Temptations* chocolates comparing the disputed area of Kashmir to the sweets: 'Chocolates you'd love to share, but won't'. Barely two months after the two countries had come close to hostilities in another of their periodic bouts of muscle-flexing over the Himalayan territory, the company published in the country's most read newspaper, *The Times of India*, the advert depicting a map of Kashmir with the slogan beneath it as an Independence Day greeting to India. Another advert ran the catch line: 'I'm good. I'm tempting. I'm too good to share. What am I? Cadbury's *Temptations* or Kashmir?' Protestors from India's governing party stormed the offices of the company in Bombay, and the Prime Minister weighed in to complain about the trivialising of a problem that had cost two wars and up to 50,000 lives. The company quickly backtracked and withdrew the advert. Global headquarters in London distanced itself, pointedly commenting, 'From time to time, local management makes mistakes. This was clearly one.' Pakistan kept a diplomatic silence.

FOR OVER THREE years, after a fit of pique about France's opposition to the US war in Iraq, Walter Jones and Bob Ney, Republican members of the House of Representatives, persuaded the House cafeteria to rename French fries 'Freedom Fries' and French toast 'Freedom Toast' to express 'our strong displeasure at our so-called ally, France'. The practice was lifted in August 2006 as relations warmed. There was a touch of irony about the announcement: Jones had now become an outspoken critic of the war, leading him to express regret at starting the name-change campaign.

FOUR DAYS BEFORE the end of the Bush Administration in January 2009, the US announced the imposition of increases to customs duties on a wide range of goods from the European Union. Commentators pointed to the possibility that Bush was still smarting from the lack of co-operation from France in the Iraq War and the new tariffs contained a parting shot. While the duties on almost all the items were 100 per cent, standing out was a 300 per cent tariff on France's iconic product, Roquefort cheese. When quizzed, no one in the Administration was willing to explain the reason for the decision.

Credence was lent to the move having had political motivation when the new Obama Administration diplomatically negotiated a dropping of the tax four months later.

A LONG-AWAITED peace gathering between two tribes in the remote New Guinea highlands convened in 1990 with the intention of having a joint feast. Members of the Puman and Mandak tribes sacrificed a pig, and proceeded to cook it. An argument broke out about the best way to prepare it, resulting in a five-day battle involving two thousand spear-wielding warriors. Five died and dozens were wounded. A subsequent peace gathering agreed to have the catering laid on.

The nadir of the summit

The United Nations' flagship conference on international development in Monterrey, Mexico, in 2002 was marred by technical difficulties over sound and translation equipment because the UN had not checked that its contractors knew the right place to go to. The German firm flew its technicians to Monterey, California, 1,500 miles away. It was halfway through the week-long conference before they reached the correct destination.

ATTENDING THE 1989 conference of the Heads of State of the Economic Community of West Africa in Ouagadougou, Burkina Faso, Gambian President Dawda Jawara arrived in what the official British observer termed 'an ostentatiously modest' propeller-driven aircraft. It was believed locally that this was designed to present an implicit contrast to the luxurious Presidential jet enjoyed by the conference host, Blaise Campaoré. The slight managed to achieve more than intended. The propellers, which were still turning as the plane halted, sucked up the red carpet, chopping it to pieces and showering President Campaoré and other dignitaries with red fluff. It was then discovered, in the words of the British envoy's report, that the airport 'proved not to possess steps of the right height to allow the Gambian President to descend gracefully to earth'.

CARDIFF'S FORAY INTO international summitry, when it hosted its first European Union Heads of Government Meeting in June 1998, almost ended in disaster when organisers spelled Germany wrongly on banners strung out in front of Cardiff City Hall. The banners spelling out each of the 15 member countries in their local languages showed the German streamer reading 'Deutchsland' instead of the correct 'Deutschland'. The slip-up was spotted by a passing German language lecturer from the local university, who described the elementary error as 'absolutely pathetic'.

A BIZARRE DIPLOMATIC ballet took place in the preparatory negotiations for the 1975 Conference on Security and Co-operation in Europe, a major milestone in managing Cold War relations between East and West. On the tricky question of who should fund the event, countries disagreed on whether the costs should be borne by the United Nations or by contributions by individual states. Tiny Luxembourg had not been able to afford to send a delegation to the talks and asked the Netherlands to represent its views. At the appropriate moment in the debate, the Dutch representative moved a few places across the conference hall to occupy the vacant Luxembourg seat and deliver a passionately argued statement demanding that the United Nations pick up the bill. Finishing the speech, he then moved back to his own seat and forcefully attacked the Luxembourg position, urging that all members should provide their own contributions.

From the history books

In 1040, Pope Benedict IX initiated a vain attempt to make war illegal by proclaiming the 'Truce of God', probably the first example of international attempts to outlaw war. It decreed that fighting was unlawful for anyone between vespers on Wednesday evening and sunrise on Monday.

THE SO-CALLED WAR of 1812 between Britain and the fledgling United States is probably history's most extreme example of war by accident. It both began and ended through error. The conflict originated in American objections to British trade blockades which were thought to be trying to squeeze the life out of the new republic. The States eventually declared war on 18 June 1812. Unknown to them, over in England, a new government under Lord Liverpool had taken office 10 days earlier. Liverpool was in favour of a more conciliatory approach to America. He had had one of the key reasons for the war removed by withdrawing controversial orders allowing the conscription of American nationals into the British Navy. These orders had been rescinded just the day before the American declaration of war. The Americans could not have been aware of this as there was no way for the news to reach Congress before it voted for war. Three more weeks, and news of the British climbdown would have been known. The war would last two and a half years and cost nearly 4,000 lives.

Its end was similarly shrouded in disastrous blunder. The culminating engagement, the Battle of New Orleans in early January 1815, took place two weeks *after* the official peace treaty ending the war had been signed on Christmas Eve 1814. News was still on its way from Europe and too late to prevent the final encounter. Nearly a thousand men lost their lives in the most unnecessary battle in history.

ONE OF THE least successful diplomatic endeavours is probably the Pact of Union signed between four Central American states intended to 'guarantee peace, maintain harmony among the states, insure the benefits of liberty and promote the general progress and welfare'. Meeting in the Costa Rican capital of San José on 19 January 1921, the governments of Costa Rica, Guatemala, Honduras and El Salvador agreed to unite the four countries in a 'perpetual and indissolute union'. A year and 10 days later, on 29 January 1922, it was dissolved.

OPTIMISM MAY ALSO have lain behind the two astonishing credentials of Sir Edward Grey, who was appointed British Foreign Secretary in 1905, a post he retained until 1916, the longest tenure of the office in the 20th century. First, he was famous for detesting foreigners. He had once written, 'These foreigners must be terrible intriguers to suspect us as they do... Foreign statesmen ought to receive their education at an English public school.' He then had what to most others might seem a second incapacitating lack of qualification: apart from a non-stop journey through the Continent some years before en route to India, and spending a few private months in the Caribbean, Grey had never been abroad, and had never set foot in Europe.

THERE ARE UNLIKELY to be many competitors better suited for the title of Britain's most embarrassing diplomat of all time than Edward Hyde, Viscount Cornbury, who was appointed by his cousin Queen Anne in 1701 as Governor-General of the New York colony. In an era steeped in the formalisms of courtly rectitude, he adopted the bizarre practice of donning women's clothes for public appearances. He turned up for his inaugural opening of the New York Assembly in 1702 dressed in a blue silk gown, a stylish diamond-studded headdress and satin shoes. When challenged on the proprieties of his choice of clothes, he replied 'In this place and particularly in this occasion I represent a woman and ought in all respects to represent her as faithfully as I can.' Described by contemporaries as a 'large, fleshy man' with a distinctly masculine face, he preferred promenading around his domain in hooped skirts, flashing a womanly fan to waft away the city odours. Amazingly, despite the outrage his transvestitism caused, he was not recalled until 1708.

RATHER MORE DIPLOMACY was shown by New York's city elders in June 1775 in the early months of the War of Independence when they faced the prospect of having to welcome both the newly appointed Commander-in-Chief of the rebel Continental Army, George Washington, and the return from England of the British Governor of New York colony, William Tryon. They both arrived in the city on 25 June. With only one main street – Broadway – available as a route for the ceremonial marching of the troops, the civic leaders laid on a welcoming reception for Washington and his force at the northern end of the thoroughfare, and for Tryon at the southern, downtown, end, ensuring that neither side managed to meet each other.

DEAD MAN WINS ELECTION

THE LONGEST RENDERING of the British national anthem occurred at the welcoming ceremony for King Edward VII when he arrived in Germany for a state visit in February 1909. As his train pulled up in Rathenau station, in Brandenburg, a military band struck up 'God Save the King' as the welcoming committee stood expectantly. No one emerged from the carriage and the anthem was played a second time. It continued to play it, eventually for 16 or 17 times – accounts vary – until the British monarch eventually appeared. He had apparently been having difficulty getting himself into the uniform of a German field-marshal.

PERHAPS THE MOST bizarre diplomatic practice was observed in Russia during the First World War when, despite the rigours of warfare, the niceties of culture were maintained. Diplomat Bruce Lockhart described in his diary how ballet and opera continued to function through the darkest periods, the war duly being noted by the orchestra playing the national anthems of all the Allies while the audience stood to attention. By the end, the number of allied hymns 'assumed the dimensions of a cricket score'. It took more than half an hour to run through the register of all the friendly nations.

A CRIPPLING PART of the 1919 Versailles peace settlement after the First World War was the reparations arrangements, which indebted all defeated powers to paying compensation to the victors. These proved too onerous and by the 1930s all the debtors had defaulted – except one, Finland, which continued to pay in full, completing its dues as recently as 1976.

PATIENCE OF ANOTHER kind was apparent in the approach adopted by the Central American state of Honduras in the same war. It became the last country to declare hostilities on Germany and join the Allied cause – in July 1918, four years into the conflict and just four months before it ended.

LABOUR FOREIGN SECRETARY Ernest Bevin, a trade union official to the core, had a typically working-class approach to the pomposities of diplomacy. Surprisingly appointed by Attlee in 1945 at a critical time of post-war reconstruction, his lack of finesse was sometimes an asset for the Foreign Office. Warned that he had to receive a puffed-up Guatemala Ambassador who was arriving at the Foreign Office to stake a claim on the British Central American possession of Belize, Bevin warmly embraced the emissary when he was shown in with the greeting: 'Guatemalia — that's where you're from, isn't it, Guatemalia...funny thing, we were just talking about it this morning, couldn't find it on the map. What a bit of luck you're here, now you can tell us where it is.'

NINETEENTH-CENTURY GERMAN Chancellor Bismarck had an equally effective but more standard diplomatic device for retaining control. The story is told of the British Ambassador who asked him during an audience how he handled 'insistent visitors who take up so much of your time'. Bismarck replied that 'I have an infallible method. My servant appears and informs me that my wife has something urgent to tell me.' At that point, there was a knock at the door and a servant entered bearing a message from his wife.

WHEN HE WAS Foreign Secretary, Lord Home adopted the practice when arriving in a new country of having his wife descend the aircraft steps right behind him whispering repeatedly the location they had just reached. He was mortified that he might announce his pleasure to be in the wrong place.

IN MARCH 1966, during the Cold War, the United States banned the importation of wigs that contained hair from people living in Communist countries.

JOHN HUMES, AMERICAN Ambassador to Austria during the same era of confrontation, finding himself facing a similar quandary, applied a more free-thinking approach. He had received a gift of a box of Cuban cigars at a time when dealing in any produce of the Communist regime would be a breach of US sanctions policy. He therefore told his chief-of-staff to dispose of them with the following instructions: 'Burn them…one by one…slowly.'

LIFE IN THE UNDERGROWTH – LOCAL GOVERNMENT

They may be a million miles from the corridors of power, and far from the glare of the national media, but those engaged in the world of local politics are no less dedicated to the wielding of what limited authority they possess. At the lower levels of the political game, a paradox frequently prevails – that the smaller the issue, the more intensely the matter is pursued. Nowhere demonstrates better the human ability to turn the blandest of subjects into a political controversy, or the capacity to come up with the most novel of solutions. The concept of pettiness, in both senses, shines through. We see the small concerns of ordinary people getting dealt with, but often with the amazingly obsessive concern for formalism embodied by the tyranny of the petty bureaucrat. Somewhere, at some time, almost every problem known to humanity has passed through the hands of a local politician. Few have reached national attention – until now. They deserve their rightful place in the pantheon of political folly.

Local issues, local approaches

The assistant head of tourism at Preseli District Council was suspended in August 1989 when he told local media that a double murder in the area the month before was good for the trade as news footage of the investigation had shown the Pembrokeshire countryside in all its glory. 'We could not have done a better marketing exercise,' said Alan Morris.

DEAD MAN WINS ELECTION

COUNCILLORS ON THE South Lakeland Council in the Lake District took time to reorganise themselves in November 1976. The changes included the Tourism, Recreation and Amenities Department becoming the Amenities, Recreation and Tourism Department.

TO THE BEMUSEMENT of local taxpayers, Cambridgeshire County Council decided in January 2006 to undertake a costly consultation exercise with residents on the subject of how it should undertake consultation exercises with residents. The council's plans for traffic-calming measures would be consulted upon once the council felt it was satisfied it knew the way people preferred to be consulted. The chairman of the committee responsible for all this said she hoped the consultation on consultations exercise would 'improve communications' between the council and the public.

AFTER THE SIGN welcoming drivers to the Sussex village of Horam had been knocked down several times by cars in 1974, the parish council solved the problem. It placed the sign safely behind a huge oak tree – and largely out of sight.

KENT COUNTY COUNCIL applied temporary parking restrictions in the village of Wateringbury in February 2008 in preparation for the start of roadworks. Instead of painting lines, or using cones, it used adhesive plastic yellow tape. The markings blew away in 5 mph gusts over a single weekend, leaving residents complaining at being unsure whether the parking restrictions were still in effect.

HAMPSHIRE'S TEST VALLEY Borough Council, whose War Memorial Park at Romsey won a nationally prestigious Green Flag for excellence in 2008, banned the park from flying the prize because councillors felt a flagpole would make the area look unsightly.

SOUTH GLOUCESTERSHIRE COUNCIL was three weeks away from completing its £2 million public library in Emersons Green, north Bristol, in March 2003 when it realised that no one had ordered – or budgeted for – any books for the new establishment. The council had to postpone the opening, and found itself needing to find another £235,000 to pay for the books, and for shelves to stack them on that had also been forgotten. Its official spokesman blamed the mistake on the council being 'a large organisation. We won't get things right a hundred per cent of the time.'

BRISTOL CITY COUNCIL launched a 'Don't Use a Padlock' initiative in 2008 that asked allotment holders not to lock their council-owned sheds so that thieves did not force their way into property and damage it. The aim was to save money because fewer sheds would need repairing after burglaries. A council spokesman said that 'where sheds have been repeatedly broken into, our advice is not to padlock them as forced entry often results in the doors being jemmied off'. He did acknowledge that the guidance offered little protection for gardeners' equipment stored inside the sheds. The initiative foundered when Avon and Somerset Police directly contradicted the scheme by telling shed owners to securely lock their premises.

Local quandaries

WESTWOOD PARISH COUNCIL, near Bradford-on-Avon in Wiltshire, found itself caught in a procedural stalemate in 1999 when 60-year-old Pat Hobbs found herself the only member returned at the council's 'election'. All eight other members had stood down and no one else had put themselves forward. Hobbs was even unable to temporarily co-opt members on to the council because, with just one member, it could not officially meet as it did not have a quorum. Fresh elections were needed two months later.

MERTHYR TYDFIL BOROUGH Council managed to disqualify its entire 33-member council in February 2002 through an administrative slip-up when introducing a new Councillors' Code of Conduct. A drafting error in the resolution formally approving the code brought it into effect before any member had time to sign it. Not signing it meant automatic disqualification. The council executive had to send letters to all members formally notifying them they were no longer eligible to do council business. All work of the council came to a halt, and at one point it appeared that a full election might be needed to regularise affairs. Three weeks into the impasse, however, a kindly High Court judge bailed the council out by ruling that as the problem had been caused by a clerical error, it could be overlooked if the right procedures were now followed. By mid-March, the red-faced council was back in charge.

CONCERNED ABOUT APATHY among local electors, Bath and North East Somerset Council launched a consultation programme in February 2002 to try to understand the reasons. Its first roadshow in the town of Keynsham (population 15,000) attracted one participant – and he was a town councillor.

ON POLICE ADVICE, Blackpool Borough Council spent £56,000 on measures to protect those attending the Conservative government's party conference in the resort in 1985. In return, the government were reported to be cutting £100,000 off the council's annual grant – for overspending.

IN 1976, BARNSLEY Council had to abandon its civil defence command post supposedly designed to survive a nuclear war because it had been wrecked by vandals.

FOUNTAINS PARISH COUNCIL in North Yorkshire managed to spend nothing during the 1999–2000 financial year, but received a bill for £61.33 for doing so. It had to pay the Audit Commission £29.02 for their costs of verifying that the council had spent no money, and £32.31 annual charge to the council's bank for handling its accounts.

LIFE IN THE UNDERGROWTH — LOCAL GOVERNMENT

ROCHDALE BOROUGH COUNCIL'S new computerised planning application system thwarted a resident's attempt to lodge an objection to his neighbour's plans because the software blocked all his e-mail messages as they contained the word 'erection'. Ray Kennedy tried three times to send his complaint. The last one arrived after the application had been approved.

AFTER A LONG campaign by residents against noisy night clubs in the small rural Somerset town of Crewkerne, South Somerset District Council's new anti-noise unit launched its first raid in October 1999 on a hall in the town centre following complaints by neighbours of a raucous party being held in the early hours of the morning. Officers discovered a birthday celebration in full swing for the husband of one of the local councillors. Among the guests were Michael Best, the town's mayor, and Hilary Leamon, who chaired the noise-abatement committee.

THE CHAIRMAN OF Pegswood Parish Council in Northumberland, who campaigned for 30 years for a bypass for the village to improve safety, became the first person to crash on the new road when it opened in 2007.

PASCHALIS FILOSOGLU, DEPUTY Mayor of Filippoi in northern Greece, who had campaigned among local farmers to keep cattle from wandering on to the highway, died in January 2009 when his car crashed into one of the cows.

HOVE COUNCIL IN East Sussex moved its official sunshine-measuring instrument in January 2000 after a resident complained it was giving bemusingly low readings. The council committee responsible for its installation discovered it had sited it in the shade.

BASILDON COUNCIL HAD to change the colour of 150 dog litter bins in 2000 from red to grey after residents began posting letters in them thinking they were post boxes.

NEWCASTLE COUNCIL REMOVED a new postbox from a city centre street in 2009 after discovering that postal collection vans could not reach it to collect mail, as they were forbidden to drive their vans down the road leading to it.

RESIDENTS IN THE CORNISH village of St Dennis finally got a council-built pavement for their narrow main street in March 2004, after having the project promised to them each year since it was first agreed in 1932. For 71 years, the project was on the county council's schedule of works, but always too low to be actioned. The quarter-mile pathway was still a compromise – the original plan envisaged a pavement on both sides of the road. Agreement had been reached in 1996 to turn the scheme into just a single side route to make the works more affordable. It had taken a further eight years before the bulldozers arrived. The village was reported to have embarked on their next request – yellow-line parking restrictions.

COUNCILLORS ON BLACKPOOL Council devoted debating time in March 2008 to deciding to lift a ban on the Rolling Stones performing in the town that had been imposed 44 years earlier following a riot. It was not clear what had motivated the council to reconsider its stance after so long a time, but council leader Peter Callow proudly told press that they were writing to the group and that 'they are welcome to play here again'.

Pole-axing poll tax payers

It was discovered in March 1981 that Liverpool City Council had continued to employ three gas lamplighters and a mate for eight years after the city's last gas lamp was extinguished. It was estimated to have cost the council £250,000 (over £1 million in 2010 prices). The city's chief engineer told journalists, 'I admit that the men have been underemployed.'

SWINDON BOROUGH COUNCIL was revealed in 2006 to have left a street light switched on, day and night, for eight years despite residents reporting the malfunction. One householder near the light had told the council of the fault as soon as he had moved into the street in 1998. 'They said they'd look into it,' Peter Brown told the media. One estimate of the pollution created by the wasted electricity put the cost at the equivalent of a car driving 14,000 miles.

AFTER A SURVEY in 1991 revealed that local taxpayers were unhappy at the state of pavements and roads, Birmingham City Council commissioned a further study, costing £6,000, to find out what people thought of potholes. The city engineer defended the decision to spend the money this way rather than mend some holes: 'It is essential that in-depth views of the public be obtained to provide detailed understanding of dissatisfaction.'

THE SAME COUNCIL spent £10,000 on writing an Albanian phrasebook for Kosovans in 1999 in preparation for receiving refugees from the conflict. It remained unused as none ever arrived. Birmingham was last heard of trying to sell the book to councils where they had.

A DISABLED WOMAN travelled across Norwich to collect and pay for a letter that had been sent to her in April 2000 without postage paid. Lynne Fisher discovered it was from Norwich City Council advising her to apply for a postal vote so she would not have to leave her house at election time.

BASSINGBOURN PARISH COUNCIL in Cambridgeshire voted in March 2005 to put £5,000 towards a bronze sculpture of a pile of dinosaur dung to commemorate the locality's wealth, which was created in the 19th century by mining fossilised dung for fertiliser. South Cambridgeshire District Council had agreed to fund the other half of the £10,000 that the memorial would cost.

DEAD MAN WINS ELECTION

COUNCILLORS IN BASILDON decided in March 2010 that the best way to advance the town's economic development was to persuade a government regional development authority to give it £90,000 to enable it to copy Hollywood's signature hillside sign. The pale imitation – five-foot letters instead of Tinseltown's 45-foot structures, and erected in a gently sloping and nondescript field next to the A127 dual carriageway – drew mocking comparisons at the Essex town's delusions of grandeur. The council was unfazed. Councillor Stephen Horgan told reporters that this 'direct investment' in the A127 'corridor' would 'address many of the key concerns that companies have'. Evidently like, 'Where's Basildon?'

LEEDS COUNCIL UNVEILED its 'Live it Love it' slogan in September 2005 at the start of an ambitious £850,000 project to market the city. It had spent £150,000 in consultants' fees to produce the slogan. Those in the trade pointed out that Hong Kong had come up with the same slogan two years earlier for its own tourism campaign. The consultants insisted they had arrived at the branding independently. Determined to get their money's worth, at the time of going to press, Leeds are still using it.

JETTISONING THE EVOCATIVE tourist slogan of its predecessor government ('The Best Small Country in the World'), the first ever Scottish Nationalist administration spent £125,000 when it came to power in 2007 on a consultancy with a top advertising agency to develop a new branding to match the new era. Six months, and much anticipation, later the new tag line was unveiled in November: 'Welcome to Scotland'.

GLASGOW ALSO CAME in for criticism in March 2010 when it unveiled its logo for hosting the 2014 Commonwealth Games. The colourful schematic, costing £95,000, played on using a large capital 'G' surrounded by concentric rings resembling the lanes of a running track. Locals, however, noticed a distinct similarity to the logo produced by the same advertising company three years earlier for a city arts festival, which also used the same symbolism. When political leaders questioned the apparent exorbitant cost, the company maintained it was an original effort and the result of 'a thorough creative process'. One MP commented with a heavy hint of sarcasm, 'The company that provided this logo deserve a medal for their entrepreneurial flair.'

A SCHEME INTRODUCED in October 1993 by Cambridge City Council to provide free bicycles for people to use and then leave at one of 15 stands dotted around the city, badly backfired when, after just four days of operation, not one of the 350 bikes could be found. The project cost ratepayers over £10,000.

AN IDENTICAL SCHEME launched by the city council in the Lithuanian capital Vilnius in the summer of 2001 had similar results. Within four days of 500 free bicycles being offered in racks around the city centre, 300 had been stolen and 200 destroyed. Some were already on sale at a local market.

AFTER COMPLAINTS IN Belper, Derbyshire, the local council set up a telephone line for the public to report vandalism, offering rewards up to £100. It ran the line for four years before closing it in 1997. It did not receive a single call.

NOTTINGHAM COUNCIL INSTALLED 215 solar-powered parking meters across the city in 2001 at a cost of over £1 million. It promptly lost a further £400,000 in the first six months as it discovered that Britain's weather was too gloomy to make them operate. Despite recording 16 per cent more sun than normal in the summer months, most units began to fail through lack of sun power to recharge batteries after use. A by-product of the investigations was a further discovery working against the success of the scheme – some meters were found to have been sited underneath trees, in the shade.

DEAD MAN WINS ELECTION

EAST HERTS COUNCIL spent £200 to get a consultant to write a 17-page report on how staff should safely make a cup of tea after the tea lady at the council's headquarters in Bishop's Stortford was made redundant in 2006.

TWO COUNCILS IN Lancashire spent £2,200 in 2008 on a 10-minute DVD demonstrating to ratepayers how they should put rubbish in their bins. Using actors carting wheelie bins to the front of houses and sorting through items, the film for Fylde and Wyre Councils was designed to help distinguish between various recycling schemes. It portrayed a man helping a women to identify a cardboard cereal box that should be placed in the paper-recycle carton, and told viewers that pieces of wood such as a twig could be classified as garden waste, whereas larger pieces ('like a door frame') could not. 'It's a complete waste of money,' campaigners against bureaucratic waste complained.

The film was distributed to householders throughout the two councils' areas. It did not go unnoticed that DVDs were one of the most difficult items to recycle. They were probably likely to be heading only for the landfill.

KENT COUNTY COUNCIL spent £15,000 on a seven-minute DVD instructing the citizens of Ashford how to cross the road. The guidance was felt to be needed in 2008 when the town experimented with a 'shared space' system in the town centre where all traffic signs and road markings were removed so that motorists and pedestrians were forced to become more aware of each other's movements. The scheme mirrored programmes pioneered in the Netherlands which had shown reductions in accidents. The film warned pedestrians to 'use all their senses' and not to 'impair their concentration' by ensuring they unplugged their MP3 players and earphones while crossing the road.

Trivial pursuits

Not only did Stroud District Council in Gloucestershire send a rates bill of 1p to pensioner Leonard Savoury in 1983, it then threatened him with prosecution for non-payment. It later blamed a computer error.

AVON COUNTY COUNCIL spent 17p on a first-class stamp in 1986 to send a 5p rent bill to pub owner David Derrick in respect of a metal grate outside his inn. When he sent £1 back to cover the rent for the next 20 years, the council spent another stamp's worth of public funds writing back to say it could not accept advance payments.

STRATHCLYDE REGIONAL COUNCIL levied a 24p poll tax charge on Joanne Laidlaw, a shop worker, for the two weeks of the 1989–90 tax year that she spent in the boundaries of the council before leaving for a new job in England.

DILIGENCE REACHED ITS apogee in Geneva in 1986 when the family of a man who died at 4am on New Year's Day received a bill from the Swiss tax authorities for 10 centimes (about 4p) as the deceased's tax assessment for the year.

STOCKTON COUNCIL EMPLOYED two bailiffs in 1992 to collect a 4p poll tax debt from Mark Allinson, who had made a mistake on the £204 cheque he had sent in payment of his bill. The bailiffs visited Allinson's house and refused to leave until he had given them two 2p coins. The treasurer of the council said: 'It might seem a small amount…if everybody got away with paying 4p less than they should, it would soon mount up.'

A BAILIFF WORKING for a council-run housing association in Wigan called on grandmother Alice Nelson in April 2006 demanding 5p for rent arrears. Although she had lived in the same property for 45 years and never knowingly been behind in her rent, she paid up. The association was apologetic but unyielding: 'We are currently having a strong push...it's important to reduce the number of people in arrears, whatever the amount.'

LICHFIELD DISTRICT COUNCIL tracked down 23-year-old zoologist Nick Coad, who had neglected to pay a £37 poll tax bill before leaving the country in 1992 for an expedition to a remote part of Nigeria. A courier delivered the final demand to Coad in his mud hut in a settlement so small it did not even have a name, after a four-hour drive from the nearest town of Apapa. The council treasurer simply told the press: 'Our message is, Lichfield Council always gets its man.'

THE LOCAL COUNCIL in the northern Italian town of Turate fined a resident in December 2001 for paying too much tax. Maria Mognoni was fined the equivalent of £20 for paying £10 too much on her local property tax. The council's payment system could only register that someone had paid the incorrect amount, but was unable to distinguish whether the error was an underpayment or overpayment. The council later generously waived the fine.

IN AUGUST 1997, councillors on Cherwell District Council's planning committee in Oxfordshire told Jonathan Ede, a local builder, to reduce the height of one wall of an office block by less than an inch. As a result, Ede had to remove the roof of the building at a cost of £10,000.

GATESHEAD BOROUGH COUNCIL ordered the wall of a new fire station to be rebuilt at the cost of £25,000 in 2005 because the bricks used were the wrong shade of red. The local planning panel had authorised a specified dark red colour to fit in with the local area. The finished wall was said to be more a shade of orange. The rebuilding work delayed the opening of the fire station, and required the council to continue to pay for fire crews to occupy temporary accommodation until the construction was completed. After the work was eventually redone, bemused local residents were reportedly unable to tell the difference.

EAST DEVON DISTRICT Council ruled in 2009 that an Axminster farmer who had spent £40,000 complying with the council's requirements to make a dilapidated cottage safe had gone too far to count the renovations as repair work. It ordered Robert Burrough to return the cottage closer to its previous dilapidation or face punishment for infracting planning permission rules.

IN AUGUST 2001, Norwich City Council surpassed its own record for creating Britain's shortest double-yellow-line parking restrictions (45 inches) by painting lines only 24 inches long between two parking bays in Theatre Street in the city centre.

THE RECORD IS now believed to be a single yellow line at Highbury Crescent, Highbury, in the north London borough of Islington. It is only 18 inches long, barely the length of a car wheel, joining two parking bays, and was painted in 2007. The council told media that no ticket had ever been issued for the location, adding that the line had been put there 'to help drivers'. Lucy Watt, an Islington councillor, explained that it separated residents' bays and pay-and-display bays, and apparently ensured that drivers did not confuse the two, claiming that 'in Islington, we take a common-sense approach to parking enforcement'.

BRIGHTON AND HOVE Council found it necessary in 2005 to paint double yellow lines just 35 inches long on a junction to prevent cars parking on a corner. A resident was quoted as saying, 'No one ever parks on that corner anyway.'

BLACKBURN COUNCIL PAINTED double yellow lines 39 inches long on a residential street in 2007. 'Only a unicycle could fit,' observed a local councillor.

DEAD MAN WINS ELECTION

BIRMINGHAM CITY COUNCIL introduced yellow-line parking restrictions in a street in the city centre in March 2006 that, on the day of the road painting, was already occupied by parked cars. Undeterred, workmen studiously painted around the tyres of the eight vehicles, and then traffic wardens ticketed them with £60 fines. One of the witnesses told media, 'The lines went pretty well as tight as they could without painting the wheel of the car.' A council spokesman later agreed that the action had been 'an error'.

A SIMILAR CASE was reported from Salford, Manchester, in October 2006. Nasser Khan had parked in a gap between two sets of restrictions. By the time he had returned, the gap had been filled and his car ticketed. To add to his woes, the machine used to burn the lines on to the roadway had partially melted his tyres, costing him £550 to replace.

IN THE TIME it took Shirley Hatcher to have her hair done in a Southampton salon in June 2006, the city council had painted a disabled parking bay around her car in the street outside, and ticketed her with a £60 fine. It later blamed 'a catalogue of errors' and rescinded the ticket.

RUTH DUCKER'S CAR was physically lifted off the roadway by Lambeth Council workers in 2009 so they could paint double yellow lines underneath it. The vehicle was then replaced, and later ticketed and towed away on the same day. It took two months and the intervention of the local Member of Parliament before the council backed down and cancelled the ticket.

CAMDEN COUNCIL SUCCESSFULLY resisted a legal challenge in November 2009 from a resident whom the council had repeatedly ticketed for parking his motor scooter on his own land. Richard Dawood, a doctor, left his bike on an area outside his clinic to which he was legally entitled to 'exclusive possession' and which was clearly signed as 'private property'. Yet he was still served with parking tickets on more than 30 occasions. The council's astute legal argument won the court's endorsement, even though the judge acknowledged it was 'counter-intuitive'. The council successfully argued that while Dawood might own the 'subsoil', the tarmacked 'surface' was subject to public access, and therefore the council's parking restrictions applied.

LIVERPOOL CITY COUNCIL painted a cycle lane that was barely four bicycle lengths long on a pavement near the Royal Liver Building in the centre of the city in 2006.

CARDIFF COUNCIL SURPASSED this with what is believed to be Britain's shortest cycle 'lane' in April 2010 when it painted an eight-foot-long box on a busy stretch of inner-city road. Less than two bicycle lengths' duration, it stuck out into the road amid an otherwise unmarked carriageway and cost £2,000 to paint.

CAERPHILLY COUNCIL INTRODUCED a 'gate-to-gate' rule in 1998 to determine eligibility for free bus travel for its schoolchildren. Only those living more than a mile and a half away from school qualified. When Dean Morris, whose two sons were deemed to have lost their entitlement, measured the distance, he discovered he lived precisely one and a half miles away. The council ruled that this was not 'more than' the required distance. Morris had to dig up his front garden, re-lay his path and reinstall his gate so that it was three yards further away from the school before the council relented.

LUTON BOROUGH COUNCIL spent £298 in legal and administrative expenses in 2006 to pursue a motorist who had flicked a crisp out of her car window. Hilary Buckland had been spotted by a council official who had been driving behind her. Her number plate was traced and she was sent a £75 fine. The council's enforcement manager for street services was unmoved by the adverse press publicity that followed: 'It does not matter if it was a cigarette butt or a [crisp]... I do not intend to let a small minority of litter louts take us a step backwards. We will take action against anyone...'

DEAD MAN WINS ELECTION

WOLVERHAMPTON CITY COUNCIL pursued a case that took three months to wend its way through the courts in 2008 against a motorist for tossing an apple core out of her car. Kate Badger refused to accept a £60 fine for wrongly disposing of 'controlled waste' and opted to go to trial before the Crown Court. The council refused to back down and formally charged that Badger had 'knowingly caused the deposit of controlled waste, namely an apple core, on land which did not have a waste management licence'. The case ended up being dropped just before the trial, saving an estimated £5,000.

HULL CITY COUNCIL spent hundreds of pounds in legal and administrative costs in 2008 to take a 20-year-old mother to court for allegedly dropping a piece of sausage roll in the city centre when trying to feed her baby daughter. Sarah Davies maintained that the 'litter' had merely fallen out of the child's mouth. It was uncontested that the morsel was quickly devoured by pigeons. Nevertheless, the council persisted in charging Davies with a litter offence and for non-payment of a £60 fixed penalty fine. When the case came before magistrates, they threw the charge out.

KIRKLEES COUNCIL IN West Yorkshire spent £2,800 in legal costs, and more than a year of court appearances, in pursuing a 10p car parking fee. Motorist Nick Newby had contested the charge for the area outside the library in the town of Mirfield in February 2005 as there had been no signs or machines to indicate payment was needed. The council slapped a £30 ticket on his car, which he refused to pay, leading to a court appearance and a £50 fine and £250 costs. He appealed and, after five further court hearings, it all ended up in the Crown Court in Leeds in April 2006, where the judge was reported to have been left 'speechless' when the council revealed that it was now allowing cars to be parked in the area free of charge. The judge promptly stopped the case.

KIRKLEES' ZEALOUSNESS RESURFACED in June 2009 when it spent an estimated £10,000 and 15 months of officials' time pursuing a litter case against a young mother charged with allowing her 18-month-old niece to drop a sweet wrapper out of her car. Larissa Wilkinson was prosecuted for depositing 'controlled waste' (namely a Murray Mint wrapper) as she was driving in Huddersfield in early 2008. After three appearances before magistrates, and one at Crown Court, a judge threw out the case, castigating the council for its pettiness. The council said it had 'noted' the judge's comment, but stood behind the decision to prosecute.

IN JUNE 2009, Herefordshire County Council refused to cancel a £75 parking ticket given to pensioner Ron Padwick in Leominster because he had displayed his disability badge the wrong way round with its details facing the driver's seat instead of the bonnet of the car. The council insisted that the instructions for displaying the permit 'were clearly laid out in the terms and conditions of use'.

Small town decisions

In 1981, Wigan Council told Harry and Esther Hough, who had successfully fostered 47 children, that they were not fit to adopt because their marriage was too happy, and that children placed with them would not be sufficiently exposed to 'negative experiences'. In a letter to the couple, the area Social Services head David Wright told them, 'It would seem that both of you have had few, if any, negative experiences when children yourselves, and also seem to enjoy a marital relationship where rows and arguments have no place.' On those grounds, they were judged unsuited to bring up children long term.

FOR A PERIOD in 1982, Dorset County Council located the Weymouth office of its Disabled Persons Resettlement service on the first floor of the Job Centre in the town, at the top of a flight of stairs. There was no lift.

DEAD MAN WINS ELECTION

IN 2002, A NEW council-installed Braille sign at the main public building in Stroud, Gloucestershire, had to be lowered after workmen had put it nearly eight feet off the ground.

IN A CRACKDOWN on muggings, Birmingham City Council decided in 1982 to plant 'thin' trees in the Newtown area of the city to stop attackers from hiding from their victims.

VILLAGERS IN PILL, near Bristol, celebrated the resurfacing of their main road in 1983 after a three-year battle with Avon County Council. The next day, council-approved gas board workers dug it up.

PENSIONER KEN STEVENSON waited a year for Weymouth and Portland Council to paint a disabled parking bay outside his home in April 2003. A day later, workmen employed by the same council resurfaced the entire street.

HAMPSHIRE COUNTY COUNCIL went one better in August 1992. Minutes after workmen had finished painting 40 mph speed limit signs on the road near Brockenhurst, another group of contractors employed by the council arrived to resurface the spot.

IN JUNE 2006, Suffolk County Council finally met the 30-year request of residents of Elmswell for a sign to direct lorries to the town's bacon factory so they could avoid clogging up the main street. The sign was erected the same week that the factory closed down.

BRADFORD DISTRICT COUNCIL redecorated and fitted new seats to the bus shelter in Baildon, West Yorkshire, in November 2000 – even though the last bus service to the village had been axed during the summer.

A LONG-RUNNING dispute on leaf clearance between two layers of local council in Cornwall in 2005 was finally resolved by an arcane compromise. The county council agreed to clear up slippery, wet leaves, on the grounds that they constituted a hazard to the public and therefore fell into its responsibilities. Dry leaves would be the responsibility of borough councils as they qualified as litter, and thus fell to the lower bodies to deal with.

THE BOROUGH COUNCIL in Colne, Lancashire, put a kitten on its 'dangerous animals' database in 2003 because it had scratched a building inspector. It also told homeowner Brian Jackson that as a result of the incident, which was formally registered as an 'attack', his address would be blacklisted for all other council workers. When he appealed, Jackson managed to have his house de-listed – but only on the technicality that the kitten was not his, but a neighbour's.

FYLDE BOROUGH COUNCIL, in Lancashire, spent £15,000 in 2006 on a 'risk assessment study' of kite-flying on local beaches after a single incident when a walker became entangled in a flyer's lines.

THE SAME COUNCIL hit the headlines again in March 2007 for another dimension of its beach management. It warned an elderly resident living next to the foreshore at St Anne's that he faced prosecution for returning to the beach sand blown into his garden after storms. The particularly severe gales that year had exacerbated the problem for Arthur Bulmer, who sought advice on the permissibility of shovelling the sand back on to the beach. The council told him it was not allowed, as moving the sand off private land to the beach would constitute fly-tipping, for which he could face fines of up to £50,000. He was told he needed to treat it as litter and take it to a council refuse tip.

A BARBER WAS ordered by Blackburn Council in 2010 to stop his 40-year practice of taking home hair clippings from his shop and using them as compost in his garden. Jeff Stone was told that the hair now constituted 'trade waste' and had to be disposed of in a landfill site, for which privilege he would also have to pay.

CHELTENHAM TOWN COUNCIL introduced a scheme in the spring of 2007 to highlight the problem of dog owners who fail to clean up after their pets. Its dog wardens began to circle each pile of dog droppings with spray paint, apparently in an attempt to shame walkers into coming back to do the honourable thing. A warden even returned a week later to paint a fresh colour around the offending pile if it was still there to embarrass offenders further. According to Rob Garnham, the councillor responsible for the local environment, 'It has the effect of allowing us to…identify if this is an ongoing problem.' Residents, however, pointed out the less than aesthetic effect for the genteel spa town of creating multiple brightly coloured circles on footpaths across the community showing up the mess. One resident observed, 'Some of the pavements look like a weird dirty protest in the Tate Gallery.'

THE COUNCIL IN Volkach, Bavaria, announced plans in 2009 to take DNA readings of all 420 dogs in the town so that wardens could trace uncleared pet mess to their owners. Mayor Peter Kornell said it would cost around €100,000 (£75,000) to compile the database but the cost of cleaning the streets worked out as a larger expense.

BOURNEMOUTH COUNCIL COURTED controversy from its thousand taxi drivers in 2008 when it became the first council in Britain to impose an eight-week training course and the taking of an exam on customer care as a condition for renewing cabbies' licences. When the content of the course emerged, the more seasoned drivers, many of whom had been plying their trade for more than a quarter of a century, objected to returning to the classroom to be taught how to 'establish a friendly rapport with customers' (examples suggested: 'Hello, Mr Smith, nice to see you again' or 'Good morning, how are you?') and how to conduct a risk assessment before carrying a heavy suitcase. While drivers called the training 'patronising' and 'mostly common sense', chairman of the council Stephen Chappell said it was 'vital' in ensuring 'our drivers are of high quality and our residents and visitors receive the best possible service'. Up to a tenth of the of town's cabbies were reported to have been suspended for refusing to take part. The cost of the courses to the council was thought to be in the region of £300,000.

It later emerged that one driver had been refused a renewal of his licence because he had misused apostrophes in an English language test he had been required to take first as a non-native speaker. Laurence Kirk would have to attend a GCSE college course funded by the council before he could resit. 'No one asked me about [routes in] Bournemouth or what I would do if I was approached by a drunk person, just where to put an apostrophe,' he told the press. 'I used to be a successful taxi driver. But now the council is telling me I can't work because I don't know how to use an apostrophe or where to put a semi-colon.'

IN RESPONSE TO complaints in May 2004 from a resident about his untidy street, North Somerset Council officials delivered a litter picker, binliners and a broom to the complainant, asking him to clean the road himself. Harold Sas, from Clevedon, told reporters that he was advised he was likely to be able to do a better job. The council explained that 'we try and clean the roads but there are nearly always cars parked there', adding 'we did go out of our way to deliver a brush and litter picker' to the concerned citizen.

RESIDENTS IN A street in Trowbridge, Wiltshire, notorious for being missed by council street cleaners, were stunned in March 2007 when a rarely seen dustcart turned up only for two workers to emerge and pose briefly with brooms for a publicity photograph for the council's magazine and then drive off. The picture later appeared on the front cover of the newsletter extolling the services provided by the council.

LEEDS CITY COUNCIL collectors refused to take away a twig cutting left out in the rubbish by pensioner Jack Hebblethwaite in July 2008 because it was thicker than the council's prescribed limits. The branch measured 3.5 centimetres in diameter, 5 millimetres too broad to be allowed to be disposed of as garden waste. He was told to order a special collection truck or take it personally to the nearest council dump, which was three miles away. He decided to keep it for posterity. The council commented: 'There are rules in place covering the size of garden waste material that can be placed in a brown bin. In the case of things like small branches and twigs, they must not be thicker than 3cm. So the advice given to Mr Hebblethwaite by our staff was correct.'

AS PART OF a new traffic scheme, Brighton and Hove Council introduced light-controlled 'puffin' crossings in the town in 2009 and at one location erected a large sign explaining to pedestrians how to use them to cross the road. It was erected in the middle of a major roundabout, meaning people had to cross the road first in order to read the instructions.

TEMPORARY TRAFFIC LIGHTS installed by Durham County Council in 1995 on the B6281 road in Teesdale in readiness for road repairs were still there three years later without any roadworks having taken place because of lack of money. In October 1998, the council announced there would be no money for at least another year.

THAT DELAY WAS nothing compared with the A494 at Drws y Nant between Bala and Dolgellau in North Wales. The local council installed temporary traffic lights when a gorge collapsed, making it unsafe for two vehicles to pass simultaneously. They were finally withdrawn after the road repair on 2 August 1999 – 28 years after the accident.

THE HIGHWAYS AUTHORITY managing the stretch of the A40(M) Westway in west London removed all street lighting in 2007. Signs were erected along the entire route pronouncing 'no street lighting'. Users of the road pointed out the futility of the investment: in day time the signs were of no value; at night time, they could not be seen by drivers because of the lack of street lighting.

IN JULY 1998, Lewisham Council in south London appointed Denis Cobell, an atheist, as its official chaplain.

WHEN WILTSHIRE COUNTY Council advertised in March 2001 for a manager of its Travelwise initiative designed to encourage local business leaders and their staff to leave their cars at home and use public transport, the perks package included a council car. The council's transport leader said in mitigation, 'It might seem a bit hypocritical to tell someone not to drive while you do…but we hope whoever applies for the job will demonstrate a personal commitment by not taking up the offer.'

TORBAY COUNCIL DESTROYED a rare wildflower meadow next to a churchyard in Torquay in April 2007 when its workers mowed the land in error. It apologised to the group of church volunteers who had raised £300 to plant the meadow, promising that it would not happen again. Within a month of the apology, council workers mowed it for a second time.

THE AUTHORITIES IN St Austell, Cornwall, put up the town's 2006 Christmas decorations in mid-September after it lost storage facilities for them. It was cheaper to install them early. While residents complained it made the town look 'ridiculous', a spokesman for the town looked on the bright side: 'They're not doing anyone any harm. It saves a job later when the weather is more inclement.'

BIRMINGHAM CITY COUNCIL printed and distributed 360,000 leaflets in August 2008 updating local taxpayers on the city's progress on recycling. Under a banner headline 'Thank You Birmingham' lay a picture of a smart and modernistic city skyline which residents quickly spotted did not look like their Birmingham. It wasn't. For unexplained reasons the picture was of Birmingham, Alabama. The council initially claimed it was meant to represent a 'generic skyline'. Suspicions fell on it more likely being the unchecked work of a less-than-geographically astute trainee: a Google search on the internet for 'Birmingham' produced exactly the same photograph.

SWANSEA CITY COUNCIL incurred ridicule in 2008 for failing to spot a wrong translation on a bilingual English–Welsh road sign that it erected in the town to bar entry for lorries to a residential area. The Welsh translation was somewhat more prosaic. E-mailing the text ('No entry for heavy goods vehicles. Residential site only') to its in-house translation service, the evidently non-Welsh speaker had taken down the reply received, which was passed on to the manufacturers, who clearly were less than proficient Welsh speakers too. What resulted was the emblazoning on the sign of the translator's out-of-office notifier. ('I am not in the office at the moment. Please send any work to be translated.').

Despite the blanket policy for translating road signs throughout the principality, in Swansea the Welsh language is actually used by only 12 per cent of the population.

FORESTRY COMMISSION OFFICIALS got a bad press in 1984 when a luncheon hosted by chairman Sir David Montgomery during a seminar on wildlife conservation was revealed to include venison and squirrel pie.

THE EAST ESSEX Health Authority launched a 'Better Health' campaign in 1986 using an expensively designed logo featuring a cardiogram. Only at the last minute did a doctor spot that the cardiogram showed that the patient would be dead.

THIRTY PEOPLE ATTENDING a conference lunch at the head-quarters of the Public Health Laboratory Service in north London in March 2001 went down with food poisoning. The conference was considering how to keep drinking water free from bacteria.

It's a small (minded) world

Councillors in Kleberg County, Texas, outlawed the use of the greeting 'hello' in 1997 and unanimously decreed that county officials should respond to telephone calls with 'heaven-o' instead. The official resolution passed cited the 'negative' connotations of 'hello', as it contained the word 'hell'. In contrast, 'heaven-o' is 'a symbol of peace, friendship and welcome' in this 'age of anxiety'.

COMMISSIONERS IN MANATEE County, south of Tampa, Florida, decided to pass a local ordinance in April 1999 to raise local community dress standards. They ruled that women in the county were banned from exposing more than 75 per cent of their breasts, and both sexes were banned from revealing more than two-thirds of their buttocks. Sheriff's Office spokesman Dave Bristow told puzzled newsmen that the law enforcement agencies needed time to work out how to implement the law. 'I don't think we'll be tape-measuring,' he said.

THEY COULD CONSULT the local ordinance passed in 1996 by legislators in St John's County, Florida, when they sought to ban nude dancing. The law required that one-third of a dancer's buttocks be covered. It then described in fine detail how this was to be calculated. The description, for legal purposes, of 'buttocks' ran to 328 words.

ITALIAN MAYORS WERE granted wider powers in 2008 to control public decency. It led to a wave of bizarre by-laws being introduced as prejudices surfaced in local council chambers. In what became for Italy's national media 'the summer of bans', holidaymaker behaviour was a particular target. In Eboli, just south of Naples, the mayor banned 'public displays of affection in a car'. In Capri, going off the beach while still wearing just a bikini was off limits, while building sandcastles in Eraclea, near Venice, was prohibited. In Porto Imperia on the country's Riviera coast, beachgoers risked a €1,000 fine for leaving a towel unattended to bag a spot.

THE MAYOR OF Mount Isa, Queensland, one of the Australian outback's most remote towns, incurred the wrath of feminists in August 2008 by issuing a public appeal for ugly women to settle in his town as part of an effort to redress a socially crippling population imbalance in the largely male mining population. The shortage of single females was a constant obstacle to development according to John Molony. 'If there are five blokes to every girl, we should find out where there are beauty-disadvantaged women and ask them to proceed to Mount Isa... Often those who are beauty-disadvantaged are unhappy in their lot – happiness awaits in Mount Isa.' Women who had found it hard to strike lucky elsewhere could be virtually assured of success among the (predominantly male) population of 22,000. 'I believe we should look after [them],' he added. 'It's an opportunity for some lonely women.'

IN 2000, THE FOUR members of Gretna City Council in Louisiana considered the weighty issue of whether it was legal to throw panties at carnival floats during the town's Mardi Gras celebrations. In a 4–0 vote, it unanimously endorsed proponents of the practice, who had maintained it was a long-running tradition of the event. Councillors did take time to differentiate on 'throws', ruling that it would be illegal to throw anything depicting 'male or female genitalia, is lewd or lascivious and includes, but is not limited to, condoms and inflatable paraphernalia'.

AS THE UNITED STATES mounted its invasion of Iraq in March 2003, Seattle City Council debated a resolution of support for the troops. What was intended to be a spontaneous act turned out to be anything but. A number of council members wanted to express opposition to the war, and the discussion on the wording of the resolution became prolonged. By the time a sufficiently bland draft had been developed so that all sides could agree on 14 April, the council had spent longer fighting over the wording than it had taken American troops to invade Iraq and capture Baghdad.

IN NOVEMBER 1983, the Planning Committee of the City Council in Chico, California, voted 6–1 to make it a misdemeanour to drop a nuclear weapon inside the city precincts, punishable by up to a year in the county jail and a fine of $1,000. The community of 28,000, lying 150 miles north of San Francisco, also barred all movement of nuclear weapons and materials through the city as well as banning the conducting of nuclear research (none of which the town had ever been involved in). When the proposed ordinance went to the full council, the only change made, it seems, was to reduce the potential fine to $500.

TO PROTEST AGAINST budget cuts, a member of the Milwaukee City Council wore a paper bag over his head at the official photograph ceremony for 1988. The picture was duly taken and still adorns the municipal offices.

THE MAYOR OF Springfield, Illinois, suffered a heart attack in 1981 during a council meeting. The council voted 19–18 to wish him an early recovery.

TOLEDO CITY COUNCIL in Ohio passed an ordinance in 2000 to deal with growing concerns about landlords who refused to do up dilapidated properties. The novel solution was to empower the local court to punish offenders by making them live in their own slums until they repaired them. The landlords would be required to wear electronic tags to ensure they complied.

FACING THE NEED to cut costs in 1992, the town council in Rotorua, New Zealand, announced a scheme that offered discounts to people willing to dig the graves of their dead relatives.

DEAD MAN WINS ELECTION

A COMMITTEE OF the city council in Wellington, New Zealand, had just begun its meeting on earthquake disaster planning in May 1992 when a 6.2-scale quake interrupted proceedings. Councillor Merrin Downing had just declared, 'If an earthquake struck now, I wouldn't even know what to do.' Seconds later, he had dived under the table.

A $1 MILLION fire station in Charleston, West Virginia, could not open when building work finished in January 2000 as the city authority which commissioned it discovered that it failed to comply with its own fire regulations.

CONSERVATIONISTS IN THE district of Marchegg on the Austrian–Slovakian border spent three fruitless years in discussion with the local council over their application for permission to build a small dam to divert water to a nature reserve. Overnight in January 2002, a single beaver did the job for them. 'The little fellow did a proper job,' said Sepp Wedenig of the local Forestry Authority. 'We found a beautifully clean dam of branches, twigs and tree trunks.'

COUNCILLORS IN THE small Dutch town of Culemborg, 10 miles south of Utrecht, introduced a controversial traffic-calming scheme in September 1996 – sheep. Initially, six were let loose in the town to wander at will through the busy roads, leaving it to drivers to slow down to avoid hitting them. There were plans for up to a hundred to be released if the experiment proved successful. Animal welfare groups declared themselves outraged at the project.

DAVE HEILMANN, MAYOR of Oak Lawn, a suburb of Chicago, introduced an unorthodox traffic-calming measure in the middle of 2007 by winning the town council's approval for adding non-standard warning messages to STOP signs at more than 50 junctions around the area. Designed to catch the attention of drivers, residents were invited to submit their ideas. Among those that got erected directly underneath the octagonal STOP boards were 'In the

Naaaame of Love', 'Whoa, Whoa, Wait a Minute', 'Billion Dollar Fine', 'And Smell the Roses' and 'Means You Aren't Moving'. After concerns were raised by the Federal Highway Administration and the Illinois transport department, the council was forced to take them down in April 2008 under threat of losing infrastructure funding.

THE DANISH ROAD Safety Council attracted global attention and opprobrium in equal measure in 2006 for its speed reduction campaign which comprised a video of topless models standing by the roadside waving 50 kph speed limit signs and jiggling their breasts at drivers. It became a hit on the internet and a spokeswoman for the council reported it had had a 'very positive reaction' for drawing attention to the problem of speeding drivers in Denmark. She claimed feedback showed that half of drivers would think more about the dangers of speeding.

AFTER THE SEVERE winter of 2010 left nearly half the roads across Germany damaged by potholes, the council in the eastern village of Niederzimmern tackled the problem by a scheme which enabled residents to meet the cost of an individual hole repair and have a personalised message placed on the finished smooth surface. For €50, the council would fill in a designated pothole and leave whatever message the 'owner' of the hole wanted. A number of businesses were reported to have bought up holes as cheap advertising space.

HANOVER CITY COUNCIL released an advent calendar for Christmas 2007 intended to portray all aspects of the city's culture – literally. Amid the singing children and Santa Claus distributing presents, the windows also revealed a depiction of the city's most notorious serial killer, Fritz Haarmann, hiding behind a tree with a meat cleaver in hand. Haarmann was executed in 1925 for the murder of 24 people, whose bodies he dismembered and sold as meat on the local black market. The tourist board defended the inclusion, saying the killer was 'part of our city's history'.

DEAD MAN WINS ELECTION

THE TOURISM BOARD of the US state of Rhode Island included in its 1992 'Top 20 Tourist Attractions' the state rubbish dump, which features the largest man-made hill in the state. In the two years since being opened to the public, it had received over 100,000 visitors.

TOWN COUNCILLORS IN Rajneeshpuram, a community of 500 in Oregon, passed a resolution in 1982 making joke-telling obligatory at every council meeting. At least one councillor had to tell a joke at the start and end of each meeting. Officials said the aim was to make humour an integral part of council business.

TOWN COUNCILLORS IN Avon, Colorado, held a public contest in 1992 to name a new bridge over the Eagle River which runs through the town. After sifting through 84 proposals, they rejected suggestions such as 'Eagle Crossing' and chose as its official name, 'Bob'. It is still so named to this day.

TOWN LEADERS IN Ismay, Montana (population 22, the smallest town in the state), were persuaded by a Kansas radio station in 1993 to rename their hamlet 'Joe' in honour of Joe Montana, the celebrated American football star who had just arrived at the Kansas City Chiefs. For a year, the town basked in local fame as Joe, Montana. Although it soon lapsed back to calling itself Ismay, as late as 2002 the old signs were still proclaiming the adopted name.

THE TOWN COUNCILLORS of Halfway, Oregon, a tiny settlement of 362 people in the east of the state near the Idaho border, agreed in January 2000 to rename their community Half.com in a commercial tie-up with a newly launched second-hand goods internet site based in Philadelphia. In exchange for $100,000, 20 free computers and the prospect of tourist fame, Mayor Dick Crow promoted his town as the world's first 'dot-com' city. 'It'll put our name on the map. By changing our name to Half.com, our community can greatly benefit from the success of the internet.' In fact, the town saw little change. By contrast, the owners of

Half.com the company sold out to eBay later in the same year for a staggering $350 million.

IN NOVEMBER 2005, the two town councillors of Clark, Texas (population 125), agreed unanimously to accept a challenge from Echostar Communications, the second-largest satellite TV company in the US, that promised ten years of free TV service to any town that agreed to rename itself after the company's Dish Network brand. The town had to agree to change its name legally and permanently, and on all government buildings, official letterheads, and road signs. In return, every single residence would be equipped with a reception dish free of charge. So Clark became DISH, Texas, amid much local controversy, as the mayor responsible for leading the change had defeated the town's founder and namesake L.E. Clark only months earlier.

As the PR stunt had been budgeted to cost the company $4 million per thousand households, the fact that there were a mere 55 residences in the township gave the company reason to be content on its side too. The rural outpost, north of Dallas, hoped to attract growth by the move. It seemed to work – a mere five years on, the population had risen by half as much again, to 181.

From the history books

According to the *Guinness Book of Records*, Henry Winn (1816–1914) served as parish clerk for Fulletby, near Horncastle, Lincolnshire, for 76 years.

MATTHEW ANDERSON WAS a member of Abingdon Borough Council in Oxfordshire for 69 years from April 1709 to August 1778.

MAJOR SIR PHILIP BARBER served as a county councillor in Nottinghamshire for 63 years from March 1898 to April 1961.

DEAD MAN WINS ELECTION

ALDERMAN G.T. Paine served as Mayor of Lydd in Kent for 29 consecutive years from 1931 until 1961.

WHEN COUNCILLOR Denis Martineau became Lord Mayor of Birmingham in 1986, he was following in the footsteps of his father, grandfather, great-grandfather and great-great-grandfather.

EVEN THAT ASTONISHING achievement pales against the familial service given in Germany. When Baron Ulrich von Holzhausen became Mayor of Frankfurt in 1800, he became the 36th member of his family to have served in the office.

ROBERT LINN SERVED as Mayor of Beaver, Pennsylvania, a community of 5,000 near Pittsburgh, for 58 years from 1946 until his death at the age of 95 in 2004, in the middle of his 15th term of office.

HILMAR MOORE WAS elected Mayor of Richmond in southeast Texas in 1949 and, as of going to press, was still in office in mid-2010, 61 unbroken years later.

HE STILL HAS some way to go to beat the astonishing feat of Edmond Mathis, who was mayor of the commune of Ehuns in eastern France for 75 years from 1878 to 1953.

MAYORS HAVE SOMETIMES shown an unwillingness to be confined to local matters or, in some cases, even earthly ones. During a UFO 'flap' in October 1954 which saw dozens of reports of unidentified flying objects over southeastern France, Lucien Lejeune, Mayor of Chateauneuf-du-Pape, issued a formal decree prohibiting 'the overflight, the landing and the takeoff of aircraft known as flying saucers' anywhere within his community. It also threatened that any landing in breach of the decree would end with the occupants being put in jail 'immediately'. The edict was to be enforced by a single rural policeman assisted by the local forest keeper. Of particular note was the added information that the announcement had even been sent to, and approved by, the Département's Prefect, the next most senior official in the region.

TIMES CHANGE. By 1976, the mayor of another southern French town, this time in the southwest, declared his community to be the world's first UFO-port, welcoming landings by any visitor from outer space. On 15 August, the Mayor of Ares, near Bordeaux, along with all his village councillors and an air force officer, formally inaugurated the landing strip. The mayor gave the rationale for the opening: 'The reason that flying saucers have never landed on Earth is because there are no airports for them.' He promised the UFO-port would remain open 24 hours a day, and offered a special bonus for the first arrival – it would be exempted from landing fees. Nearly four decades on, it has still to receive any business.

OTHER SMALL COMMUNITIES have marked critical moments in their development in equally bizarre ways. The local council of the cotton-growing town of Enterprise, Alabama, erected a monument to the industry's principal enemy, the boll weevil, in 1919. It is the world's only monument built to honour an agricultural pest. They did so because the devastation of the local cotton plantations by the bug forced the community to diversify its economy, which in the long run ensured the future of the town. The plaque on the statue of a woman holding aloft a huge weevil foresightedly dedicates it 'in profound appreciation of the Boll Weevil and what it has done as the herald of prosperity'.

ONE MONUMENT THAT never got built was given protracted consideration by Kent mayors shortly after the Second World War. It would have given the Channel coast skyline one of the most remarkable sights ever conceived. The idea broke through all the norms of national custom, design and, probably, taste. It was for nothing less than the erection of a giant statue of Winston Churchill on top of the cliffs at Dover to overlook the English Channel.

Modelled on the Statue of Liberty, it was to be more than 150 feet high. If that was not bizarre enough, the scheme's proponent proposed that the statue should portray Churchill with his famous cigar in mouth, its tip permanently illuminated a deep red as a guide to shipping.

It was the brainchild of a Margate man, a Mr H.A. Marsh. He had managed to interest American politician Charles Davis, whose hopes for political mileage in support of his bid for the Presidential nomination in 1948 gave the scheme a greater impetus than it might otherwise have had. In September 1946, Davis announced the establishment of a $100,000 fund to pay for the statue and Marsh formally put the proposal to Margate Town Council.

Like an increasingly hotter potato, the council passed it on to the ruling body of the Cinque Ports and the Cinque Ports decided it was too big an undertaking for it alone and so brought in the mayors of nine other towns. They all met in Sandwich in November to juggle with the idea.

This exercise in spreading the fame – or the blame – for the project was understandable. The principle of a permanent tribute to the now revered Churchill was unquestioned, but the proposal in front of them hardly conformed to anything the country had ever seen before. This first meeting unanimously agreed that Churchill's services should be commemorated in some form but expressed the doubt whether a giant statue was in keeping with Britain's tradition and dignity. They were to meet again when Mr Marsh had a proper design.

They did so on 14 December, along with more Kent mayors, 14 in all, at Hythe, where they were presented with a photograph of a model of the proposed statue. Marsh and Davis had taken note of the earlier doubts and modified their plan. According to press reports, it still however drew gasps of astonishment as the civic leaders appreciated for the first time the magnitude of the project.

The monument was now envisaged as a three-stage affair – a huge 34-foot-high square base from which a 60-foot column would project, on top of which would stand a 75-foot-tall statue of

Churchill. The base would have two huge doors in its front over which would be inscribed the tribute 'Never was so much owed by so many to one man.' The bizarre touch was not however to be extinguished. On top of the base, at each corner, in the tradition of Nelson's Column, there would be four bronze British bulldogs, each 14 feet high and 18 feet long.

Still stuck in the cleft stick, the mayors acknowledged that approval of any design would have to be given by the Lord Warden of the Cinque Ports, who fortuitously had been since August... Churchill himself. The outcome of the meeting was another rapid casting of the potato – into the lap of the great man. And there it sat for many months.

Public interest in the scheme waned as the whole matter seemed to have disappeared into a black hole of indecision. A year later, in November 1947, it was publicly revealed that Churchill had responded in diplomatic terms to the proposal, saying that he would prefer the matter to be discussed after he had left active politics or after he had died. The project went into abeyance and as the old man lived for nearly another twenty years, by the time he died it had all been quietly and thankfully forgotten.

MAKING A MEAL – OFFICIALDOM

Sometimes, politicians should simply not get involved.

Until the mid-1980s, politicians in Belgium dictated what parents could call their children. The choice could be made only from an official register of 1,500 accepted monikers dating from the Napoleonic era. The government announced its intention to abolish the list in 1984. In future, families would have free choice except for names that were judged 'absurd, shocking or ridiculous'.

FRANCE, WHICH HAD a similar law limiting parents to names of saints or historical figures, abolished its restrictions only in 1993 – mostly. Authorities kept a reserve power to forbid a name if it was judged likely to be against the interests of the child. In 1999, a prosecutor in Besançon invoked the powers to prevent a couple naming their child Zebulon, on the grounds that it was the Gallic version of Zebedee from the children's television series, *The Magic Roundabout*. This was judged to be likely to cause the child 'inevitable sarcasm and mockery'. Despite the parent's protests that it had an ancient and esteemed Biblical origin, the French authorities prevailed.

IN 2003, NORWAY replaced its own list of approved names with a ban on swear and sex words, illnesses and negative names. Argentina, Denmark, Germany, Portugal and Spain all still maintain official lists from which parents must choose. Portugal's list comprises 39 pages of officially sanctioned names and 41 pages of those which are banned.

LOCAL AUTHORITIES IN Japan have powers to vet the suitability of names. In 1993, Tokyo city hall rejected a couple's attempt to register their baby son as Satan. After a six-month battle, the parents gave up and announced he would be called God.

A GERMAN COURT ruled in 2000 that five names plus a surname are the maximum permissible for a child. Upholding a 1993 law banning long names, it denied a mother's attempt to give her son 12 — Chenekwahow Migiskau Nikapi-Hun-Nizeo Alessandro Majim Chayara Inti Ernesto Prithibi Kioma Pathar Henriko.

IN 2009, THE German constitutional court upheld the government's laws that prohibit any German from having more than a double-barrelled surname. It ruled that a ban in force since 1993 was valid and prevented the wishes of one Frieda Thalheim, who wanted to add her surname to that of her husband's, Hans-Peter Kunz-Hallstein.

SWEDISH COUPLE Sara Lindenger and Johan Leisten were banned by the authorities from calling their son 'Staalman', Swedish for 'Superman', in 2003. The government disallowed the registration, saying it would be 'unpleasant' for the boy in later life.

ANOTHER SWEDISH COUPLE, unidentified in news reports, managed to have a ban overturned by the Court of Appeal in 2008 after the authorities had tried to stop them naming their son Lego, after the toy brick.

FOR 689 YEARS, Korean law banned people sharing the same surname, even though unrelated, from marrying. Introduced in 1308 to prevent in-breeding, it caused particular hardship in a country with an unusually restricted range of names — 20 per cent of families are called Kim. The law was finally declared unconstitutional in July 1997.

DEAD MAN WINS ELECTION

BELGIUM IS UNIQUE in never having exercised any censorship of films for adults.

AUSTRIA'S NEW SOCIAL Democrat Minister for Women's Affairs, Helga Konrad, announced plans in August 1995 to introduce legislation to force men to do equal amounts of domestic chores as women. Failure to do so would become a ground for divorce. Compulsory courses at 'marriage schools' covering housework, child-care, wage distribution and fidelity were envisaged to prepare prospective spouses for their obligations. Konrad also proposed that legally binding pre-nuptial contracts would be introduced for all marrying couples. Opposition commentators ridiculed the idea as overly intrusive into families' private lives. The proposed law never materialised, and by 1997 Konrad was no longer a minister.

THE OTHER END of the political spectrum in Austria also dabbled in the tricky world of social advice in 2001 when the far-right Freedom Party issued a crime prevention booklet blaming scantily clad women for causing rapes. It claimed that more than half of sex offences occurred outside, mainly because of the clothes women wore. It warned women going out to 'take clothes with them to change into or to cover themselves up'. It also advised that women should 'avoid seeming too permissive' when walking alone at night. Opposition parties condemned the publication as 'an affront to all women'.

THE UK DEPARTMENT of Education spent £50,000 producing a 'Dad Pack' of guidance for fathers in 2006 which, according to critics, contained 'astonishingly obvious' advice. It told them how to play with their children ('take them to a playground') as well as suggesting 'hide and seek and making paper patterns'. It contained a poster with a hundred phrases on how to praise a child, as well as advice on fidelity ('don't have an affair').

THE MAYOR OF the Italian coastal resort of Diano Marina proposed in the summer of 1995 that only slim and beautiful women should be allowed to wear bikinis in his town. Andrea Guglieri was reported by Turin's La Stampa newspaper as declaring, 'I don't want people who don't have good physiques walking the streets in their swimming costumes.' The mayor had commissioned a Professor of Aesthetics from the University of Milan to draw up a 10-point guide to help officials decide who was and was not beautiful.

FOR TWO YEARS between 1997 and 1999, the mayor of the wealthiest district in Venezuela's capital, Caracas, banned kissing in public. Irene Saez, a former Miss Universe, introduced the restrictions after claiming to be outraged at 'overpassionate' antics in the city's public parks. Residents complained that the campaign had gone too far, with police taking action if kisses went on for more than a few seconds. Saez's successor instructed the police to concentrate on more pressing concerns.

RICHARD EVANS, A member of the Australian House of Representatives, proposed in 1996 that all domestic cats in the country be eradicated by 2020. He claimed that they had been responsible for killing off nine native species of wildlife. His plan would see feral cats destroyed by releasing a fatal virus among them, and pet cats gradually eliminated by being compulsorily neutered and allowed to die out naturally. His idea provoked a storm of protest from animal lovers and Evans, who had only been elected in 1993, lost his Western Australia seat at the next election in 1998 with the fourth-largest swing against a sitting member in the whole election.

AT THE OTHER end of the spectrum, the city council in Girona, near Barcelona, introduced by-laws in 2009 to improve animal protection by forcing dog owners to walk their pets for at least 20 minutes a day, or face a €400 (£350) fine. There would also be fines for owners who tie up their animals for more than six hours a day, or keep them in cramped conditions. It was not a complete free-for-all for pets' rights – letting one's dog off the lead or allowing it to splash in a public fountain could lead to a €500 fine. And feeding stray animals in the street attracted a fine of €150.

From the history books

In the earliest years of parliamentary development in England, trust between the king and his nobles was not a guaranteed state of affairs. When King John held a Parliament in 1205, he required the children of the barons to be held as hostages to ensure the allegiance of those attending. To this day at the annual State Opening of Parliament, to guarantee the monarch's safe return, a Member of Parliament – a government whip – is required to stay at Buckingham Palace as a hostage while the sovereign attends Westminster.

TO PROTECT THE national wool industry during a downturn in the economy, Parliament passed an Act requiring that from 1 August 1678, every person buried in the country had to be wrapped in a shroud made of English wool. The penalty for transgressing was a fine of £5 (about £650 in modern values).

PETER THE GREAT, Tsar of Russia, banned his people from wearing beards in 1698 as part of his modernising programme for the country. He decreed that they were a sign of backwardness. The legal prohibition clearly had less impact than he desired and in 1705 he dreamed up a simpler way of disincentivising the growing of beards – he put a tax on them.

IN 1910, LAWMAKERS in France banned the practice of separating couples kissing on railway station platforms because of the delays to train services it caused.

THE SALE OF cigarettes to adults in the US state of Iowa only became legalised in April 1921.

TO PREVENT ALLEGED alcoholism in wartime industries, emergency regulations introduced in October 1915 made it illegal for anyone in Britain to buy rounds of drinks. The penalty for 'treating' another person was a £100 fine or six months in jail.

IN APRIL 1939, Glasgow City Council banned the playing of darts in pubs for being 'too dangerous'.

IN NOVEMBER 1948, London County Council banned tenants with television sets. It rationalised that as their accommodation was subsidised, those who could afford a television were sufficiently well-off to be able to live elsewhere.

LURKING DANGER – HEALTH AND SAFETY

The rise of a litigious society in Britain has generated over the past 20 years one of the greatest expansions of officialdom in our history – the seemingly ubiquitous and all-pervading concern for 'health and safety'. From the 1990s, up and down the country councils began to assess 'risks', churn out official guidance and issue injunction after injunction to curtail previously unremarkable activities which were now judged acute hazards to public safety. A pernicious world of petty rules has been spawned, and shows no sign of abating. Here we document some of the most ludicrous decisions that have blighted the daily lives and practices of common folk.

The public highway

A 15-foot row of pansies four inches high on the front verge of a garden in Wiveliscombe was judged by Somerset Council in September 1999 to be a hazard for drivers as the flowers would restrict visibility at the nearby road junction. Lesley Grist, the homeowner, was ordered to remove them.

DESPITE COUNCILS UP and down the country being encouraged to generate revenue by introducing 'sponsorship' for roundabouts and erecting advertising boards, a Cornish parish council which wanted to prettify a weed-strewn new roundabout was told by the Highways Agency in 2009 that it could not do so because the floral display could cause a distraction to motorists. It refused the plans put forward by the villagers in Dobwalls, and insisted on installing 'low maintenance' grass instead.

CARMARTHENSHIRE COUNTY COUNCIL produced a road safety leaflet in 2001 helpfully explaining for road users the meaning of 'daylight' ('all times other than darkness') and defining what pedestrians were ('road users on foot').

NORWICH CITY COUNCIL achieved notoriety in the field for its zealous concern for public safety. In June 2001, officials announced they planned to chop down 20 horse chestnut trees in time for the autumn because of fears that conkers could fall on passers-by, and that drivers were put at risk by the distraction of falling conkers. Children collecting them could also be in danger of being run over. The trees had been in their location for over 25 years. No one locally could recall any incident that had caused danger in the past. After an outcry in the national media, the council relented and put the issue to a public consultation.

A month later, the council hit the headlines again when it told council-house tenants in a block of flats in the city to remove their window flower boxes 'without delay' for fear they could fall on people below. Residents pointed out that some boxes had been installed for more than a decade without incident. Local insurers expressed bemusement at the risk. 'It's not a problem we are aware of,' said a representative of one company.

THE ROYAL MAIL told Marie Zadeh, a householder in Hove, East Sussex, to trim a lavender bush in her front garden, as it contravened health and safety regulations, or she would have to collect her own post from the sorting office. The Mail said: 'The safety of our staff is of prime importance'.

MAIDSTONE COUNCIL BANNED its mayor from flying the town's flag on the official mayoral car in 2008 because of the risk it might blow off and cause a danger to other cars. The flag, measuring eight inches by five, had never been known to come loose before.

In November 2009, Solihull Council told a shopkeeper who tied balloons to the outside of his shopfront to attract customers to remove them, as they constituted a safety hazard. Derek Betts was told that there was a risk that a balloon could come free, blow into the road and lure a child into danger. They could also distract drivers, a council inspector told him, threatening legal action if they were not taken down. A council spokesman defended their approach: 'We have responsibility for ensuring people can use our footpaths safely, something we cannot and do not take lightly.'

The Manifesto Group, a libertarian campaign group, published a highly successful photo collection of unnecessary safety signs in 2009, the result of a two-year project to highlight the blighting impact of modern health and safety warnings. It revealed that in the 100 yards between the Royal Festival Hall and Waterloo Bridge in south London there were 95 safety signs, and that a double-decker bus displays 24 separate cautions.

Taking no chances

In March 2003, Norwich Council banned doormats at a block of flats as a trip hazard, leading to the inch-high coconut mat outside one resident's door being removed by an official. When the owner, Michael Watling, replaced it, it too was removed and he was told he would face legal action if he continued to lay down a mat.

GOSPORT COUNCIL IN Hampshire also banned doormats in 2008. Council safety officers told tenants in its properties that mats were potential hazards if other residents needed to evacuate the building in an emergency. When publicity about the issue spread, the council denied there was a total ban: each mat would be assessed on an individual basis.

BOURNEMOUTH COUNCIL IMPOUNDED a newborn baby's pram left in the communal porch of a block of council flats in 2009 because it represented a safety hazard to others who might need to flee in the event of a fire. The pram belonging to Lee-Anne Futcher had been left in the hallway for less than two hours while Futcher awaited her partner's return from work to lift the pram up the stairs to their flat. The council told them they would need to pay £50 to have it returned, and had four weeks to do so otherwise it would be disposed of.

AS A CONDITION for allowing Richard Wearn to keep pot plants outside his house, officials from Portsmouth City Council in 2008 required him to sign a disclaimer form indemnifying the council and undertaking to pay compensation to anyone who tripped over them.

THE BRITISH STANDARDS INSTITUTE decreed in November 2005 that fountain pens were too dangerous for children under the age of 14. Despite generations having grown up with nothing else, the pens were now judged under a rewrite of British Standard 7272 to be a safety hazard because of the sharp nib, and the absence of the now obligatory hole in the pen cap in case a child swallowed the top.

AFTER EIGHT CENTURIES of practice, and without any record of accidents, Wymondham Abbey found itself obliged in April 2006 to ban the use of a stepladder in the twice-yearly lighting of the 24 candles in the ornate chandelier after a risk assessment condemned the contraption as a safety hazard. Despite being done only at Easter and Christmas, it had to invest in a £6,000 pulley system to lower and raise the chandelier instead.

CLOCK WINDING AT St Michael's church in Helston, Cornwall, which had been done by hand since 1793 by a warden standing on a ladder, was judged by the local council as being 'too dangerous' in

September 2009 because no one was available to hold on to the bottom of the ladder. The church faced raising £5,000 for a self-winding mechanism.

PAPER NAPKINS WERE withdrawn from Meals on Wheels services provided in Tewkesbury, Gloucestershire, in 2006 after fears that the elderly or disabled might choke on them.

POSTAL SERVICES IN the remote Scottish township of Ardmore at the northern tip of Sutherland were withdrawn in July 2006 after a relief postman tripped on the one-and-a-half-mile rugged pathway which had been used without incident for more than a hundred years. The path was now deemed 'fundamentally dangerous' by the Post Office, although residents used it daily and the regular postman had never suffered problems. 'It's punishing and tiring, but I enjoyed it,' said George Mackay. The Post Office now had a different view: 'This route…would not only put the health, but the lives, of Royal Mail staff at risk. It is unreasonable to expect Royal Mail staff to take such risks.'

SIXTY YEARS OF postal deliveries to the remote Yorkshire Dales village of Booze ended in 2008 as Royal Mail followed up the findings of a risk assessment that condemned the track, which had been safely traipsed by generations of postmen, as 'an accident waiting to happen'. Despite being a council-maintained road, and deemed perfectly safe for residents and other service providers, the review concluded that the road was in such a poor condition that post-van drivers could suffer 'long-term injury' by driving up and down it. The residents of the 11-home hamlet were given 24 hours' notice of the withdrawal of deliveries and now faced a 30-mile round trip to collect mail at the sorting office in Richmond, the nearest main town.

IN 2010, Royal Mail excused postmen in Bideford, Devon, from delivering to the last cobbled street in the town because of health and safety concerns about the surface. Despite having been there for 280 years, the Post Office declared it 'unsafe' when it rained.

ROYAL MAIL ANNOUNCED in March 2010 that it was to stop all postal deliveries by bicycle because it was now 'too dangerous' to use Britain's roads. In future, deliveries would be by van or a trolley pushed by a postal worker on foot.

EAST CHESHIRE NATIONAL Health Service Trust approved the actions of one of its hospitals in 2007 when Congleton War Memorial Hospital removed from public view knitting needles that had traditionally been left with a box of wool in its waiting area for use by visitors to knit small squares for a local charity to make into shawls. The box had been on display for three years without incident. They were now described as a 'safety hazard' and hidden behind the reception desk. The box was, however, still available 'on request'.

Training required

FIREMEN IN GREATER MANCHESTER were instructed by their management in 2006 not to use new reclining chairs in their rest areas until they had been trained in how to use them. Every member of the fire crew had to digest a four-page manual giving guidance on how to manoeuvre the seat into the various positions. A spokesman for the fire service explained that the training was required for health and safety reasons. 'There are moving parts,' he said.

A PROGRAMME TO install more road speed indicators in Lancashire to improve adherence to speed limits came to a halt in mid-2007 when the council discovered it did not have enough workers who were qualified to use ladders. Needing to comply with the 2007 amended Working at Height Regulations from the Health and Safety Executive, it faced a £5,000 fine for anyone working more than three feet off the ground who had not been formally trained to climb a ladder. Thirty signs were waiting to be erected when the stricter rules came in. According to safety experts, speeding was the cause of some 350 deaths on the road in the previous year. In the same period, 14 people died from falling off ladders.

POLICE CALLED IN response to a broken stained-glass window at a Rochdale church in 2005 told the churchwarden they could not investigate as they had not had specialist 'ladder training'.

NICK BARKER, a village police community support officer in Halstead, Kent, was banned by his force in 2008 from riding his bicycle until he had attended Kent Police's two-day Basic Police Cycle Skills course. Having ridden a bike since he was a small boy, Barker was now required to travel between the villages he patrolled by bus and walk several miles to reach outlying farms. Kent Police insisted that 'all officers must complete a bicycle training course before they can ride a bike on duty. It is about ensuring their safety and the safety of those around them. If you have a civilian driving licence you can't drive a police car. The same applies to a bike.'

LANCASHIRE POLICE CONSTABLE Tony Cobban refused to ride a bicycle for a publicity photo shoot in 2009 because he had not passed the constabulary's proficiency test. He even declined to sit on the saddle with the bike stationary. Sent to Preston's Halfords store to publicise the company's donation of bicycles to the police, Cobban rebuffed press requests for a shot of him riding one of the gifts, explaining the bicycle 'hasn't been risk assessed or insured'. His caution was backed up by his inspector, Nick Emmett: 'Our officers are required to be appropriately trained and assessed prior to using bikes to comply with insurance and for the safety of themselves and the public.'

IN NOVEMBER 2009, the Association of Chief Police Officers published, reportedly at the cost of several thousand pounds of taxpayers' money, the Cycle Training Doctrine, an official guide for police forces on how to ride their bicycles safely. It ran to 93 pages.

IN MARCH 2010, the introduction of a scheme by Northamptonshire Constabulary for cycle patrols in Northampton had to be delayed for more than three months because the officers had not attended a 10-hour training course on how to ride their mountain bikes.

FIRE EXTINGUISHERS INSTALLED at blocks of flats in Bournemouth were removed on the advice of Dorset Fire Service in 2008 because they were judged to be a fire risk by encouraging residents to attempt to fight a fire by themselves, and thus endangering their safety. Residents were informed that unless each and every one of them had been trained in their use, the extinguishers would be removed as a potential hazard. Peter Whitaker, 'Protection Policy' chief at the fire service, said: 'We do not want to encourage people to leave their flat to fetch a fire extinguisher from a hallway and then return to a blaze. We want them to get out safely.'

THE *Cambridge News* reported in 2009 that a porter at Addenbrooke's Hospital refused to help a wheelchair-bound blind woman into the premises as he was 'not trained' to push wheelchairs into the hospital from the outside. He was only covered to push wheelchairs inside the building.

FIVE WEEKS AFTER Craig Hodge, of Paignton, Devon, stepped in to volunteer as his school's crossing 'lollipop man' in 2009 when the regular attendant went on extended sick leave, he was banned from continuing when the local council found out. Having undertaken the duties without complaint from parents or the school, Hodge was barred by Torbay Council because he had not been trained for the post.

Care of others

Midlothian Council was revealed in 2007 to be keeping the lights on in a disused school in Dalkeith so that vandals were not at risk of hurting themselves if they broke in. The council told the media: 'Some lights are left on during the winter months to protect potential intruders from hazards.'

POLICE IN BATH refused to pursue a thief who had stolen a £1,200 moped in June 2006 because they feared they would be sued if he fell off as he was not wearing a helmet. The bike's owner, Max Foster, was told by the officers they could not instigate a chase if doing so put the fleeing thief's safety in danger. Avon and Somerset police confirmed that the officers were acting within police rules and that the decision was in line with normal practice.

IN 2008, BROMSGROVE District Council told a gardener to remove barbed wire he had put around his council-owned allotment to deter thieves because of the risk that intruders would injure themselves. Bill Malcolm's allotment in Marlbrook, Worcestershire, had been robbed three times in four months, with thieves getting away with equipment worth £300. The single strand of barbed wire, three feet off the ground, was judged a health and safety hazard. The council confirmed that 'We are obliged to request its removal or remove it on health and safety grounds to the general public, as this is a liability issue.' Mr Malcolm's suggestion of inviting any injured thief to sue him, 'as at least I would know who was breaking into my allotment', was declined by the council.

PRISONERS HAD TO be transported nearly 40 miles from Cambridge Magistrates' Court to Peterborough's court for three weeks in 2009 because guards refused to escort prisoners up the Cambridge court's stairs after the lift broke down, claiming it broke safety procedures.

FRENCH AUTHORITIES AT Calais were reported in January 2008 to be refusing to allow British border police to use X-ray scanners to search lorries arriving at the Channel port for illegal immigrants because it breached European health and safety directives if they did not obtain the written permission of those being subjected to the scanning in advance. France had outlawed the use of the scanners on safety grounds.

THE HEALTH AND SAFETY Executive issued guidelines in July 2008 to carpenters and woodworkers not to use brooms to sweep up sawdust because of health dangers from inhaling particles. It advised carpentry firms to buy vacuum cleaners and air purification systems. Representatives of small businesses complained that most would not be able to afford the costly investment.

TWO LOCAL RADIO presenters taking part in a BBC Essex programme in 2009 on acquiring new skills were required by the Corporation's safety rules to have a paramedic and first aider present before they endeavoured to change a car tyre. The wheel change demonstration taking place in the radio station's car park in Chelmsford was halted by the producer until a St John's Ambulance team had arrived. The BBC defended the precautions, saying: 'The presenters were working against the clock using unfamiliar equipment.'

A CLEANING COMPANY in Chippenham, Wiltshire, employed 16-year-old Karl Walker for a week in 2008 before terminating his job when it realised it was breaching official government guidelines for employing 'minors'. While the student was old enough to join the Army, drive a motor vehicle and get married, the guidelines deemed it unsafe for him to be in charge of hot water, cleaning fluids or an industrial vacuum cleaner.

CANN HALL PRIMARY School in Clacton-on-Sea, Essex, was ridiculed in 2008 for publishing photographs of school activities on its website having blanked out every child's head with a cartoon smiley face, ostensibly to protect their identities. In one scene, a group picture of a class marking a school visit had stickers covering every one of the 25 pupils. Even the National Society for the Protection of Cruelty to Children judged that the school 'may have gone too far', adding that schools needed to take 'sensible precautions that strike a balance between protection and celebrating children's achievements'.

WESTFIELD COMMUNITY COLLEGE in Watford imposed in March 2010 what was believed to be Britain's first blanket ban on any parent taking photographs of any child during school events, in the interest of 'pupil safety'.

THE POLICE FORCE'S watchdog, the Independent Police Complaints Authority, issued instructions to every policeman in April 2010 that they must ensure they follow up every complaint from the public, no matter how outlandish it seemed. It required the complaint to be investigated fully, even if 'bizarre, implausible or intrinsically without foundation'. One anonymous officer cited the case of a local man 'who claims that police implanted a microchip in his brain and use it to control him' as an example of the complaints that would now have to be given police time to examine.

No ball games

Burnham Grammar School, Buckinghamshire, banned football in the playground in 2007 after a teacher was hit by a stray ball crossing the play area. The head teacher defended the action, saying pupils were generally kicking the ball 'quite hard'.

JOHN F. KENNEDY Primary School in Washington, Tyne and Wear, had to ban the three-legged race and sack race at its sports day in

2008 because of safety fears that children would fall over. The event, ironically themed on Edwardian times, was held at a museum which demanded the changes to conform with its insurance arrangements.

CHESHIRE COUNTY COUNCIL removed children's goalposts from a park in 2007 because it straddled a public right of way and officials feared that walkers could stumble into them at night. Although local residents observed that the field was so muddy that few walkers were likely to opt for the route, the council went ahead on the advice of a 'rights of way' officer who had visited the scene and insisted that the public right of way took precedence.

A SURVEY OF nearly 600 teachers by the *Teachers* TV satellite channel in 2009 revealed that almost half had experienced instructions or practices on health and safety in schools that negatively affected children's learning. Of the most extreme examples of overly restrictive regulations, teachers cited a requirement for children to wear goggles when using Blu-Tack to affix posters to walls, the banning of eating sweets as a choking hazard, and a bar on traditional conker and snowball fights. Also reported was the issuing of a five-page warning note about using glue sticks.

No longer innocent pleasures

Steve Wood, who planned to sit in a bath of baked beans to raise £100,000 for his local lifeboat charity, was told by Swansea City Council that he could not go ahead with the stunt unless he took out a £5 million public liability insurance policy.

OAKLEY AND DEANE Parish Council in Hampshire banned the feeding of ducks in Oakley village pond in 2007. It said it feared toxins in the birds' droppings could harm children.

DEAD MAN WINS ELECTION

ORGANISERS OF THE 2007 Christmas pantomime at Great Yarmouth instructed the performers not to partake in the traditional throwing of sweets into the audience for fear of lawsuits from injured children.

A 600-YEAR-OLD tradition of pancake racing on Shrove Tuesday in the precincts of Ripon Cathedral, North Yorkshire, was abandoned in 2008 because of the amount of work needed to undertake 'risk assessments' and public liability insurance requirements.

THE 200-YEAR-OLD tradition of cheese rolling on Cooper's Hill, near Gloucester, finally met its end in 2010 on health and safety grounds. The famous event, which annually saw hundreds of competitors chase a seven-pound Double Gloucester cheese down the precipitously steep hill, was cancelled by the local council because of alleged crowd-control issues.

A TRADITION DATING back to 1680 was banned in 2008 because it was deemed that children should not be exposed to loud noise. Wimborne Council in Dorset opposed the performance by the town's Militia re-enacting the tradition of firing their muskets over the Christmas tree during the annual switching on of the High Street's festive lights.

COUNCIL AUTHORITIES IN Southwold, Suffolk, objected in 2008 to a planned Christmas Day swim in the sea to raise money for charity because the wearing of fancy-dress costumes was a safety risk. The organisers were also required to ensure adequate insurance cover running into the millions, an adequate police presence, and a lifeboat. They eventually called off the event, saying, 'there are too many barriers'. One hundred and thirty people had taken part in the previous year's swim without incident, raising £8,000 for local causes.

ORGANISERS OF THE fancy-dress 'World Walking the Plank' championships held on the Isle of Sheppey, Kent, in August 2009 were required by Swale Borough Council to demonstrate they had obtained scientific advice that the sea was clean enough to jump into. They had to get water samples tested before permission for the event was granted.

ESSEX HIGHWAYS, the local authority responsible for road safety, issued the tiny village of Hatfield Broad Oak with a six-page list of rules in May 2008 when the local trades association wanted to put up bunting to decorate the main street during their annual festival. The tradition of flying tiny flags, which had been preserved for over a hundred years, came to an abrupt end that year because the rules stipulated that the lines could only be attached to 'fixed points on buildings and by tolerance-tested steel eyebolts'. Deciding it was impractical, the association banned the bunting.

THE ANNUAL SUMMER carnival in Ferndown, Dorset, suffered the same fate in 2009 when the county council refused to approve the traditional bunting stretched across the road for fear it could sag and become entangled in traffic, despite the event being held for more than 20 years without any incident.

ANGLIA RUSKIN UNIVERSITY, based in Cambridge, issued a request to students attending the annual graduation ceremony in 2008 for them not to throw their mortar boards into the air in the decades-old celebratory style. It cited the risk of injury from the sharp edges of the hats as the reason.

WILTSHIRE COUNCIL INSTRUCTED a gardener who had been mowing a communal area of grassland outside his home for 43 years to desist in 2009 because of the risk of injury to himself or a neighbour. Graham Alexander had been tending the 40 feet by 30 feet land in the village of Harnham near Salisbury without incident since the 1960s. He was now required to leave it to council contractors.

'To comply with regulations...'

A fleet of 28 new trains destined for a busy overcrowded commuter line was mothballed in April 2006 when disability advisers noticed that the electronic matrix signs announcing routes and stops were three millimetres too narrow. South West Trains, which faced daily complaints from rail users for the lack of trains on the Reading to Waterloo line, was forced to stop their planned introduction into service because the lettering which should have been 35mm high to comply with new disability legislation was found to be only 32mm tall. The cost of rectifying the problem was estimated at £750,000, even though the change was deemed by the company as likely to have 'no discernible impact on journey quality for the majority of passengers'.

JOHN SNAPE, a church minister from Blackburn, Lancashire, was refused travel on a Northern Rail train in March 2009 because the mobility scooter he used was 1.6 inches longer than the company's length limit and thus breached its health and safety regulations.

ORGANISERS OF THE Christmas parade in Halesowen, West Midlands, were told by their council as they prepared for the 2007 Christmas season that the sleigh they had used for the past 20 years had to be modified to enable Santa to wear a seatbelt for the 5 mph procession.

ORGANISERS OF THE annual carnival in Wombourne, Staffordshire, announced in 2009 they were abandoning the use of their 5 mph motorised floats, in use for more than 30 years, because of a requirement that anyone riding on them had to be physically tethered to comply with safety rules. They were dropping down to smaller, hand-drawn trolleys.

WHEN PERFORMING A production of *Robinson Crusoe* in its Christmas season in 2007, the amateur dramatics club in Perranwell, Cornwall, was required by health and safety guidelines to report its two plastic spears, six wooden swords and a toy gun to the local police. They had to be kept under lock and key when not being used on stage, and have a 'responsible guardian' appointed to ensure their safe keeping. Elaine Gummow called the rules 'farcical', adding 'in other scenes, we hit each other with frying pans and saucepan lids but there's no problem with them'. The Health and Safety Executive, responsible for developing detailed rules for theatrical performances, defended the arrangements, saying they were designed to make risks 'sensibly managed'.

SOLDIERS HAD TO remove the 'snaps' from 650 boxes of Christmas crackers being sent to troops in Afghanistan and Iraq in 2007 because they contravened the British Forces Post Office's safety regulations. The cracker snaps were classed as explosives, in the same category as flares, nitroglycerine and fireworks. Major Iain Dalzel-Job told the press that 'it was quite tricky to get them out. It took us two hours to get through them all.' The Ministry of Defence confirmed the need: 'The safety of our aircraft and personnel is paramount. Large numbers of Christmas crackers are classified as dangerous air cargo and therefore require special handling.'

HEATHER WELSH, a 22-year-old student, was refused permission to buy a box of Christmas crackers by the York Marks and Spencer supermarket in 2008 because she had no ID to prove she was over 16. The shop cited the need to comply with the 1875 Explosives Act and the 1997 Fireworks Safety Regulations.

THE LOCAL BUSINESS association planning decorations in Walton-on-the Naze, Essex, was told in 2008 that in order to safely install its Christmas tree, which it had bought for £400, it had to buy a 20-ton concrete base to ensure its stability, costing £1,500. The town went treeless.

RAILWAY STAFF AT Wadhurst station in East Sussex in November 2009 told Vicky Pachner, a mother struggling with her 10-month-old baby son, that they could not help carry her pushchair up the stairs of the footbridge because they were not insured to do so.

KATHY CHRISTOPHER, a 71-year-old pensioner, was left without heating in February 2010 when the company who delivered her two gas canisters refused to take them into her house because they would have to be lifted up the three steps of her porch. The driver told her this now breached the company's safety regulations.

THE MARITIME AND COASTGUARD AGENCY, in charge of Britain's inshore rescue services, issued instructions to its rescue crews in 2009 that before attending emergencies they had to fill out a 'vehicle pre-journey risk assessment' form. The form required them to detail the type of rescue and journey being made, the 'reason for journey' and to list any risks they could face. They had to explain any 'actions taken to mitigate risk' and assess whether the risk was 'acceptable'. The Agency responded to criticism by denying that the form-filling could delay responses to emergencies, as the paperwork 'can be done at the same time as the rest of the team prepares equipment'.

It was not the first safety-related regulation to irk the crews. The Agency had just banned the traditional practice of firing off flares during emergencies on safety grounds.

A MUNICIPAL RECYCLING tip in Blandford, Dorset, refused to allow in a couple who had brought their rubbish on foot 400 yards from their home. David and Katie France were advised they needed to return home and drive to the site, as health and safety rules forbade pedestrians entering. Mr France left his wife and the rubbish at the entrance, walked back home, brought along his car, packed it up with the refuse and was then allowed entry to dispose of the load. 'Whatever good we did in recycling our waste was probably counteracted by the CO_2 emissions we used in our car,' said the bemused Mr France.

BOLTON COUNCIL RESPONDED to a resident's request in March 2010 to remove a double mattress that had been dumped down an embankment at a local beauty spot by sending a risk assessment team, which concluded that to comply with health and safety rules, the job needed a mechanical digger and a four-person crew to mount the operation. On being told it would take another week to arrange the recovery, two local men took four minutes to drag the mattress on to the nearby road, which enabled a council van to take it away immediately.

We end with perhaps the most emblematic illustration of our modern drift to high anxiety about risk.

A PHOTO SHOOT in September 2004 to launch a year-long programme of events marking the bicentenary of the Battle of Trafalgar had an actor resplendently rigged out in the costume of Lord Nelson sail up the Thames to Greenwich. The drama of the scene was much diluted by the requirement for Nelson to don a bright orange, high-visibility life jacket.

From the history books

While the modern obsession with the welfare of the public is fixated on the supposed threat of personal hurt and injury, the longer past is full of equally wayward concerns for the safety of the nation.

WHEN WALT DISNEY'S seminal first feature-length cartoon *Snow White and the Seven Dwarfs* was released in Britain in 1938, the British Board of Film Censors gave it an adult certificate because the depiction of the enchanted forest and the witch were deemed too disturbing for children to see. The *Daily Mail* film critic agreed. In a piece headlined,

'Snow White Censor Did Not Blunder', he wrote, 'I do agree with the British Board of Censors in having given this film an Adult certificate. The scene in the dark forest where animals with glaring eyes and trees with clutching arms…is definitely eerie. The transformation of the Queen to the Witch with the death's head on the poisoned apple and the skeleton in the dungeon is even more so.'

DEBATING VOTES FOR women in the House of Commons in May 1905, arch opponent Henry Labouchere broadened the question to consider the merits of women performing traditional male professions. He expressed disbelief on the question 'could a policeman be a woman?' The public safety would immediately be put at risk because 'they have no sense of proportion. They exaggerate one thing and despise another.' Fellow MP Frederick Banbury concurred that women would never make good politicians. 'It would be useless to debate any point at all because the women will have made up their minds before the debate begins.' John Bryce, in 1910, averred, 'By their constitution, they are more liable to be affected by gusts and waves of sentiment…their very emotional nature make women an easier prey to showy argument [and] to the influence of an attractive personality.'

THE NATIONAL ASSOCIATION OF SCHOOLMASTERS, the main representative group of teachers in Britain at the time, passed a resolution at its annual conference at Manchester in April 1930 deploring the increase in women teachers and demanding that only men should teach in boys' schools. Among the claimed problems associated with females teaching boys was: 'boys need strong control shorn of emotion, petting or jealousy'. The fate of the nation was at stake as 'the boy who comes only under women's influence cannot become a 100 per cent he-man… You cannot feminise boys without feminising the nation.' The resolution was agreed with only two dissenting votes.

Even some women agreed. In October 1933, the Women's Council to Advocate Masters for Boys held its inaugural meeting at which speakers claimed the Board of Education's approval of women teaching was because they were cheaper to employ. A Miss F.M. Lowe declared that 'the public must be awakened to...the growing feminisation of the nation.' Referring to boys' developmental needs, she went on, 'the influence of nothing but women during those crucial years has a definitely softening effect on his character'.

AS LATE AS March 1932, the French Senate rejected a proposed law allowing women to become solicitors on the grounds that women were congenitally incapable of keeping secrets and therefore unable to perform duties which required them maintaining discretion.

THE FRENCH LOWER HOUSE was not averse to taking action either. In March 1926, it voted 370–153 to ban the manufacture of babies' dummies after the proposer claimed, and successfully persuaded his fellow members, that the dummy was one of the chief causes of child mortality.

THE DECISION BY judges in the London High Court in 1910 to stop sitting on Saturdays provoked a public debate on the increasing practice of a two-day weekend. The Daily Mail suggested the development was a sign of 'national decadence'.

THE CORONER AT Hackney, east London, hearing a case in 1912, pronounced deep concern at the potential suicidal influence of the new phenomenon of cinemas after. 26-year-old George Porter had shot himself apparently after neglecting his job and having 'gone mad about picture shows'. The coroner warned that 'exciting shooting and stabbing illustrations' were the frequent fare of film shows, said it was a pity there was not more censorship, and asked the jury to consider adding a rider to its verdict on the health impact of movies. (The jury, perhaps wisely, declined.)

POLITICIANS WERE STILL concerned as late as 1946 at the impact of the mayhem regularly involved in Saturday morning children's cinema. Thomas Skeffington-Lodge told the House of Commons of his anxiety at the 'atmosphere of mass hysteria which is induced by the communal shrieking. I think we shall develop citizens with a false set of values. We shall have a nation of robots and automata for whom "glamour" offers an escape from the duties and responsibilities of life.'

THE CHANGING FASHIONS for women piled up a constant stream of professional opinion about their deleterious effects. High-heeled shoes were widely condemned by doctors for their deforming impact on feet. But it did not stop there. An eminent orthopaedist, Sir Herbert Barker, voiced his conviction in 1923 that 'most of the internal ills from which women suffer are caused by the wearing of high-heeled shoes, which displace the most vital organs of the body by curving a woman's back in an unnatural way'. An unidentified biologist added to the alarum by predicting that women would eventually end up with fewer toes: 'With the high heels now worn three toes are sufficient for progressing, and as nature always gets rid of superfluous organs it seems likely that in the course of time women's toes will be reduced to three and perhaps later to two or even one.'

As recently as 1947, a South African Association for the Advancement of Science meeting blamed high-heeled shoes for 'divorces, hysterics, spinal diseases, sick headaches and moodiness'. E.S. Priester, the country's top foot doctor, claimed that the shoes created in a woman 'depression, desperation, irritability, laziness, loss of jobs through lack of concentration, failure to find husbands through moodiness, [and] mental instability contributing to [a] high divorce rate'.

The short, bobbed, 'shingle' haircut, which became fashionable in the mid-1920s, was said by doctors to have given rise to a new complaint, 'shingle headache', as women began to suffer from neuralgia brought on by the 'sudden removal of the warm, protective covering of hair above the nape of the neck'.

In 1927, a new threat appeared. The chairman of the Hairdressers' Registration Committee warned of the dangers of the modern fashion of wearing tight hats. Women would find that these restricted the circulation of blood to the head and 'secretions' to the hair, leading to loss of growth and eventual loss of hair.

And men were not immune either. As late as 1929, the Men's Dress Reform Party campaigned for the abolition of men's shirt collars on the grounds, according to its secretary, Alfred C. Jordan, that 'there is more than a suspicion that baldness from which men suffer more than women is due to collars which restrict the flow of blood to the cells from which the hair grows'. Another doctor, one C.W. Saleeby, claimed further that collars also hid the thyroid gland from the air. As it was a source of growth, 'men might well be taller if collars were abandoned'.

Even more alarmingly, a meeting of the Design Industries Association in February 1963 was told of recent Swedish research into the dangers for men of the current fashion for narrow trousers, which potentially had 'far-reaching genetic effects'. The editor of the trade journal *Tailor and Cutter* warned that tight trousers were a greater threat than all the radiation now in the atmosphere. Restrictive underwear or narrow, tight-fitting trousers were responsible for raising the 'local temperature', adversely affecting men's fertility.

The 'Swinging Sixties' woman was faring no better. The general secretary of the Motor Schools Association came out in the same year with a condemnation of female learner drivers and their choice of clothes, arguing that women who wore bras were hazardous. Patrick Murphy said that too often women drivers corseted and strapped themselves so tightly that it restricted their movements behind the wheel. 'Too often some of the undergarments they wear affect their breathing and they are not able to relax properly.' He particularly took exception to bras, tight skirts, dangling jewellery attached to bracelets and high-heeled shoes.

At its conference in 1961, the Royal Society for the Prevention of Accidents warned women that wearing nylon panties could cause a fire or an explosion. A Mr J. Howlett of the Distillers Company told the gathering that tests conducted on women wearing nylon pants and leather shoes revealed charges of 600 volts after walking 25 yards. He warned them that 'conducting footwear should be the rule in dangerous locations'.

MODERN FASHION WAS not the only threat to human well-being. The introduction of new technology was fraught with dread. French nerve specialists warned in 1928 that the new-fangled calculating machines, increasingly used by bank tellers, were 'anti-biological, and their continued use, involving intense mental application, can only result in nervous breakdown and sometimes dangerous mental maladies'. Electric light, New York oculists claimed in 1896, was a cause of blindness. 'Great injury is caused to the eyes of those who work in offices,' one claimed. 'The proper thing to do,' asserted one Dr Houghton, 'is to abolish electric lights altogether.'

The United Nations Educational, Scientific and Cultural Organisation, UNESCO, published in 1953 a study of television and education. Its author, Professor Charles Stepmann, included the views of an unidentified 'prominent US teacher' who claimed: 'Under the impact of television, I can contemplate a time when people can neither read nor write but will be no better than a form of plant.'

A 1960 study of British children's television by a respected research group, the Nuffield Foundation, expressed concern that two shows were too 'violent', naming the Westerns *Laramie* and *Rawhide*, and that pop music was 'drivel'. It reserved its deepest concern, though, for quiz shows, registering its worry that 'the nightly gloating over rich rewards for puny efforts must, in the long term, encourage the development of a false set of virtues'.

THE HEAD OF Children's Television at the BBC, Freda Lingstrom, revealed to a film festival audience in 1953 that the corporation had a strict policy for protecting children's sensitivities. The showing of dragons and witches was permitted provided that they never had teeth, 'for children find teeth terrifying'.

A Harley Street child psychiatrist condemned the highly popular *Dr Who and the Daleks* when the film was released in 1965. Dr Ellie Stungo told the press that his objection was not just a matter of artistic taste: 'These horrible things are enough to upset a stable child, let alone one who is not so well balanced. Even adults are likely to be disturbed by them.'

NEW ZEALAND LIBRARIES banned all of Enid Blyton's Noddy books in 1960 because, in the opinion of the authorities, they were 'pervaded by feuds, jealousies, mean triumphs and revenges, idle ridicule and name-calling'.

We end with two examples of activities which certainly would not now be sanctioned by modern stewards of public office. Read, and feel for a bygone age.

DURING AN INFESTATION of wasps across Britain in the spring of 1912, some local councils came up with imaginative schemes to tackle the problem. Town councils in Hythe and Marden in Kent offered children a bounty for each queen wasp killed and delivered to the council offices. Hythe offered a penny per queen, and received 4,000 in just 19 days. Marden children killed over 3,000, being paid at the rate of three penny.

BUT PERHAPS THE most extreme illustration of the distance travelled by the modern world from just a couple of generations ago, Britain's 'ratting clubs' offer a stark picture of a lost way of life. In Kent in the 1930s, hunting vermin was a popular pastime for young and old. So much so that in November 1933 the county newspaper instituted the first of what became a bizarre annual competition which ran before the Second World War to help clean up the county's streets and houses. The practice involved quite simply the systematic and methodical hunting in alley ways and rubbish dumps for as many rats as one could find.

The paper offered a prize of £10 to the rat club that collected the most rats inside the month and £3 to the most successful individual effort. The entrants were instructed to 'notify' the newspaper of their total catch and retain the rats' tails for subsequent inspection and verification.

DEAD MAN WINS ELECTION

A month later the results were announced, producing an astonishing insight into what passed as a healthy pastime 80 years ago. No fewer than 6,802 rats were recorded as having been caught in the competition. Pride of the county was the Rat and Vermin Club of Southborough and Bidborough, between Tonbridge and Tunbridge Wells, which returned the highest catch, a massive 1,872. A special runners-up prize was awarded to the second place in view of its being far ahead of the remainder of the field – 1,492, collected by the Eynsford Club from near Swanley.

The top prize for an individual went to an indomitable character, Mr Constable of Tonbridge, who single-handedly accounted for 547 rats. He seems to have led a particularly unattractive life, according to the paper, spending most of his days on top of the town's refuse dump hunting. He was the mainstay of the local ratting club. The tradition was a long one in Kent. Rat and sparrow Clubs had been in existence for decades. One, in Sevenoaks, was over a hundred years old and believed to be one of the oldest in the country.

PARTING THOUGHTS

We have witnessed the extremes that politics can produce. Actions, they say, speak louder than words. But the motivations of politicians can be just as entertaining and thought-provoking. To round off our collection of political foolishness, we leave some parting thoughts.

Politics observed

Politics is derived from two words – 'poly' meaning many and 'tics' meaning small blood-sucking insects.

(Anon)

Political promises go in one year and out the other.

(Anon)

Politics is the skilled use of blunt objects.

Lester Pearson, Canadian Prime Minister

Never mistake motion for action.

Ernest Hemingway

Man's capacity for justice makes democracy possible; man's inclination for injustice makes democracy necessary.

Reinhold Niebuhr, 'The Children of Light and the Children of Darkness'

DEAD MAN WINS ELECTION

If people have to choose between freedom and sandwiches, they will take the sandwiches.

Lord Boyd-Orr

People bribing the government – that's corruption; the government bribing the people – that's democracy.

John Fortune, 2001

Let us never forget that we can never go farther than we can persuade at least half of the people to go.

Hugh Gaitskell, Labour Party leader, 1955–63

Democracy is the art of saying 'nice doggie' until you can find a rock.

Wynn Catlin, US columnist

I take a balanced view of the government – I like it less than last week and more than next week.

Graffiti, London 1979

There is nothing more disgusting in British political life than a Conservative who thinks he has public opinion behind him.

Auberon Waugh

Ninety per cent of politicians give the other 10 per cent a bad name.

Henry Kissinger, former US National Security Adviser and Secretary of State, 1978

A number of anxious dwarfs trying to grill a whale.

English critic J.B. Priestley defining politicians in action, 1974

Today's ministers are a bit like actors in a huge, dark theatre, initially delighted at the absence of heckling or booing, but beginning uneasily to ask themselves whether anyone is still watching.

Andrew Marr, BBC political editor, on the growth of British political apathy, 1999

PARTING THOUGHTS

A newspaper poll found that fewer than one in twenty people could explain the government's 'third way'. Some thought it was a religious cult, others a sexual position, and one man asked if it was a plan to widen the M25.

Keith Waterhouse, columnist, quoted in the Observer, *a year after Tony Blair's New Labour came to power, 1998*

The quickest way to become a left winger in the Labour Party today is to stand still for six months.

Dave Nellist MP, on the Blair revolution

To be a good campaigner, you have to be prepared to be a bore and to be labelled a bore. I have never flinched from boring people.

Tam Dalyell, veteran controversialist Labour MP, 2000

When your opponent is drowning, throw the son of a bitch an anvil.

James Carville, Democrat campaign strategist, 1994

Many a poor political speech had been saved by throwing in a few lines about patriotism.

Bismarck

The difference between an EU Commissioner and a supermarket trolley? – You can get a lot more food into a Commissioner.

Former EU Commissioner Neil Kinnock, 1999

If the newspapers of a country are filled with good news, the jails of the country will be filled with good people.

Daniel Moynihan, US Senator and Ambassador to the United Nations

No one stays apolitical for very long once they have experienced a charge by the French riot police.

Anonymous French university lecturer, after Paris street disturbances, December 1986

We have very little power beyond the ability to make noise.

> *Austin Mitchell, Labour MP, on the decline of backbench MPs' influence,*
> 2000

The Civil Service

I compare it to a rather stupid dog that wants to do what its master wants and, above all, wants to be loved for doing it.

> *Sir Richard Mottram, Permanent Secretary, Department for Local*
> *Government, Transport and the Regions, on the British Civil Service,*
> 2002

You do not need brains to be Minister of Transport because the civil servants have them.

> *Sir Ernest Marples, Minister of Transport 1959–64*

It's like watching an elephant get pregnant. Everything's done on a very high level, there's a lot of commotion, and it takes 22 months for anything to happen.

> *US President Franklin Roosevelt, on working with the State*
> *Department*

A difficulty for every solution.

> *Viscount Samuel, High Commissioner for Palestine, on civil servants,*
> 1922

They will answer the question you asked, but won't volunteer the answer to the question you should have asked.

> *Bruce Smart, US Undersecretary of Commerce, on civil servants, 1988*

What you have to remember is that civil servants use vagueness and ambiguity with razor-sharp precision.

> *Anonymous senior civil servant, quoted in letter to Daily Telegraph, 2006*

PARTING THOUGHTS

Civil servants have not got the expertise at their disposal which a merchant bank has. If they had such expertise, they would probably be working very successfully for a merchant bank.

Margaret Thatcher, then shadow Fuel Minister, Queen's Speech 1967

There's nothing which cannot be made a mess of again by officials.

Konrad Adenauer, German Chancellor 1949–63

The only thing that saves us from bureaucracy is its inefficiency. An efficient bureaucracy is the greatest threat to freedom.

Eugene McCarthy, US politician, 1979

The single most exciting thing you encounter in government is competence, because it's so rare.

Daniel Moynihan, US Senator, 1976

One of the enduring truths…is that bureaucrats *survive*.

US President Gerald Ford, memoirs, 1982

The Civil Service is a self-perpetuating oligarchy, and what better system is there?

Sir Robert Armstrong, Head of the British Civil Service, 1977

The requirements of a successful Governor of the Bank of England are the tact and skill of an ambassador and the guile of a Romanian horse thief.

Harold Lever, Labour cabinet minister, 1974

The Prime Minister said it was a loose classification by the Board of Trade. 'Locomotives, ships and aircraft' should have read 'wire, mattresses, tacks, nails and manhole covers'.

Daily Mail report, date unknown

In developing our industrial strategy for the period ahead, we have the benefit of much experience. Almost everything has been tried at least once.

Tony Benn, a fortnight after becoming Secretary of State for Industry, 1974

Governments don't retreat; they simply advance in another direction.

Geoffrey Rippon, former Conservative cabinet minister, 1981

Many journalists have fallen for the conspiracy theory of government. I do assure you that they would produce more accurate work if they adhered to the cock-up theory.

Bernard Ingham, Press Secretary to Margaret Thatcher, 1985

Political perspectives

It's a mistake to judge people by their friends. Judge them by their enemies. I am very proud of my enemies.

Former Conservative cabinet minister Norman Tebbit, 1991

I ask you to judge me by the enemies I have made.

Franklin D. Roosevelt

Change your friends.

Charles de Gaulle, advice to his Governor-General of Algeria, who had complained that all his friends were attacking him for supporting de Gaulle's Algeria policy, 1955

It is never wise to try to appear to be more clever than you are. It is sometimes wise to appear slightly less so.

Willie Whitelaw, Conservative Deputy Prime Minister 1979–1988

I'm not particularly interested in becoming Prime Minister. It's a lousy job. I don't want it, and others can do it.

Norman Tebbit, 1987

PARTING THOUGHTS

The most dangerous animal in politics is the politician with no more personal ambition.

Norman Tebbit, 1987

The secret is to always let the other man have your way.

Claiborne Pell, US Senator, 1987

The free market has done more to liberate women than all the political posturing in the feminist movement.

Teresa Gorman, Conservative MP 1998

I have always thought that a stuff-'em-all party would poll a lot of votes.

Maverick Liberal MP David Penhaligon, 1981

Mr Tony Banks: The minister's first reply was a lot of old bull –
Mr Speaker: Order. That is not a very elegant word.
Mr Banks: I am not a very elegant person.

Exchange, Defence Questions, 13 June 1989

A wet is someone who would use North Sea oil to build community centres all over the North of England; a dry doesn't know what a community centre is.

John Butcher, Conservative MP, 1981, on the defining divisions of the early Thatcher era

Every solution needs moisture.

Badge appearing at the 1981 Conservative Party conference

Most Conservatives believe that a crèche is something that happens between two Range Rovers in Tunbridge Wells.

Caroline Shorten, Social Democrat politician, 1993

I admire her, but it's like sitting next to electricity.

Robert Runcie, Archbishop of Canterbury 1980–91, on Margaret Thatcher

He's a great ex-President. It's a shame he couldn't have gone directly to the ex-presidency.

Thomas Mann, Brookings Institute, on ex-President Jimmy Carter's
success in mediating with North Korea, 1994

Political life

The main advantage of being famous is that when you bore people at dinner parties they think it is their fault.

Henry Kissinger

Well done. You'll find lots of problems in your new job. I caused many of them.

Keith Joseph, Conservative cabinet minister and former Housing
Minister responsible in the 1960s for expanding tower block development,
congratulating one of his successors in the 1980s, recounted in Joseph's
obituary, 1994

Chief Secretary, I'm afraid there is no money. Kind regards and good luck.

Outgoing second-in-command of the Treasury, Liam Byrne, leaving a
message for his successor, David Laws, after the British general election,
2010

Leading the Labour Party is like driving an old stage coach. If it is rattling along at a rare old speed, most of the passengers are so exhilarated – perhaps ever seasick – they don't start arguing or quarrelling. As soon as it stops, they start arguing about which way to go. The trick is to keep it going at an exhilarating speed.

Harold Wilson, Labour Party leader, 1963–76

The Conservative Party does not like brains. Thank God I don't have any.

Willie Whitelaw, Conservative Deputy Prime Minister 1979–1988

PARTING THOUGHTS

One thing about a pig. He thinks he's warm if his nose is warm. I saw a bunch of pigs one time that had frozen together in a circle, each one's nose tucked under the rump of the one in front. We have a lot of pigs in politics.

Eugene McCarthy, US politician, 1968

There are no true friends in politics. We are all sharks circling and waiting for traces of blood to appear in the water.

Alan Clark, MP and diarist, 1990

When I was standing for Greenock in the early 1970s, I was scheduled to speak at a local school. Unfortunately, no one turned up except for the headteacher and the caretaker. To my surprise the headteacher brought some extra chairs into the hall and announced we were going for a pint. The next day a headline in the *Greenock Telegraph* read: 'Extra Chairs Brought Into Meeting.'

Liberal Democrat Menzies Campbell, 1999

I was at a big international conference, when a woman who seemed vaguely familiar asked me where I was from. 'I'm Tony Blair from the British Labour Party,' I replied. 'And you are?' 'My name is Beatrice and I'm from the Netherlands.' 'Beatrice who?' 'Just Beatrice.' 'What do you do?' I asked. 'I am the Queen.'

Prime Minister Tony Blair, in a 1999 interview to Woman's Journal,
revealing his worst social gaffe.

Jack Straw, Home Secretary, visiting an old people's home in 1999, introduced himself to a resident with the greeting, 'Do you know who I am?' The elderly lady replied, 'No, dear, but if you ask matron, she will tell you.'

I would never do anything to deride the profession of politics – although I think it is a form of madness.

Lord Home, former Prime Minister, 1983

If I go on TV and look grim, they say the situation must be even worse; if I smile at all, it's complacency.

> Harold Wilson, 1975

Keep your sense of humour about your position. The higher a monkey climbs, the more you see his behind.

> Donald Rumsfeld, US Defence Secretary, on serving President Ford
> 1974–76

I too was a rowing blue. It is, of course, an extraordinarily apt sport for men in public life – because you can face one way whilst going the other.

> Gough Whitlam, Prime Minister of Australia, speech to
> Lord Mayor of London, 1974

It is in the national interest for me to take an afternoon nap because I cannot initiate anything while I am asleep.

> Calvin Coolidge, US President 1923–29

If you've got 'em by the balls, their hearts and minds will follow.

> Sign on desk of Charles 'Chuck' Colson, special counsel to
> Richard Nixon 1969–73

I don't think Prime Ministers go until they're pushed.

> Jo Grimond, former Liberal Party Leader, 1973

To stay in No 10., most Prime Ministers would eat their own grandmothers.

> New Society (political weekly), 1986

Parliament

The less people know about how sausages and laws are made, the better they'll sleep at night.

> Bismarck

PARTING THOUGHTS

Working at Westminster is like having the nutters on the bus beside you every day.

Amanda Platell, former Conservative spin doctor, 2001

Show me a quiet parliament, and I will show you an undemocratic country.

George Thomas, Speaker of the House of Commons, 1976–83

All is fair in love, war and parliamentary procedure.

Jonathan Aitken, Conservative MP, during filibuster, House of Commons, April 1989

Nowhere in the world has radical social change ever been accomplished by Parliament.

Rights activist Peter Tatchell, 1983

Mr Hardy: I asked Lech Walesa... Lech Walesa does not speak English, but he stuck his thumb up and gave me a broad grin...
Mr Speaker: Order. I think that the Hon. Gentleman is on the wrong Pole.

Exchange during filibuster on the Antarctic Minerals Bill, July 1989

Anyone who enjoys being in the House of Commons probably needs psychiatric help.

Ken Livingstone, former Leader of the Greater London Council and newly arrived as Labour MP for Brent East, 1988

Being an MP is not really a job for grown-ups – you are wandering around looking for and making trouble.

Ken Livingstone, 2000

Like a bunch of 11-year-olds at their first secondary school.

Newly arrived MP Liz Lynne describing her fellow members, 1992

DEAD MAN WINS ELECTION

Being an MP is the sort of job all working-class parents want for their children – clean, indoors and no heavy lifting.

Diane Abbott, Hackney North and Stoke Newington MP, 1994

The only safe pleasure for a parliamentarian is a bag of boiled sweets.

Veteran backbench MP Julian Critchley, 1982

Sir Geoffrey Howe, debating with whom was famously likened by Denis Healey in 1978 to being 'savaged by a dead sheep', was patient in his riposte:

I was sorry to miss [Healey's] speech. The House may recall that the Rt Hon. Gentleman said that he had read so many obituaries of himself in the past few weeks that even he thought that he was already dead. Rather disconcertingly, the Rt Hon. Gentleman makes increasingly benevolent remarks about me. If I may respond in kind to one of his more memorable phrases, I feel rather as though I am being cherished by a dead savage. [Laughter] I hope the House will think that that was worth waiting for.

Howe, Leader of the House, debate on the Queen's Speech, November 1989

When I go down to the Lords, the only way I can keep awake is by making a speech myself. Otherwise it is almost impossible; it is so soporific down there.

Labour peer Lord Shinwell, 1975

The House of Lords is a perfect eventide home.

Baroness Stocks, 1970

We are nothing much to look at and most of us are not very young any more. We are not very exciting to listen to and many of us are not great orators, but we do have dignity.

Lord Denham, ex-government Deputy Chief Whip, 1975

I have been in favour of Lords reform almost since I have been there, because any House which has me in it really needs its head examined.

7th Earl of Onslow, 1998

We haven't said they're all hopeless, but quite a few of them are.
> *Baroness Jay, Leader of the House of Lords, on the reforms that would*
> *expel all but 92 hereditary peers, 1998*

When I gave my big speech on the Lords, the longest letter I received was from a lady who wanted to know where I had bought my blouse.
> *Baroness Jay, 1999*

If 'pro' is the opposite of 'con', then 'progress' is the opposite of 'Congress'.
> *William Howard Taft, US President 1909–13*

If Parliament were an airport, it would have been shut down long ago because of fog.
> *Carlo Vizzini, leader, Italian Social Democratic Party, after the 11th*
> *round of voting failed to elect a new President, 1992. It eventually took*
> *16 ballots before Oscar Scalfaro won.*

Elections

It's not who votes that counts, but who counts the votes.
> *Anonymous graffiti, 1980s*

Polls are like bikinis: what they reveal is interesting, but what they conceal is vital.
> *Len Murray, Trades Union Congress General Secretary, 1980*

Trust is not having to guess what a candidate means.
> *Gerald Ford, US President, 1976*

Be thankful only one of them can win.
> *Bumper sticker, Nixon–Kennedy contest, 1960*

In your heart, you know he's right.
> *Campaign slogan, right-wing Republican candidate Barry Goldwater, 1964*

DEAD MAN WINS ELECTION

In your guts, you know he's nuts.

Democratic Party riposte

Governments are like underpants. They start smelling pretty bad if you don't change them once in a while.

Margaret Murray, Toronto Star, 1981

The voters have spoken – the bastards.

Morris Udall, defeated US Presidential primary candidate, 1976

You campaign in poetry; you govern in prose.

Mario Cuomo, New York Governor, 1985

People never lie so much as after a hunt, during a war or before an election.

Bismarck

Democracy has at least one merit, namely that a Member of Parliament cannot be stupider than his constituents, for the more stupid he is, the more stupid they were to elect him.

Bertrand Russell

Tranquillity

Conservative Party general election slogan, 1922

Safety first

Conservative Party general election slogan, 1929

International affairs

American democracy is like a palaeolithic dinosaur which is slow to arouse, but which, once aroused, lays about itself with such force as to wreck its own habitation. [Often retranslated as America being 'difficult to get mobilised, but once mobilised almost impossible to stop'.]

US diplomat George Kennan

PARTING THOUGHTS

The US presidency is a Tudor monarchy with telephones.

Anthony Burgess, 1977

With these few words I want to assure you that I love you and if you had been a woman I would have considered marrying you, although your head is full of grey hairs, but as you are a man that possibility does not arise.

Perhaps the most bizarre diplomatic exchange of modern times, Ugandan President Idi Amin writing to Tanzanian President Nyerere, August 1972

What a terrible revenge for Pearl Harbor.

Samuel Hayakawa, US Senator 1977–83, on the success of McDonald's in Japan

Using the veto is rather like adultery. The first time you do it you feel a bit guilty, but after a while it becomes tremendous fun.

Sir Anthony Parsons, British Ambassador to the United Nations, recalling the views of his Soviet counterpart after a contentious debate – and veto – on the 1979 Soviet invasion of Afghanistan

I have been a Kremlinologist for 42 years and I still cannot guess what the Russians will do next.

Sir Fitzroy MacLean, diplomat, 1979

Workers of the world – we apologise.

Banner carried by reformist protesters, annual commemoration of the Bolshevik Revolution, Moscow, during democracy upheaval in Eastern Europe, November 1989

And now for a round-up of the Lenin monuments attacked today...

Start of segment on Vremya, Soviet official TV news, during the collapse of Communism, December 1990

263

DEAD MAN WINS ELECTION

The disintegration of the collectivised economies of the former Soviet Union was a rare example of an historical experiment testing a theory to destruction.

> *Former Conservative Chancellor of the Exchequer, Norman Lamont*

What is the USSR now? The USS *were*.

> *Quip in America during the collapse of the Soviet Union, 1990*

When you're dealing with the Middle East, 2,000 years is the normal wait for things to happen.

> *Marlin Fitzwater, White House spokesman, on the Palestine problem, 1989*

Forgive me for saying so, but no.

> *Margaret Thatcher, asked by a French television interviewer, at the Bicentennial celebrations, whether the French Revolution had a message for today's world, July 1989*

Seriosification.

> *Andrei Gromyko, Soviet Foreign Minister, describing the phase his talks with British Foreign Secretary, Sir Geoffrey Howe, were going through, January 1984*

I have not had major experience of talking with people once pronounced braindead, but I think we could be safe in saying he did not have great zip.

> *Sir Howard Smith, British Ambassador to Moscow 1976–79, on meeting Soviet Premier Leonid Brezhnev*

It's like carrying frogs in a wheelbarrow.

> *Lord Robertson, Secretary-General of NATO, on the difficulties of securing consensus in the enlarged organisation, 2002*

Anybody whose idea of relaxation is rolling in a barbed-wire duvet would love to do this job.

> *Neil Kinnock, on being a Vice-President of the European Commission, 2002*

PARTING THOUGHTS

I seriously doubt if we will have another war. This [Vietnam] is probably the last.

US *President Richard Nixon, March* 1971

And to conclude:

Don't tell my mother I'm in politics. She thinks I play piano in a whorehouse.

*Anon, c*1930

INDEX

INDEX

INDEX